Intimate Divisions
Street-Level Orthodoxy in Post-Soviet Russia

Since the early post-Soviet period, the understanding of the place of the Russian Orthodox Church in Russian society has been challenged by two developments, often considered contradictory. On the one hand, the Church has become an important player in the political arena and has become part of overall social life. On the other hand, however, statistical surveys continuously point to low levels of attendance and observance. Similarly, active parish religiosity has remained insignificant from the point of view of statistics. Nonetheless, obviously, the parish churches are dynamic places. Based on ethnographic fieldwork in a town in Saint Petersburg Region, this book addresses the dynamics of Russian Orthodoxy by focusing on highly variegated participations and interactions that make up the everyday life of the Church at its basic territorial level. The parish is approached through the lens of 'street-level Orthodoxy', a conceptual and methodological tool that concentrates on the physical margins of the church and its thresholds; on people who usually appear as unimportant to church life; and on practices that often fall out of the scholarly investigation of 'religion'. It is at the street-level that we can find important channels through which the relation between the Church, as an ecclesiastic organization, and society-at-large is actively constructed.

    The argument for a street-level approach is further supported by following the ethnographic thread of inequality and social distress. In post-Soviet Russia, socio-economic and gender disparities are embedded in routinized, even trivial, forms of Orthodoxy. They are not articulated as problems to be solved. Several such disparities are examined through different topics: inter-parish differentiations, social stratification, the church economy, women's teaching and technical support in parish schools, almsgiving, and grassroots charities. The book trains a spotlight on a variety of characters: parish clergy, churchgoers, occasional droppers-in, official staff and informal personnel, but also church beggars and non-churchgoers. These people experience inequality, differentiation, social disruptions, and distress as inbuilt simultaneously in the life of local churches and in the encompassing world. As they interact around these issues, they actively contribute to the mutual embedding of Church and society.

Halle Studies in the Anthropology of Eurasia

General Editors:

Christoph Brumann, Kirsten Endres, Chris Hann, Burkhard Schnepel, Lale Yalçın-Heckmann

Volume 35

LIT

Detelina Tocheva

Intimate Divisions
Street-Level Orthodoxy in Post-Soviet Russia

LIT

Cover Photo: Easter service in an Orthodox church in the Saint Petersburg Region (Photo: Detelina Tocheva, 2007).

This book is printed on acid-free paper.

Bibliografische Information der Deutschen Nationalbibliothek
Die Deutsche Nationalbibliothek verzeichnet diese Publikation in der Deutschen Nationalbibliografie; detaillierte bibliografische Daten sind im Internet über http://dnb.d-nb.de abrufbar.

ISBN 978-3-643-90873-5 (pb)
ISBN 978-3-643-95873-0 (PDF)

A catalogue record for this book is available from the British Library

©LIT VERLAG Dr. W. Hopf
Berlin 2017
Fresnostr. 2
D-48159 Münster
Tel. +49 (0) 2 51-62 03 20
Fax +49 (0) 2 51-23 19 72
E-Mail: lit@lit-verlag.de
http://www.lit-verlag.de

LIT VERLAG GmbH & Co. KG Wien,
Zweigniederlassung Zürich 2017
Klosbachstr. 107
CH-8032 Zürich
Tel. +41 (0) 44-251 75 05
Fax +41 (0) 44-251 75 06
E-Mail: zuerich@lit-verlag.ch
http://www.lit-verlag.ch

Distribution:
In the UK: Global Book Marketing, e-mail: mo@centralbooks.com
In North America: International Specialized Book Services, e-mail: orders@isbs.com
In Germany: LIT Verlag Fresnostr. 2, D-48159 Münster
Tel. +49 (0) 2 51-620 32 22, Fax +49 (0) 2 51-922 60 99, e-mail: vertrieb@lit-verlag.de
e-books are available at www.litwebshop.de

Contents

	List of Illustrations	ix
	Acknowledgements	xi
	Note on Transliteration	xv
1	**Introduction: Binding Divisions**	**1**
	An Ethnography of the Margins of Religion	3
	Elusive Definitions: A Note on History	5
	Post-Soviet Conundrums	7
	Thinking through the Edges of the Parish	9
	Street-Level Orthodoxy	11
	Street-Level Orthodoxy through the Lens of Inequality and Social Disruption	13
	Protestant Denominations and Social Distress: A Different View	15
	A Qualification	17
	The Structure of the Book	19
2	**Local Configurations Face the Instituted Rule of Unequal Churches**	**21**
	Engaging the Field	21
	Profane Landscapes	25
	Religious and Ethnic Diversity	27
	Thriving Orthodoxy	30
	The Instituted Rule of an Unequal Church	33
3	**Rebuilding the Church: A Key Moment in the Shaping of Street-Level Orthodoxy**	**43**
	An Enthusiastic Church Rebuilding	45
	'We Were Building with Our Hands'	47
	A Community with Two Cores	48
	The Moral Worth of Material Limitation	51

4	**Inter-Parish Differentiation**	57
	Hidden Transcripts	57
	Cultivating Distinct Connections to the Divine: A Priest with 'Strong Prayer'	63
	And, a New Martyr Saint	67
	From Troubled Past to New Disparities	73
5	**The Economy of Street-Level Orthodoxy: Struggling over Moral Values, Power, and Equity**	77
	Inside Church Commerce	79
	The Differential Moral Valence of Gift and Commerce	84
	Malleable Pricing and the Ethics of Equity	89
	Organizational Image and Power	91
	When Gifts Undermine Honesty	94
	Conclusion	97
6	**Women in Orthodox Schooling: Living an Ordinary Life and Making Society Better**	99
	The Bottom of the 'Hierarchy': Little Old Ladies	101
	Women at the Middle and Top	104
	Work at the Top	105
	Below the Teachers	107
	Valentina: The Challenges of Low-Paid Jobs and the Normalcy of Single Motherhood	109
	Tamara: Practising Orthodoxy 'Out of Love'	115
	Coming to Love	117
	Conclusion	118
7	**The Alchemy of Almsgiving: How a Persistent Social Problem Prompted New Ethics**	121
	Ethics, Morals, and Values	123
	The Dilemma of Charity	125
	Characters and Spaces	128
	Ethics as Interaction	131
	Orthodox Almsgiving	134
	Soviet and Early Post-Soviet Morals of Work	137
	Crafting Ethical Responses: Accepting while Rejecting	139

8	**Secular Relatedness in Orthodox Churches: Grassroots Charities**	**141**
	Insiders' Views on Giving Help	143
	From Foreign Aid to Local Patterns	145
	'The Cleaners Know Who Is in Need'	146
	'People Bring, Others Take'	148
	Perceptions of the *Lavka* Activity	150
	Gifting and the *Lavka*	151
	Privileged Recipients	152
	A Procedure of Appropriation	154
	Discrimination in the *Lavka*	155
	Conclusion	158
9	**Conclusion**	**161**
	Bibliography	167
	Index	183

List of Illustrations

Plates

1	In the vicinity of the city	30
2	Easter cakes awaiting the priest's blessing	31
3	Offerings of eggs for Easter	32
4	Pilgrimage	39
5	Pilgrims waiting to bathe in a holy spring	40
6	Ordering prayers for the living and dead	62
7	Unpretentious Christmas supper	64
8	Accompanying Saint Lidia's relics to the church	70
9	A church stall	81
10	A smaller church shop	82
11	A box for prayer orders and money gifts	85
12	A price list	90
13	A church cleaner	102
14	A cleaning lady of a parish school	103
15	A parish school library	108
16	Elderly women collecting alms	129
17	Bags of donated clothes	149

(all photographs by author, 2006–2007)

Acknowledgements

This study began as part of the project 'Religion and Morality in European Russia' based at the Max Planck Institute for Social Anthropology in Halle and led by Professor Chris Hann between 2006 and 2009. My colleagues from the MPI – the scientific members and administrative staff, guests and associates – have all contributed to creating the stimulating and friendly atmosphere that enlightened my work during my nearly seven-year affiliation with this project and a subsequent one.

Chris Hann was keen to consider the manuscript for publication in the Halle Series in the Anthropology of Eurasia. From accepting me as a member of the 'Religion and Morality in European Russia' project group to supporting me in the final stages of publication eleven years later, Chris has played a key role throughout my intellectual upbringing. I deeply thank him.

Jennifer Cash, a dear friend and colleague, deserves a special note here. She offered to this study an impressively efficacious pair of editorial eyes and an outstanding anthropological brain. The idea of putting together this book burgeoned in a conversation that we had over a coffee in the German city of Magdeburg on a rainy day in October 2015. Since that moment, she embraced the idea of completing the manuscript as much as I did myself. She did much more than editing the original manuscript. She drew my attention to ideas that were buried under the presented material. In other places, she pointed to me possible analyses that I had not articulated clearly or simply had never thought about. With great subtlety, she made the entire manuscript by far more reader-friendly than it was before. Jennifer's unlimited intellectual and human empathy is the greatest gift I have received throughout the completion of this book.

I wish to warmly thank several individual colleagues from the Max Planck Institute. Tobias Köllner, Tünde Komáromi, Agata Ładykowska, and Jarrett Zigon, as well as Nathan Light, Miladina Monova, Monica Vasile, and Bea Vidacs created the intellectually stimulating and friendly atmosphere that I have enjoyed throughout the years. They influenced my thoughts in numerous ways. Some of them read different parts of the manuscript at earlier stages. My thanks go also to Milena Benovska-Sabkova, a temporary external advisor on the 'Religion and Morality' project, for the stimulating discussions we had.

At different stages of the project, I have benefited also from dialogue, constructive suggestions, and numerous readings and re-readings generously offered by Aliki Angelidou, Christoph Brumann, Melissa Caldwell, James Carrier, Stephen Gudeman, Patrick Heady, Deema Kaneff, Douglas Rogers, Michael Stanley-Baker, Vladislava Vladimirova, and Lale Yalçın-Heckmann. I thank the participants of the weekly seminar of the Department

'Resilience and Transformation in Eurasia' who, over the years, patiently read, commented, and helped improving hundreds of papers, including mine. Barbara Karatsioli too made valuable suggestions on an earlier version of the introduction.

I am endlessly thankful to Anke Meyer and Berit Westwood who played the role of kingpins in a variety of areas. Among innumerable other things, they helped me in organizing trips, offered advice and timely support, and even helped me settle when I first arrived in Halle. Berit finally prepared the manuscript for publication with great efficacy and devotion. What makes their assistance definitely unparalleled are their wonderful smiles and unlimited patience.

Kathy Rousselet offered her wonderful friendship and critical comments that helped me make the introduction more clear and focused. Kathy Rousselet and Alexander Agadjanian have been outstanding colleagues, advisors and friends for many years and I will never be able to express how much I learned and continue to learn from them.

My work has benefited immensely from Jeanne Kormina and Sergey Shtyrkov's expert knowledge of issues pertaining to religion in Russia and elsewhere, and from their critical eyes. While I was working on the final manuscript, the awareness of their kindness, open-mindedness, and infinite friendship have been always on my mind.

I thank Julia Andreeva who provided great assistance, useful guidance, and local expertise in Russia. My friend Larissa Zakharova and her family in Russia generously assisted me at the early stages of my field study. Elena Guseva, her children, and Babushka Nina guided my first steps in Russia. They did much more too, offering a friendship and support that knows no boundaries. They helped me settle down and made my life in the field pleasant and comfortable. Elena introduced me to the people from the largest local parish. I will never be able to fully express how much I admire the infinite patience and deep empathy with which this family met my awkward questions and reactions. I express my gratitude to dozens of informants and friends in the field whose open arms, but also sometimes discontent, helped me understand how things work in the parishes and in the surrounding world. In this book, I have tried to describe most of what I understood from the explicit information and implicit teachings I was granted.

In spite of these much valuable supports, all shortcomings are, of course, mine.

Parts of chapters 3 and 4 draw from my earlier publication, Ot Vosstanovleniia Khrama k Sozdaniiu Obshchiny: Samoogranichenie i Material'nye Trudnosti kak Istochniki Prihodskoi Identichnosti. In A. Agadjanian and K. Rousselet (eds.), *Prikhody i Obshchiny v Sovremennom Pravoslavii: Kornevaia Sistema Rossiiskoi Religioznosti*, pp. 277–297. Moscow: Ves' Mir, 2011. Chapter 5 is a revised version of The Economy of the Temples of God in the Turmoil of Changing Russia. *European Journal of Sociology* 55 (1): 1–24, 2014. The unchanged parts are reprinted with permission. Most of Chapter 7 was previously published as Crafting Ethics: The Dilemma of Almsgiving in Russian Orthodox Churches. *Anthropological Quarterly* 84 (4): 1011–1034, 2011. Chapter 8 largely draws on An Ethos of Relatedness: Foreign Aid and Grassroots Charities in Two Orthodox Parishes in North-Western Russia. In J. Zigon (ed.), *Multiple Moralities and Religions in Post-Soviet Russia*, pp. 67–91. New York: Berghahn Books, 2011. I thank the publishers for permissions to reprint.

Note on Transliteration

The Russian transliterations used in this book follow the Library of Congress system, excepting some names for which the usual transliteration is different: Patriarch Sergius, Patriarch Alexii, Saint Xenia, Nadieszda Kizenko, Sergey Shtyrkov. All translations from Russian are mine.

Chapter 1
Introduction: Binding Divisions

Natalia occupied an administrative job in City Hall when I first met her in 2006. For a few years already, she also had been teaching occasionally in the Orthodox school of the main local parish, organizing sewing workshops on several weekends per month for the children who attended Sunday classes. Natalia had pushed open the door of the school for the first time because, she said, she 'lacked socializing'. As she knew a bit the woman who acted as the head of the school, she was quickly integrated into the team and began organizing workshops.

Natalia's engagement with the school can be explained from various directions. On the one hand, the parish school is well known for its many activities and the quality of education it offers. On the other hand, Natalia benefitted from the extra income. Her administrative job was stable, but the salary was inadequate. She had been struggling with money shortages since the harsh 1990s, and – a single mother – she had been supported heavily by her own mother. It was true that when I met her in 2006, Natalia's children no longer represented the same financial burden as they had when they were younger. Her daughter had graduated recently from the university and had immediately found a job. Her younger son was about to graduate as an engineer. Yet the small amounts that Natalia received on an informal basis from the parish school for her sewing classes were a welcome addition to her tiny salary.

In the years following our initial meeting, Natalia continued to teach occasionally at the parish school. She kept a good relationship with the school's personnel. Sometimes she participated in pilgrimages organized by the parish school, and sometimes she attended Easter and Christmas services in the church, often in the company of her parish school colleagues. But not always. On some years, when the weather was particularly harsh on Christmas's Eve, Natalia 'attended' the religious service at home by watching it on television.

In 2016, having reached retirement age, she left her administrative job at City Hall. Not long before her retirement, a private Orthodox school had opened in Ozerovo, and the head of the parish school had been appointed as its director. She offered Natalia a position as a part-time secretary on an official contract. Natalia accepted. The chance to add a salary to her meagre old-age pension was a desirable one, and the position offered her the opportunity to continue sharing in the friendly company of Orthodox teachers. This is a company that Natalia appreciates highly. As I am writing, Natalia works still as the part-time secretary of a private Orthodox school in Ozerovo.

Natalia does not consider herself to be a strictly observant Orthodox. Nor is she an active parishioner in any church. She does confess, and she takes communion, usually, on Easter and sometimes at other occasions too. For many years she has partaken of these 'services' at Ozerovo's central church (to which the first parish school where she worked belongs). But, she sometimes drops by another local church to light a candle and order prayers (*podat' zapisochku*) because it is cheaper than the central church.

I begin this chapter with a sketch of Natalia's participation in different local organizations affiliated with the Russian Orthodox Church (ROC) because it draws attention to the plethora of ways of being Orthodox in contemporary Russia. Natalia's case also exemplifies conjunctures between engagement with Orthodoxy and common sorts of social distress, gender disparities, and economic inequalities. In Russian society, such conjunctures are also multiple. Their study allows insights into the large spectrum of participations and interactions that make the basic territorial level of the post-Soviet ROC extraordinarily dynamic.

This book is precisely about the intertwined aspects of inequalities and the social life of parishes. It is also about how the Church has become part of Russia's social fabric and how, reciprocally, the Orthodox Church at the parish level has been shaped by larger dynamics of social differentiation and distress. The present work is based on a case study of parishes in a small city. The ethnographic material, and the analysis and conclusions that follow, reflect the specificities of this field site. The propositions formulated here should nevertheless contribute to broader debates concerning Russian religiosity, religious organizations, and the anthropology of religion.

The understanding of the role of the post-Soviet ROC, the main ecclesiastical organization in Russia[1], has for a long time been a challenge for scholars of religion. The puzzlement derives from a persistent paradox. On one side, statistics point endlessly to low levels of religious observance

---

[1] I describe the ROC as an 'organization' instead of an 'institution', drawing on the distinctions elaborated by Halemba (2015).

among those who declare themselves to be Russian Orthodox. The numbers of active Orthodox culminate, at best, at eight per cent, but are often lower. On the other side, accounts of the ROC's power and influence (e.g. Knox 2005; Mitrofanova 2005; Garrard and Garrard 2008; Curanović 2012), as well as more nuanced analyses stressing the ROC's ambivalent position in society and *vis-à-vis* political power (Mitrokhin 2004; Dubin 2005; Filatov and Lunkin 2006; Papkova 2011; Richters 2013; Rousselet 2013a) all converge on one point: they find the importance of the ROC in present-day Russia incontestable. Models inspired by empirical studies of the Western world are of little help. The classical sociological template of 'believing without belonging' (Davie 2003) and its opposite, 'belonging without believing', hardly offer a way out of this conundrum (Köllner 2012), not least because in post-Soviet Russia the notions of believing and belonging are bewilderingly complex. Applying a Western-biased concept of 'public religion' to Russian Orthodoxy also seems inappropriate. If primarily defined in terms of civil society, human rights, and a free religious market (Casanova 1994), 'public religion' is poorly equipped to account for the 'de-privatization' of historically dominant religions in many places. The problems of applying it to the postsocialist world generally and in Russia specifically have been made clear (Dragadze 1993; Hann 2000).

How then are we to understand the manifest presence of the ROC in Russian society against the low numbers of active parishioners? Rehearsing the existing debates will fail to bring new light. Re-examining figures of attendance and observance does not seem promising either. A different approach is needed. We can start by decentring the attention given to the master topics in the study of religion. We must shift our attention to problems other than those of attendance, observance, belief, and ritual. Instead, we can, as I do in this study, turn our attention to the large variety of *participations* and *interactions* that make up the everyday life of the Church in society. We must look at the parish level, but not be misled into looking for a formally organized parish.

An Ethnography of the Margins of Religion

The post-Soviet Orthodox parish is most commonly defined by the centrality of the temple, clerical office, and a community of faithful. The following chapters devote much attention to these classical components. But the ethnographic scope goes beyond. The reason for that is empirical. In my field site, life is effervescent in spaces that are considered somewhat marginal to the heart of the church, such as the church porch and yard, a parish school, church shops located inside and in the vicinity of the church, the yard and immediate surroundings, even the streets nearby. Very different kinds of people interact in these spaces. Some are most obviously church insiders, such as the clerics and the most committed church workers and churchgoers. Some are occasional visitors to the church. Some are among those who may believe but 'never go to church'. Others are never considered as 'church people' in any meaningful way, but are nonetheless usual actors in the life of the churches. For instance, beggars are among the ambivalent characters typically present around urban churches. Clerics and church workers expect that they stay on the physical edges of the church, keeping them neither really inside, nor entirely outside.

When viewed from the perspective of the people who approach it, the parish evidences a large spectrum of everyday forms of participation that cannot be described easily in terms of belonging, believing, or observance. These apparently marginal participations form a large and complex field. And it is here, I argue, that we can find important channels through which the relation between the Church, as an ecclesiastic organization, and society-at-large is actively constructed.

In order to bring to light some of the multiple ways in which very different people and practices are part of church dynamics, I ethnographically follow the thread of social inequalities. Beggars embody one of the most conspicuous forms of social distress in Russia, but there are other forms of social distress that are much less eye-catching and much more culturally accepted, such as gender inequalities. In post-Soviet Russia, socio-economic and gender disparities are embedded in routinized, even trivial, forms of Orthodoxy. In the subsequent chapters, I examine several of them by looking at specific topics: inter-parish differentiations, social stratification, the church economy, teaching and technical support in parish schools, almsgiving, and grassroots charities.[2]

The choice to focus on kinds of participation in church life (as opposed to formal degrees of membership), coupled with a preference for inequalities as a thematic thread, means that the focus of this book is on a double margin. This choice is motivated, first of all, as I pointed out, by my empirical findings. Theoretically, it builds on an important claim put forward by Frances Pine and João de Pina-Cabral at around the time I completed my fieldwork. That is, what is usually reckoned as being on the 'margins' in the study of religion is, in fact, socially structuring. Thus the analysis of such margins is theoretically fruitful (Pine and Pina-Cabral 2008). As Pina-Cabral and Pine put it, 'The grey areas are the best place to study both what we call religion and the place which it holds in the larger social context' (ibid. 2).

---

[2] Of course, the official hierarchy of the parish clergy is also a locus of embedded inequalities, but it is deliberately left out from the present work except to the extent that it overlaps with the informal arenas of church activities examined here.

They continued: 'Although neither religion nor margins is an easily definable concept, the two consistently interrelate in anthropological theory. In this sense, concentrating on the margins of religions [allows us] to think in terms of places/spaces where overlap and fuzziness of categorical distinctions is not only unproblematic but is in fact anticipated and even integral to the complex processes of sociality' (ibid. 3). They further defined the 'margins of religion' as a limit (i.e. as 'being "a margin" of something'), as a 'higher level of relatedness' and, finally, as a process that unfolds in time (ibid. 5). While each of these three aspects appears in the present work, greater attention is devoted to margins as encapsulating a sense of relatedness.

Elusive Definitions: A Note on History

Debates over the definition of the Russian Orthodox parish were frequent in pre-Soviet times.[3] Historians of the pre-Soviet Church, especially those focusing on the nineteenth and early twentieth centuries, show that the parish (*prikhod*) was associated with a territorial unit, a liturgical community, and a church (*tserkov'*) or temple (*khram*) (Freeze 1983; Chulos 2003; Shevzov 2004). Since the Great Reforms promoted by Peter I (the Great) in the seventeenth century, religious belonging was de facto defined by the state administration. The parish priests recorded in registers the births, marriages, and deaths for all Orthodox subjects of the Russian Empire on the territory of their parish. This administrative function of the parish clergy supported the common idea that a parish community was congruent with a territorial community. However, no inclusive register of all parish members has ever been put in place by the Church. While this absence did not seem to raise problems in smaller settings and in the countryside, it proved problematic in cities with many churches where the territory of the parish was not clearly delimited and especially when urban centres begun to grow dramatically. For instance, at the end of the nineteenth century, when migrants from peasant origin came to work in Saint Petersburg's factories, parish priests perceived the parish affiliation of these workers as uncertain. The priests, in principle obliged to celebrate weddings for all couples belonging to their parish, sometimes felt confused and even refused to marry such members of the emerging working class (Dixon 1995, cited in Kenworthy 2006: 12).

---

[3] In Orthodox milieus and most writing on the history of the Church, it is common to refer to the pre-Soviet period as 'pre-revolutionary' (*do Revoliutsii*). But, the revolution lasted only a short period and the changes in relations between church, state, and society occurred more properly over the subsequent 70 years of Soviet government. For this reason, 'pre-Soviet' appears more often in this text.

Historians of the late nineteenth and early twentieth centuries note some commonsensical definitions of the parish that went along with the practical absence of legal and theological definitions in the context of multiple inflamed debates about the role of the parish. Chris Chulos was particularly specific about how peasants defined the parish in Voronezh Province (some 500 kilometres south of Moscow): 'In the eyes of worshipers, the parish community (*prikhod*) consisted of a spiritual realm of living and deceased Orthodox Christians and a physical territory comprising land, buildings, and sacred objects' (Chulos 2003: 54). In spite of these deeply rooted perceptions, controversial debates often broke out. Particularly vivid in the period 1905–17, they mainly revolved around the roles of the laity and clergy in the ecclesiastical structures, their internal relationships, the place of the parish within the organization of the state, the duties of the lay community, and the delimitation of its specific responsibilities (Shevzov 2004: 12–53). Vera Shevzov noted the legal and theological 'elusiveness' of the concepts of parish and Church (ibid. 22). Throughout the history of the Russian Church and notably in the late imperial period, dozens of regulations were adopted, as projects for reforms and impassioned debates proliferated. Shevzov underlined 'the lack of any single systematized set of legislation or bylaws delineating official parish identity' (loc. cit.). Generally, in the bulk of regulations, the notion of the Church was equated with that of the clergy, while documents conveyed the view that 'lay involvement was extrinsic to the "essential" activity of the Church' (ibid. 25). Despite the lack of clear legal definition of the parish and the overall marginal or passive role granted to the laity, Shevzov demonstrated that the lay Orthodox had a strong sense of belonging to their temple (54–94)[4], thus matching Chulos's (2003) findings.[5] In brief, the pre-Soviet parish was an important source of identification, even though parish identity remained elusive in theological and legal terms. Indeed, this disjuncture between localized claims and Church attitudes foregrounded the parish as a subject of heated debates. The pre-Soviet parish was a complex, controversial, and elusive unit. In its post-Soviet re-emergence, the parish has been no simpler or easier to define.

---

[4] Vera Shevzov (2004) also argued that chapels, icons, and feasts were devotional centres along with parish temples.

[5] The introduction of parish councils (*popechitel'stva*) in 1864, bodies that were not legally subordinate to the parish, led to the involvement of numerous lay Orthodox in decisions regarding the organization of local church life: e.g. charity, church upkeep, the material sustenance of the clergy (Freeze 1983). They remained active after the 1917 Bolshevik revolution, until 1928 (Young 1996).

Post-Soviet Conundrums

Clergy, clerical office, and the temple have remained central to popular post-Soviet definitions of the parish. Sometimes, the three points of definition do not coincide because more than one church or chapel is placed under the responsibility of a single head priest. It is, however, deceptive to search for traces of continuity with the strong sense of parish belonging, best documented for the case of Russian peasants in the pre-Soviet period. Seventy years of forced Soviet secularization profoundly shook the Church. State-driven repression decimated the parish clergy, closed down churches, and – as a result – almost completely destroyed the notion of belonging to a parish community for most Soviet citizens. The Soviet policies of massive and frequent dislocations for various purposes further contributed to this destruction.[6] If the post-Soviet Church has actively reasserted the centrality of the temple and that of the parish clergy, the post-Soviet Statute of the Parish formulates a markedly loose definition of parish membership.[7] Moreover, the territorial principle was taken out from the latest Statute of the Parish adopted in 2000.[8] The last Statute that mentions the territorial principle dates back to 1918. Although post-Soviet Church sympathizers commonly speak of the 'revival' or 'renaissance' (*vozrozhdenie*) of Russian Orthodoxy, and even when we take into account the highly influential theological concept of Tradition within Orthodoxy, the contemporary parish is by no means the blueprint copy of its pre-Soviet predecessor.

Such a position is what Alexander Agadjanian and Kathy Rousselet argued for in their edited collection *Parish and Community in Contemporary Orthodoxy* (2011a), published in the Russian language. At the time of my book's publication, their work remains the most comprehensive study of the complexities concerning post-Soviet parishes. Much of the debate around the post-Soviet resurgence of parish life, especially among clergymen and laity,

---

[6] In the twentieth century, radical transformations of the parish have also occurred in Western Catholic parishes. Yves Lambert's study of French Catholicism is a famous example. Lambert claims for the French region of Brittany that the Catholic 'parish civilization' came to an end with the Council of Vatican II and the modernization of agriculture (Lambert 1985). But parallels with Russia are hardly relevant. In Russia, very different social and political processes unfolded in the Church and society before, during, and after the Soviet period.

[7] The Statute of the Parish was entirely revised in 1988 and 2000. Important amendments were adopted in 2008, 2011, 2013, and 2016. http://www.patriarchia.ru/db/text/133141.html, accessed on 5 April 2017.

[8] Point 1 of the general dispositions of the Statute defines the parish as 'the community of Orthodox Christians, composed of the clerics and the laity, united around the temple'. Point 2 specifies the 'voluntary basis' of membership for the laity. The eparchy council defines the limits of the parish. But no general territorial principle is mentioned. These aspects are further discussed in relation to the economy of the post-Soviet parishes in chapters 2 and 5.

has concentrated on the tensions and overlaps between two definitions of the parish: as an administrative unit and as a community of the faithful. In order to shed light on these tensions, and more generally in order to appreciate the significance and role of the parish in post-Soviet Orthodoxy, Agadjanian and Rousselet brought together a large range of individual case studies. These studies propose typologies of parishes and communities; sociological analysis of the clergy, laity, and their respective types of authority; analysis of church rituals and subculture, of parish formation and identity, of relations between parish communities and the surrounding society. On this basis, Agadjanian argued that the ecclesial ideal of 'Eucharistic community' defined as a group of clergymen and laypeople who form a sacramental community, does not describe accurately the empirical reality of post-Soviet parishes. In the beginning of the 1990s, a period when longings for an Orthodox rebirth drew on romantic images of the first Christian communities, some religious activists found this ideal particularly appealing (Agadjanian 2011: 29–30). In reality, the post-Soviet parish has unclear territorial boundaries and undefined membership.[9] Moreover, there are various degrees of participation and observance, different types of core communities (*prikhozhane*), and occasional visitors (*zakhozhane*). Arina Tarabukina (2000) brought attention to the existence of such marked differences already in the mid-1990s in her study of particularly committed and conservative Orthodox whom she called 'the temple milieu' (*prikhramovaia sreda*). The idealistic model of local belonging to a parish is thoroughly challenged by the increasingly popular practice of pilgrimage religiosity (see also Kormina 2010; Naletova 2010; Rock 2014). In short, a viable definition of the Orthodox parish community cannot be tailored after the 'Eucharistic community' model. In general, the measurement of different canonical forms of observance, such as attendance at Sunday services, communion, fasting, or the regularity of prayers, steadily finds that the levels of observance are insignificant (Filatov and Lunkin 2006). Pointing to the equivalence that the majority of people see between being Russian and being Orthodox is often used to explain the persisting popularity of the Church in the context of low levels of observance. But this perceived equivalence, however strong and enduring, does not explain the continuous existence of a dynamic parish life.

Are there alternative analytical categories that can allow us to grasp the different ways to be part of Orthodoxy? The ideal of 'Eucharistic community' has much in common with the definition of the strictly obser-

---

[9] This observation should be tempered if we look at rural areas. The possibility for multiple parish 'membership', or rather alternate visits to different local churches, de facto drops out when there is only one church within a reasonable distance.

vant parishioners whom Jeanne Kormina called the 'structural Orthodox' – an 'exotic minority' in twenty-first-century Russia (Kormina 2012: 196). In contrast, wrote Kormina, there are at least four distinct 'regimes of Orthodox sociality'. The first one is determined by participation in a local parish community and is formed by the structural faithful. The three other regimes, which she calls 'nomadic', are represented by the pilgrimage, the network, and the flash mob (temporary gatherings aiming at the veneration of travelling shrines and occasional participation in Orthodox fairs, that engender particularly popular and ephemeral religious practice). Each of these regimes is defined by a specific understanding of where religious charisma is located, how it is legitimated, and how it is accessed (ibid. 199–200). This model of a variety of regimes of religious sociality in Russian Orthodoxy is particularly insightful. However, it again reduces the study of the local parish to its structural members – while displacing all other forms of Orthodox participation well outside ordinary church grounds.

Thinking through the Edges of the Parish

In a certain sense, Kormina's investigation of different regimes of Orthodox sociality follows in the steps of Thomas Luckmann's much earlier critique of the positivist approach developed by 'church sociology' (Luckmann 1967). Founding his critique in the Western world, Luckmann accused church sociologists of failing to grasp forms of religion beyond church walls. The problem with Luckmann's critique is that it gives too little attention to the variety of practices surrounding churches themselves. Churches are still strongly present in the physical landscape, in the West and in Russia, and this means that they still matter regardless of how low levels of attendance drop. It is no doubt important to look beyond them, but is also important not to overlook them. Physical churches remain important even to practices 'beyond their walls': each of Kormina's four regimes of religious sociality evolves in a complex relationship with the official ecclesiastical organization and, often, local churches (Kormina 2012). This local base of a post-Soviet ecclesiastical organization is a central issue, and not only in the case of the ROC. As Agnieszka Halemba persuasively argued in her ethnography of a deanery belonging to the Greek Catholic Church in Transcarpathian Ukraine, interest in the organizational character of religion in the recent 'anthropology of Christianity' has been notably sparse (Halemba 2015: 20–21). She wrote further, that 'What has happened in the twenty years after the collapse of the Soviet Bloc seems to suggest that the challenge was not to restore a will to believe and experience religiously, but to revive organizational religion' (ibid. 26). But is the 'revival' nothing more than a resurrection of the Church as an organization? This argument might well be made if one looks only at the organization's efforts: the ROC has indeed re-instantiated its centrality as an organization, and it has done so notably through policies supportive of church construction; by underlining the pivotal role of the clergy and priestly service at the parish level; and by stressing the utmost importance of the continuity of canonically sanctioned ritual. But is there not more to say about the revival in terms of people's kinds of participation in parish life? I take inspiration from Halemba's organizational analysis and propose to look more closely at the parish. Neither the study of the post-Soviet Orthodox Church nor that of Christian churches in general can afford to conceive of churches, parishes, deaneries, and eparchies as closed units. Neither can the sociological and anthropological analysis be grounded in canonical definitions. Indeed, Halemba's (2015) emphasis on the faithful's feeling of being faced with the challenge of globalization evidences the need to rethink the organizational approach in order to be able to account for the connections between large-scale challenges and processes unfolding in the churches and their sub-units. In this sense, Halemba's demonstration of the vibrancy with which the local level of the organization experiences global transformations does not really contradict Luckmann's critique of the parochial concerns of 'church sociologists'. It underlines the need to see the interactions and mutual influences of practices *inside* and *outside* church walls.

To build that bridge, we must enlarge our vision of which kinds of people form a parish. The parish community is formed not only by clergy and structural believers. These groups claim to be the parish, but they are not the only claimants – neither historically nor in contemporary practice. Our view has to be more comprehensive than that taken by the putative unit formed by the clergy and 'the people who see themselves as privileged members of [the religious] organization' (Halemba 2015: 33).

I follow too in the steps of Agadjanian and Rousselet who argued that a study of the post-Soviet Russian Orthodox parishes should begin with the understanding that they are not 'isolated enclaves'. 'Parishes and communities are inbuilt in the fabric of values and relations of their social surrounding through their members' (Agadjanian and Rousselet 2011b: 9). In other words, parishes are not distinct from society-at-large. I take this insight as a premise, but find it necessary to conceptualize further, to the point of dissolving the porous membranes of parish and society altogether. That is to say, the invocation of 'membership' cannot be sustained. Membership is an elusive category in the post-Soviet parishes because there is no way to define, record, or delimit official membership. Nor does a consideration of the relationships between devoted churchgoers and 'outsiders' sufficiently account for the composite character of church life.

Parishes are entrenched in broader social dynamics through much more complex intertwinements than are suggested by a taxonomy of people's relations to the church. Finally, the taxonomy that appears in some accounts is a model of concentric circles, with the most active churchgoers in the centre.[10] This model refines the popular typology of 'parishioners' (*prikhozhane*) and 'droppers-in' (*zakhozhane*), but it still does not leave space for the types of people whose presence is instrumental to the practical operation of the church, such as (female) doorkeepers and cleaners, or people who voluntarily participate in church reconstruction, but never really participate in religious services or other church activities. And of course, this model does not leave space for beggars. A more largely inclusive model is needed. 'Street-level Orthodoxy' can serve that purpose.

Street-Level Orthodoxy

The notion of 'street-level Orthodoxy' is not an alternative to 'parish'. I use it instead to provide a more comprehensive frame for the analysis of the parish. I use it for the study of the post-Soviet Church specifically; I cannot speculate about its applicability to earlier periods. Street-level Orthodoxy trains a spotlight on the composite character of Orthodox parish life as manifest through a plethora of participations and interactions in many places in, near, and related to local churches.

The composite character of parish life that can be perceived through a focus on 'street-level Orthodoxy' is not in conflict with the rules of the Church as an ecclesiastic organization, with its rigid hierarchical structures, or with the stiff Church canon. Street-level Orthodoxy is rather integral to the Church. In this respect, I draw inspiration from the concept of 'street-level bureaucracy' coined by political scientist Michael Lipsky (2010 [1980]). Lipsky was concerned with understanding how state policies in the United States, idealistically defined at the top level of the state, were actually implemented by front-line civil servants, such as policemen, teachers, and lower court judges, in their 'face-to-face encounters' with citizens. For Lipsky, it was these 'street-level bureaucrats' who effectively conducted state policies. What makes Lipsky's idea of street-level bureaucracy particularly appealing for my analysis of the ROC is its ability to account for two dimensions of reality that seem incompatible at first glance, but are actually deeply interconnected. As Lipsky wrote: '"Bureaucracy" implies a set of rules and structures of authority; "street-level" implies a distance from the center where authority presumably resides' (Lipsky 2010: xii). Individual judgment and discretion, and the production of 'routines of practice' at the

---

[10] I am grateful to Kathy Rousselet for having pointed out this model to me.

street level are totally absent from the official texts and from formal instructions of the organization. They are nonetheless instrumental to the perpetuation of the official organization. It is this central idea – that there are many essential practices and relations that are nowhere described, located far from the centre of authority, that in practice smoothly combine with rigid official hierarchies and rules – that I have borrowed from Lipsky. For the rest, it is obvious that the American state and the Russian Orthodox Church are not comparable in terms of structure, legitimacy, or the nature of their authority; neither is the relation between street-level civil servants and citizens truly comparable to that between parish clergy and the laity. Nevertheless, the character of Russian Orthodoxy, just like the character of American society, is created through many 'invisible' actions and discretions.

A constellation of different people participate and interact in the frame of the parish and through it. This is the second aspect defining street-level Orthodoxy. That is, at the 'street-level', parishes depend on the activities of many people whose roles are not imagined in the official organization of the Church. Sometimes, such people can be described collectively as the 'laity', but this term is most useful only for distinguishing them from the 'clergy'. There is no other term that accounts for the variety of groups, positions, and roles found in contemporary Orthodox churches. In the constellation of actors, ordained clergy stands out as a noticeable exception; only they are part of the Church's official hierarchy. They are referred to collectively as 'servants of the sacred' (*sviashchennosluzhiteli*), but the differences between the deacon (*diakon*), priest (*ierei*), and archpriest (*protoierei*) are also recognized by their distinct titles.[11] The Church does recognize a number of other key positions occupied by non-ordained people under the collective term 'church servants' (*tserkovnosluzhiteli*). In practice, the differences between them are substantial, even if viewed only on the economic plane: some *tserkovnosluzhiteli* are granted an official working contract and receive a declared salary; others are paid or otherwise compensated according to various, often strictly local arrangements; others work on a totally benevolent basis. Among the *tserkovnosluzhiteli* are psalm chanters and choir singers, helpers at the altar, church stall sellers, lay parish elders, bookkeepers, church school teachers, (female) cleaners, and yet others who hold more or less stable positions in the parishes. In addition, there are a number of what we might call 'activists'. These people work more generally on behalf of the church, taking up various tasks and responsibilities as they emerge. Some such people are the heads of the lay parish council, also called

---

[11] The common word for a priest of any rank is *sviashchennik*, and it is usual to hear people refer to a priest affectionately as *batiushka*.

parish elders (*starosty*), or its members, but not always; some are just committed churchgoers. Beyond the kinds of people who 'work' for the church, there are also those categories that are more often mentioned: active and less active churchgoers; occasional visitors, and outsiders who nonetheless participate in church life in one way or another. In the subsequent chapters, I show how street-level Orthodoxy is populated by low-rank parish clergymen and heads of parishes, former construction workers at a church rebuilding site, church bookkeepers and parish elders, stall sellers, librarians, choir directors and choir singers, gatekeepers and cleaners, pilgrimage organizers, parish school teachers and lower-task school workers, devoted parishioners, casual droppers-in, as well as beggars, common and less noticeable groups of the needy.

Finally, street-level Orthodoxy defines a heterogeneous physical area. According to common sense, the church stands as a central element of parish Orthodoxy. But if this material centre is a matter of common agreement, the official regulations do not define its territorial boundaries. Moreover, inside the church and in its surroundings, there are many limits and transitional spaces. There are various physically circumscribed 'insides' – inside the church, but also inside the parish school, inside an adjacent building used by the clergy and laity for mundane purposes, inside the churchyard, inside a church shop, even inside a bus rented for a pilgrimage. There are various 'outsides' too. There are thresholds, doors, and porches separating the church from the churchyard; and gates that separate the yard from the street. Some types of people, most noticeably beggars, are restricted to the 'outside' and experience regularly its expansions and contractions. The churchyard, a space on which the church radiates its monumental presence, expands and contracts. For example, during cross processions and in periods of higher attendance, such as the time around Easter and Christmas, the yard is assimilated with the 'inside' of the church. The presence of the church is, in some places, etched durably in the surroundings; the street in front of the main church of Ozerovo is called Sobornaia ulitsa (Cathedral Street). Street-level Orthodoxy is the locus of geographical edges and places of juncture between insides and outsides.

Street-Level Orthodoxy through the Lens of Inequality and Social Disruption

After 1991, deep inequalities took root in Russian society along the lines of income, wealth, status, gender, ethnicity, housing, geographical region – and all with interlocking aspects.[12] A quarter of a century later, reports noted that 'Russian society faces unprecedentedly high levels of income and wealth inequality, which is exacerbated by high levels of spatial and social inequality' (Oxfam 2014: 31). Oxfam further assessed that actually implemented state policies were unlikely to remedy the situation, and substantiated this assessment on the basis of rich statistical data. In fact, Oxfam's report only underscored what has long been part of common knowledge in Russia. The place that one occupies in relation to the market and to the political authority, and one's belonging to a specific category of the population, largely determine an individual's position within Russian society. This applies as well to disparities within the parishes and among them. Yet, 'inequality' has not been a popular word among Russians. Neither is it among the actors of parish life with whom I worked. Sociologist Olga Shevchenko argued that 'crisis' (*krizis*), in its cultural and pragmatic dimensions, proved more meaningful than 'inequality' (*neravenstvo*) when, back in the harsh 1990s, Russians saw rampant unemployment and the sharp decline of their income (Shevchenko 2009). The Muscovites among whom Shevchenko conducted research defined their household as the only island of stability. Their references of 'normal' and 'stable' configurations nevertheless underplayed gender divisions that were embedded in the functioning of the household (ibid. 90–101). Similarly, they preferred to speak of 'the people' (*narod*, ibid. 7), as if it were (or should have been) homogenous. They did not use terms that conveyed the perception of actually increasing inequalities. Rather, their expressions of desired unity overshadowed deeply rooted and culturally accepted forms of inequalities. My informants, as Shevchenko's, did not commonly speak of 'inequalities', 'disparities', 'differentiation', or even of 'social distress' or 'poverty'. They rather experience these phenomena as inbuilt simultaneously in the life of the churches and in the encompassing world.

The reinvigoration of parish life in the post-Soviet period took place in a context of overarching socio-economic and gender inequalities. Their widespread forms have become inbuilt in the ecclesiastical organization at the parish level. Overall, their examination has mostly remained peripheral to the study of post-Soviet Russian Orthodoxy. However, a few particularly stimulating anthropological studies have been conducted. For example, in

---

[12] Although inequalities along the lines of material well-being and status existed in the Soviet period (see McAuley 1979), Soviet Russia was far more homogenous than post-Soviet society. Sociological surveys conducted in the 1990s found that a large majority of Russians expected 'equality of material life' (Shlapentokh 1999: 1172) and social justice, while polarization was thriving, with the political elites disdainfully looking at popular ideas of equality (Shlapentokh 1999).

their research on the worshippers of Saint Xenia the Blessed, the most venerated saint in Saint Petersburg Region, anthropologists Jeanne Kormina and Sergey Shtyrkov (2011) interpreted the appeal of this saint to middle-aged and elderly women in relation to the women's social suffering. Kormina and Shtyrkov showed how through the veneration of Saint Xenia, ordinary women take recourse to Orthodoxy and turn the saint into an intimate ally from whom they expect help in their difficulties. Furthermore, in her studies of popular pilgrimages, Jeanne Kormina multiplied the examples of entanglements between social inequalities and Orthodoxy, all located at the edges of organizationally sanctioned practice (Kormina 2010, 2012). This approach directly resonates with my own interest in social disparities as embedded within a religion which, at the street-level, is highly dynamic and composite, and which evolves in the context of rigid official hierarchical structures.

Protestant Denominations and Social Distress: A Different View

The relation between Orthodoxy and socio-economic inequalities, analysed in the above-cited works, significantly differs from the one that anthropologists have found in Protestant movements within the former Soviet Union. Since the early 1990s, Protestant groups have evidenced concern with poverty and disenfranchisement. Immediately after the collapse of the Soviet regime, Protestant, mostly proselytizing movements, quickly put in place programmes for poverty relief. Most of them started converting new members, to whom the community of faithful provided support and social upgrading. Melissa Caldwell (2004), for example, addressed inequality through the lens of poverty in her study of a Protestant-run Moscow soup kitchen. In the second part of the 1990s, large numbers of the population were 'making do' with scarce material resources. Like most sociological studies of this period, Caldwell claimed that 'making do' required relationships, rather than material resources as such. Those who came for soup, thus valued even more the new relationships that could be built through the Protestant congregation and its outreach activities. Caldwell described specific groups of recipients: the elderly, who made up the majority, but also mothers of large families, disabled veterans and mentally ill persons. Progressively, Protestant faith-based organizations in Moscow moved their focus from poverty relief to various sorts of support; by the 2010s, practical collaborations between different faith-based organizations provided programmes including juridical advice and the defence of human rights (Caldwell 2017).

Protestant movements, above all proselytizing evangelicals, Pentecostals, and charismatics, have acquired a solid reputation for being more active in helping the needy, as well as for strongly supporting their own members. For the case of Protestant evangelical communities in Orthodox-dominated Ukraine, Catherine Wanner argued: 'In the face of a crumbling state social service sector, to the extent that they can, church communities attempt to provide a safety net of sorts for members' (Wanner 2009: 171). According to Wanner (ibid. 170), the success of Protestant movements in post-Soviet Ukraine can be explained largely by the ability of evangelical communities to address marginalization. Indeed, she documented the significance of female conversions to the growth of these communities. Elsewhere, Wanner wrote about the evangelical 'charitable impulse': 'Sometimes the plight of a single person or family becomes a cause célèbre and the entire congregation mounts an effort to help out' (Wanner 2007: 184–85). Elsewhere too, Protestant charismatics and evangelicals have deployed a variety of tools in order to address dislocation and economic disruptions: altruistic gifts among charismatics in Lithuania (Lankauskas 2009); support and friendship for women in Kazakhstan (Clark 2009) and for rural migrants in urban settings in Kyrgyzstan (Pelkmans 2009a).

Mathijs Pelkmans most clearly formulated the idea that Protestantism stands in contrast with mainstream religions in the post-Soviet region. Protestant communities provide not only the warmth of a community of fellow believers, but also practical tools, social networks, and suitable moral responses to the disruptions of the post-Soviet era. 'These movements', he wrote, 'were quick to jump on what they perceived to be the ripe fields of atheist rule; their plain and concrete answers to terrestrial problems often proved more attractive than Orthodox Christianity and mainstream Sunni Islam (in their various local forms)' (Pelkmans 2009b: 2). This assertion also resonates with a view, widespread in Russia in the 1990s and early 2000s, according to which the Orthodox Church should have helped the population, but that it refused to do so, being instead self-interested (Caldwell 2010). This view unwittingly replicates Max Weber's blatant opposition of historically established churches to Protestant sects (Loader and Alexander 1985; Weber 1985 [1906]). Weber pictured the old churches as nearly fossilized, entrenched in a tradition of Caesaropapism (Weber 1985 [1906]: 9), 'bound by the parochial fixation of their "office"' (ibid. 10), in contrast to the 'Protestant sects' that he painted as vehicles of modernity.[13] But, even if the ROC has always been concerned with tradition and the continuity of ritual, and even if it did not 'jump' to respond to the pressing material needs of the population, this does not mean that disruptions and inequalities have

---

[13] For a critical assessment of Weberian stereotypes in relation to Orthodox Christianity, see Makrides (2005); Hann (2007, 2014); Hann and Goltz (2010).

remained outside of the scope of Orthodoxy. Simply, disruptions and inequalities are embedded in Orthodoxy as it works on the ground. At the street-level, they are not primarily designated as social problems that the community of faithful should try to solve; they are above all integral to its functioning.

A Qualification

Here I need to make one qualification. A growing body of historical research claims that the Church did engage in charity work and social activism, in particular during the nineteenth and early twentieth centuries, in rural areas (Young 1996) as well as in Saint Petersburg (Kenworthy 2006; Kizenko 2006; Hedda 2008). The contemporary ROC has responded to its critics on the points of social distress and poverty, but I do not take up those responses in this work. I do not examine systematically ROC's official statements on social support because they had almost no impact in the parishes where I worked. Neither do I describe any of the formal projects or programmes run by the ROC because I did not encounter such initiatives in the field. Nevertheless, it is important to provide a cursory overview of the ROC's official position and programmes before continuing with an account of what was visible and tangible in my field site.

Within the ROC is the Synodal Department of Church Charity and Social Service. Through this department, and not only, the hierarchy of the ROC has issued several programmatic official documents focused on charity and social work. Declarations of top leaders also emphasize the need to develop social service. But, overall, issues of inequality and social disruption are not prioritized as official concerns. *The Basis of the Social Concept of the ROC*, a major document dealing with theological, ecclesiastic, and social issues does not express a clear position concerning socio-economic distress (ROC 2000) – a point I discuss more extensively in relation to almsgiving (chapter 7). The most comprehensive and ambitious document that approaches the subject, 'On the Principles of Organization of Social Work in the Russian Orthodox Church', was adopted in its final version on 4 February 2011 at the Council of Archbishops. In this document, the top hierarchs stated that social service (*sotsial'noe sluzhenie*), love, and mercy cannot be 'contained or limited by religious, national, state-political or social frames' and that service must be delivered also to those who do not belong to the Church. The document emphasizes the centrality of social service for the cultivation of Christian values, such as love, self-abnegation, and patience. It offers a comprehensive list of positions that Orthodox Christians can occupy in the exercise of social service. It stresses the need for close collaborations to be developed between the Church, civil servants, and experts, drawing such individuals to become members of the Church. Finally, it defines specific tasks for each level, from the Synodal Department of Church Charity and Social Service, through the eparchy and deanery, to the parish. The parish is expected, among other things, to hire a parish social worker on an official contract (*v shtate*), form groups of volunteers, list the needy parishioners (such as the elderly, sick and disabled, large families), collect resources and advertise its work in the public media, collaborate with social and medical staff from the secular sector, and educate children and youth.[14] This list of expectations stands out as overly ambitious.

In recent years, the official declarations have become more modest and focused on specific points. For instance, on 3 September 2015, at the Fifth All-Church Council on Social Ministry, Patriarch Kirill launched an appeal to the eparchies and parishes to make use of opportunities for providing social work offered to non-state organizations by the Federal Law on the Foundations of Social Service to the Citizens of the Russian Federation (entered into force on 1 January 2015). According to Patriarch Kirill's statement, the Church should develop organized social work on the basis of the already existing Orthodox volunteer networks. Among the specific issues identified as needing redress, the Patriarch called attention to sustainable anti-abortion work and intervention in alcohol addiction. Work with disabled persons should focus on making the churches accessible to them.[15]

According to data made available by the ROC in 2015, on the territory of the Russian Federation, the Church runs 70 drug rehabilitation centres, 72 centres for the homeless, 54 alcohol rehabilitation centres, and 232 centres that work with alcoholics and their relatives. There were more than 400 charity groups and more than 200 benevolent associations mostly helping families with children, all under the umbrella of the ROC.[16] Relatively little has been written about any of these initiatives. One study that does exist is that by Jarrett Zigon (2011a), who conducted fieldwork in a ROC-affiliated drug rehabilitation centre. Zigon argued that the ROC has become an active agent of neoliberalization in Russia because he found evidence that a neoliberal sense of individual responsibility was being promoted among the studied centre's rehabilitants. I doubt that this monolithic picture can accurately describe a Church that is so internally bewilderingly diverse. But Zigon's conclusions can be taken as evidence that different ways of looking

---

[14] http://www.patriarchia.ru/db/text/1401894.html, accessed on 14 May 2017.
[15] http://www.pravmir.ru/patriarh-kirill-nam-nuzhna-obshhetserkovnaya-blagotvoritelnost/, accessed on 19 June 2017.
[16] http://www.diaconia.ru/vicepremer-rossii-olga-golodec-vstretilas-s-uchastnikami-v-obshhecerkovnogo-sezda-po-socialnomu-sluzheniyu, accessed on 10 January 2017.

at the ROC bring to light very different facets of Orthodoxy and the Church as an organization.

The Structure of the Book

The seven chapters hereafter have been written at different stages after the completion of my main field research. In the first part of chapter 2, I introduce the field site and discuss aspects of methodology. In the second part, I bring into discussion the economic situation of the parishes, legal dispositions, and formal church decisions that led to the establishment of material inequality between the city's parish churches in the post-Soviet period. In chapters 3 and 4, I offer an ethnography of a local case of inter-parish differentiation. In chapter 3, I discuss the case of a rebuilt church and the ascetic motives that led to the creation of a specific parish identity; both continue to pervade local narratives about the city's churches. In chapter 4, I depict how the past hardship of this church became a cornerstone in the coexistence with the main local church, considered far more prosperous, and how these premises have given way to the promotion of a distinct connection to the divine in each of these two churches. In chapter 5, I concentrate on various uses and meanings of the church economy which make this vivid component of street-level Orthodoxy a sensitive arena on which different actors make statements about power, social stratification, equity, and honesty. In chapter 6, I discuss the role of laywomen in Orthodox parishes, with a special focus on low-level jobs in parish schooling. These women face the usual structural gender disadvantages of low payment, unstable jobs, and single motherhood, while simultaneously transforming the Orthodox school into their own spiritual enclave. Chapter 7 addresses the variety of ways in which clergymen craft ethical responses in day-to-day interactions with beggars, a conspicuous group of the indigent who are an inseparable part of street-level Orthodoxy. Chapter 8 presents an ethnography of parish grassroots charities open to everyone, where givers and recipients range from active parish members and church workers to people indifferent to religion.

I identify the city of my fieldwork with the pseudonym Ozerovo to maintain some confidentiality for my informants. I use pseudonyms for the city's three parishes too: Trinity, Saint George the Warrior, and Saint Michael the Archangel.

Chapter 2
Local Configurations Face the Instituted Rule of Unequal Churches

This chapter is organized in three sections. I first present the context in which I conducted ethnographic research, address aspects of methodology, and briefly outline the 'profane landscape' of the city. Then I turn to describing the past and present situation of the religious landscape in Ozerovo. The three main local parishes are perceived differently by Ozerovo's residents. Indeed they differ as to their history, geographical location, and degrees of material well-being. The latter aspect derives from past and present local configurations, and from specific parish choices. But there are also choices and policies that belong to the national level of both the post-Soviet state and the ROC. These choices and policies are crucial for understanding the ongoing inter-parish differentiation in Ozerovo, as on the level of the ROC as a whole. I introduce them in the last section.

Engaging the Field

While the ROC, headed by the Patriarchate of Moscow, is the most prominent religious organization in Russia, in fact it has long been a white spot on the map of contemporary ethnographic studies of post-Soviet religion. Thus, my choice to settle in an urban setting was determined by the objective to focus on mainstream Orthodoxy. Urban settings of European Russia have been central places of the Orthodox resurgence since the fall of the Soviet regime (Benovska-Sabkova et al. 2010). I chose a relatively small city in Saint Petersburg Region. I had a connection there through a Russian friend based in Paris whose aunt occasionally taught in the religious school belonging to the main local parish. This school became the gateway to the rest of my study (chapter 6). Some of the school teachers and school workers I met there have remained close acquaintances to this day; some of them and their family members visited me in Germany. In spite of the fact that personal and professional trajectories have shifted over time, some still work together in Ozerovo. Two of the parish rectors with whom I conducted interviews and conversed in a more casual way still occupy their position as I am writing. Sadly, a third rector has passed away; he was the youngest among Ozerovo's Orthodox rectors.

In the religious school where my research began, as in other places, my integration went overall smoothly. Here is the place to specify that I did not participate in communion, neither did I cross myself, light candles, kiss icons, order prayers or bathe in the holy springs during pilgrimages (which often raised the question, 'If you don't bathe, why did you come?' among pilgrims who did not know me in advance). I did observe the minimum dress code for women in church by wearing a skirt that covers the knees and a headscarf. I was fortunate to be accepted by most of my interlocutors without practising their religion. Teachers and workers from the parish school, parents with their children, and grandparents became my privileged interlocutors from the beginning. The priests and church workers of Ozerovo's main church, Trinity Church, let me spend as much time inside as I wanted making observations during feasts and on normal days. Spending time in an urban church to make observations did not raise problems in itself, given that more or less anonymous droppers-in make most of the daily visitors. Indeed, everyone can enter a church and stay inside, with the notable exception of beggars who are expected to remain outside (chapter 7). Observing anonymous people and overhearing conversations was fundamental. In addition, this freedom proved critical for collecting data, among other things, about the day-to-day operation of the church economy (chapter 5). Talking to occasional church visitors and family members of children who attended Sunday classes took me beyond the milieu of church workers and active members, and allowed me to learn about the ways Orthodoxy matters to people who may never be identified in statistical surveys as practising or belonging to the ROC in any structurally defined form.

I was also granted some extra freedoms. Here I have space to mention only a few of the friendly and fruitful relationships established in the field. For instance, during an Easter celebration in Trinity Church, I was the only one authorized by the rector to take pictures. This was an extraordinary privilege, since in this church as in most churches, using a camera is prohibited for all visitors, as a placard at the entrance usually announces. In the parish of Saint George the Warrior, I spent countless hours asking questions and making observations of what I call 'grassroots charities', thanks to the women who run them (chapter 8). The rector of Trinity Church allowed me access to part of the parish archive containing documents about the distribution of humanitarian aid which had taken place a few years earlier (chapter 8). The woman who acted as the Sunday school teacher of the smallest parish was immensely open and hospitable, as were many active members in each of the three parishes. Attending casual gatherings in these people's homes, and drinking tea in the parish school of Trinity Church and in the lower temple of the Church of Saint George the Warrior were moments of warm socializing. The main problem I encountered was in conducting interviews with clergymen themselves. Oftentimes, they are overloaded with work inside the church or have to pay visits outside. They had to organize their schedules in advance to have a bit more than a casual chat with me. They also had to make sure that we would not be interrupted, as they are constantly addressed for an impressive variety of managerial, pragmatic, and spiritual issues. I am grateful that many of them, including often the parish rectors, found time to answer my questions.

I made, however, a number of abrasive encounters, in particular when some people viewed me as an ambivalent foreigner. That I was born in Bulgaria and baptized in my early childhood in the Bulgarian Orthodox Church helped me open some doors, although I suspect that the people who were friendly knowing these aspects of my biography would have been so without such 'evidence' of my trustworthiness. In several cases, these biographical facts proved definitely insufficient for overcoming my putatively ambivalent status in local and church society. I was seen partly as a harmless person because of my Bulgarian name and origin, and because of my good command of the Russian language. But I also introduced myself as an ethnographer (and sometimes a sociologist if the situation required it) working for a German research institution, and having a long background in France. These biographical details made me immediately suspicious, and the fact that I was to stay in Ozerovo for one year added to that suspicion.

My Bulgarian and Orthodox credentials could work against me too. Once, a man who had begun to engage actively with Orthodoxy only recently asked me if my first name was the name of a saint canonized in the Bulgarian Orthodox Church. I replied that there was no such saint, but – sensing his building concern – explained that the name was recognized by the Bulgarian Church as an acceptable baptismal name. This answer backfired. With a great show of irritation, the man concluded that I was baptized in a heretical church. After all, the ROC requires baptismal names to be the names of saints or biblical figures. In an effort to resolve the situation, a woman who was listening in on our conversation told that there must be a Saint Detelina, but that I did not know of her. She was obviously more inclined to accept me than was the man; both centred their arguments, however, on my name and whether or not it was properly 'Orthodox'.

In a very limited number of cases, interlocutors saw me from the outset as an untrustworthy Westerner. Such persons suspected me of being a spy – an agent of Germany or another Western power preparing to destroy the ROC and their parish in particular. Once someone also questioned whether I might be a Jew – and then himself decided I was not.

Most of the time, perceived ambivalence of my origin and intentions continued into an ambivalent relationship. For example, in the beginning of my stay, two middle-aged brothers undergoing a process of 'in-churching' (*votserkovlenie*) were first nice and open to me. Soon after, they started accusing me of being sent by George Soros's Open Society Foundation, then by other Western foundations. These were outright accusations of, at best, being unfriendly towards Russia and receiving support from obscure financial powers. The two brothers decided to stop talking to me; they would pretend not to see me in the parish school and in the church, the two places where I usually met them. I did not insist on talking to them and passed my way. Finally, during the last six months of my stay, this ostracism progressively faded away, giving way to a joking but rather distant relationship. Nonetheless, though the brothers themselves remained distant, they introduced me to some of their friends who talked about their own work and daily lives very openly. I had wonderful conversations with the wife of one of these two brothers, especially about her first spiritual and physical experiences as a person who 'knew nothing about [her] own religion' and who, a few months earlier, had participated in a pilgrimage where she had to bathe in a hole made in the ice covering a lake. My relationship with this family encapsulated much of the ambivalence I experienced, between ostracism and friendly openness.

I was able to record on an electronic device about 30 interviews. When I felt or was explicitly told that recording was undesirable, I took notes, on the spot or at home at the end of the day. My fieldwork was conducted entirely in Russian. My attempt to use a questionnaire in order to conduct a survey on churchgoers' economic and charitable practices completely failed. I had the kind support of a man who acted as a psalm chanter and librarian in the parish where I wanted to conduct the questionnaire. But when submitted to the rector, to the head of the lay parish council, and to several other active parishioners, my proposed questionnaire was countered with reactions ranging from clear hostility to a kind of compassion for the victim of a naïve idea. I could intimately appreciate then what many of those who conducted field research in Russia had experienced before me. As Dorothy Weaver wrote, Soviet memories of oppression and surveillance have remained particularly vivid to this day. They make conditions in which a questionnaire is considered invasive, unpleasant, and a means of state (or foreign) surveillance, while informal interviews and observation are interpreted as the tools of the spy (Weaver 2011a). As many researchers, I had to walk a thin line and give up part of my initial ambitions.

Following my one-year stay between August 2006 and July 2007, I returned to Ozerovo for short visits in 2008, 2009, and 2010. Since then and until April 2013, I received some of my informant-friends in Germany. At the end of April 2013, I left Germany for France. Since then, my contacts have been through phone calls and emails.

Profane Landscapes

I have silenced on purpose some detail peripheral to the argument of this book that would have made the city easy to identify. Ozerovo is located in north-western Russia, in the Saint Petersburg Region. The housing in its vast majority is typically Soviet-styled apartment blocks, some made of brick (*kirpich*), others of pre-formed cement panels (known as *panel'ki*).

Ozerovo is within commuting distance of Saint Petersburg. Buses of the *marshrutka* type are frequent. Commuter trains (*elektrichki*) are frequent too and cheaper than the buses. Some of my interlocutors drew some pride from the fact that their city is 'almost a suburb' of Saint Petersburg. Others bemoaned their daily commute; they chose to stay simply because housing is much cheaper in Ozerovo. A visitor arriving in Ozerovo after having spent some time in downtown Saint Petersburg cannot help but find that the few well-refurbished façades of neoclassical style, much appreciated at the end of the imperial period, are not more than a pale reminder of the splendid buildings that pervade the central avenues of Russia's northern capital. The streets of Ozerovo are by far narrower than those of the nearby city, and grey Soviet-era buildings prevail. The striking visual contrast between the two neighbouring cities reminds the visitor to forego comparison; Saint Petersburg and Ozerovo are not cities of the same kind.

My attempts to find figures for the number of commuters or for local unemployment rates proved unsuccessful. Employees at City Hall straightforwardly told me that they themselves had no way of knowing how many people commute to Saint Petersburg for work. There were no instruments available to measure how many of Ozerovo's inhabitants work elsewhere. Similarly, the employment office was unable to deliver true figures of unemployment rates. The woman who received me there gave me the official estimation of one per cent of unemployment. She explained that most people who are looking for a job do not bother to register as unemployed; the benefits are so ridiculously low, that there is no incentive to register. Nor does the office serve as a resource in job hunting: only announcements for the worst jobs – the kinds of jobs that no one wants to take, she said – are posted there. This unavailability of figures is not a local peculiarity; it is rather a small illustration of the situation at the national level.

If the observer relies on visual appearances and the lack of trustworthy statistics, she may conclude that Ozerovo is an economically gloomy place. The truth, however, is that it is not economically depressed. Among other towns and cities in the region, Ozerovo is considered to be dynamic. It has a dozen or so industrial plants, most of which are the privatized heirs of Soviet industry. Two large construction companies, two big plants producing metallic and plastic elements, a bread factory, and a dairy plant are important employers. Small entrepreneurship is particularly dynamic, especially in the service sector. Food stores and mobile phone stores, restaurants, coffee shops, and hairdressing shops are what one sees in the street. There are also local offices of at least five national-level banks, insurance companies, travel agencies, small newspaper and advertisement companies, a local TV-channel, and small construction work enterprises.

Farming is another significant economic activity in the region. Agriculture and animal breeding became important sources of income by the end of the eighteenth century, when the nobility, by then well-established in Saint Petersburg, started to push into the countryside for their recreational outings and to build large manors and palaces. The lifestyle of the nobles increased the market demand for dairy products, meat, fruits, and vegetables. Under Soviet rule, agricultural development continued in a radically different form – collectivized and state-run. Production significantly increased under Soviet rule. The relatively poor quality of the land and harsher climatic conditions meant that the region never reached the impressive production levels of southern Russia, with its black-earth soil (*chernozem*) and mild climate. Nevertheless, by the end of the Soviet period, several large state cooperatives encompassed a number of agricultural activities, such as growing cabbage, carrots, and potatoes. Chicken and pig breeding were also developed. A particularly large pig-breeding farm in one of the region's villages supplied the needs of much of north-western Russia. These socialist enterprises were dismantled or privatized during the Yeltsin period (1991–99). Since privatization, farming has continued on a smaller scale. Around Ozerovo, there are now two relatively large agricultural enterprises coupled with limited and small-scale private commercial farming.

Among my acquaintances, there was one family with two children that tried to make a living from producing and selling agricultural produce. They grew carrots, cabbage, and potatoes on large plots that they rented. They had entered agriculture as part of the conservative Orthodox lifestyle that they had recently embraced. But their engagement with agriculture makes them a notable exception. Most people simply buy the food they consume. Nevertheless, gardening is not uncommon. Some of my acquaintances, both those who engaged with the church and those who stayed aloof from church life, work a small plot of land around their modest summer house (*dacha*) in the vicinity of the city. This domestic production is valued for its higher quality, but it does not provide primary subsistence.

Local inhabitants consider Ozerovo as a rather privileged place in terms of the availability of good primary and secondary education. The city boasts some 15 state-operated kindergartens and 10 elementary schools and high schools. Private education has progressively emerged since approximately 2005, with the opening of one private kindergarten and later three private schools that have a reputation for offering good education and excellent material conditions to the pupils. The most prestigious school, combining primary and secondary education is, however, a state school that was created in the late nineteenth century. Over the past 15 years, this school has eagerly endorsed an Orthodox orientation, with a chapel functioning inside the building.

The city is run by a head of the city (*glava goroda*), elected by the 33 members of the city council (*sovet deputatov*), who are themselves directly elected by the population. Another important character in local politics is the head of administration (*glava administratsii*), whose nomination needs the approval of the city council. The United Russia Party has been the ruling political force in the city since the party's formation in 2001. A small but noticeable group of elderly members of the still existing Communist Party regularly celebrate important dates by gathering around Lenin's statue in the city centre. The most active civil type of organization is the Society of Friends of the Park who organize cleaning weekends and take care of the trees. The cinema and theatre hall organize events on an almost weekly basis.

Religious and Ethnic Diversity

In addition to the churches belonging to the ROC, introduced at the end of this section, Ozerovo also has a Lutheran church (*kirkha*). Lutheran Protestantism was the religion of most local Estonians[17] and Ingrian (Ingermanlandian) Finns, and that of some local Germans. Before the 1917 Revolution, the Estonians outnumbered by far the two other ethnic groups in

---

[17] Estonia became an independent state from Russia for the first time in 1918. The Estonian language was first codified at the end of the nineteenth century, with the beginning of the so-called national awakening. Therefore, being Estonian before this period should be understood in terms of linguistic identity and as belonging to the 'country people' (*maarahvas* in Estonian).

parish membership. Since 1994, the church has belonged to the Evangelical-Lutheran Church of Ingria, an officially registered religious organization, treated by the political authorities as among those constituting the 'traditional' religions of the Russian Federation.[18]

The existence of a Lutheran parish in Ozerovo has been attested since the end of the eighteenth century. But today's stone church, able to host more than 200 visitors, was built only in the beginning of the nineteenth century. Local inhabitants consider it one of the city's most beautiful buildings. It was closed under Stalin's anti-religious repressions in the 1930s and heavily damaged during the Second Word War. After the war, it was thoroughly renovated and reopened as a sports school. Some of my informants had attended the school ignorant of the building's previous religious function.

Not all ethnic Estonians were Protestant in the pre-Soviet period. Russian Orthodox Estonians were also a significant group. Trinity Church, Ozerovo's central church since 1852, employed from 1897 a priest and a psalm chanter (*psalomshchik*) to conduct religious services in the Estonian language. And a smaller Estonian Russian Orthodox church was erected around 1907.

This smaller church was closed in 1938 during a wave of violent religious repression. Two successive rectors of the church were sentenced to death and killed. The closed building burned during the Second World War, definitively ending the life of the parish community, and erasing any sign of the Estonian Orthodox community until around 2000. After 2000, activists from Trinity Church, with the support of self-trained local historians (*kraevedy*), initiated archival research to make publicly available information about pre-Soviet Orthodoxy in Ozerovo. The results are a few books and a well-furnished website. Nevertheless, Ozerovo's historical Estonian communities, both Protestant and Orthodox, have little impact on the contemporary city. It is the Finns who are felt to still be present.

Ozerovo is located on territory that was long disputed between Sweden and Russia. In 1702, at the beginning of Peter the Great's Great War of the North, this territory was included into the possessions of the Russian Empire. Russification followed. Before Peter the Great's initiatives, the local country people were mostly Ingrian (or Ingermanlandian) Finns. The local ethnic Estonians were, in Russian eyes, roughly the same as the Ingrian Finns. Some of my informants claimed that their elderly parents and grandparents where still able to speak the local version of Finnish. But I myself never met an actual speaker, including in villages surrounding

---

[18] The Law on the Freedom of Conscience and Religious Association adopted in 1997 mentions explicitly four 'religious traditions': Christianity, Islam, Judaism, and Buddhism.

Ozerovo. The contemporary names of some villages are said to be derived from earlier Finnish names. Finland is now considered a relatively accessible country; it is easy for Russian citizens in Ozerovo to acquire a visa to Finland and – because Finland takes part in the Schengen Agreement – to the rest of Europe. In contrast, Estonia, which is only a few kilometres and accessible by bus, feels like the real 'abroad'. Political animosity between the Russian and Estonian states since the fall of the Soviet Union, and the subsequent independence of Estonia, engendered a strong sense of separation and loss, despite the geographical proximity of Ozerovo's inhabitants to the Estonian border (Tocheva 2009).

Roman Catholics were also present in Ozerovo since the eighteenth century, although they were a small minority. A church was erected in the beginning of the twentieth century. It had a short life: closed in the 1930s as a result of Soviet repression, the building was left in ruins after the Second World War. Post-Soviet attempts to renovate it have been rather unsuccessful so far. However, a small community of around 20 faithful attends Sunday services held in a house near the former church building.

Ozerovo also boasts new religious denominations and congregations. Once I visited an American-sponsored Protestant evangelical church, located in a private apartment. The Russian pastor and his wife, who spoke no other language than their native Russian, told me about their efforts to support and convert impoverished people in Ozerovo. Entirely funded by its American mother church, the local congregation was very recent and totally invisible from the outside. I found it through the recommendation of an elderly woman who used to clean occasionally at Trinity Church. She herself had converted to the new church, and offered to bring me to this 'Christian church that helps the needy' (chapter 6). These evangelicals went unnoticed in public space. They preferred to keep a low profile because of the prevailing atmosphere of politically-driven campaigns of suspicion against 'imported' religious movements; many new churches were accused publicly of extracting money from Russians.

Only once did I meet with Jehovah's Witnesses, and then in the persons of two middle-aged women who were selling *The Watchtower* journal. They were selling on the street, but away from the main streets of the city. When I bought the journal, I was invited to join a meeting on the next Sunday morning. I asked in turn if their attempts to attract new adherents were met with success, and they confessed that attendance at their Sunday meetings was rather low.

Jews, Muslims, and Buddhists were totally absent from the visible religious landscape of Ozerovo. I occasionally saw people in the street who were probably from the Caucasus and Central Asia. They may have been of

Muslim origin, but I did not collect data from or about them. In Ozerovo, it is widely known that people from the Caucasus and Central Asia come to do construction work, but such workers do not integrate into the fabric of the city's social life.

Thriving Orthodoxy

Ozerovo has three main parishes. These are attended by local residents with extremely variable degrees of commitment and knowledge. All three parishes belong to the Ozerovo deanery (*blagochinie*). Trinity Church acts as the centre of this deanery which was comprised of 24 parishes at the time of my main field research (the 3 parishes that feature in this work, 18 parishes in nearby villages, and some 6 smaller chapels and churches under Trinity's direct supervision). Two of the chapels overseen by Trinity are in other institutions: one in the hospital and one in a school. The church's priest rector is also the priest-in-chief, or superintendent, of the deanery.

Plate 1. In the vicinity of the city.

Built in 1852, Trinity Church has remained open ever since, with the exception of a four-year closure during the Second World War. It is located at the top of Ozerovo's main pedestrian street. Its visibility and almost continuous operation mean that the church is well known to local inhabitants. Indeed, it is the most visited of all local churches, and accordingly has the largest staff. Trinity employs about forty people, but only six (mainly priests) work full-time on proper contracts.

Church attendance grew rapidly in the 1990s. When I conducted my field research, churchgoers and above all less observant droppers-in were no longer a deviant minority among urban Russians. The local churches were actively visited on days of major religious celebrations. Trinity Church claimed between 500 and 600 regular parishioners, counting as 'regular' those people who come to church at least once every three weeks.[19] Since there is no parish register – only a few parishes have introduced this practice in recent years based on their own initiative – it is impossible to check these figures. In the absence of official parish membership, the status of parishioners is conferred only orally and flexibly, by the clergy and by fellow churchgoers.

Plate 2. Easter cakes awaiting the priest's blessing.

---

[19] The standard of 'regular' attendance of once every two or three weeks appears to be shared between churches. The most committed churchgoers refuse to consider occasional visitors as parishioners or churchgoers (*prikhozhane*) and dismiss them as 'passers-by' (*zakhozhane* or, less commonly, *prokhozhane*).

The number of occasional visitors to Trinity Church is difficult to estimate. According to the priests, during important feasts up to 4,000 visitors attend per day. The most active churchgoers whom I met are former and current factory workers, medical staff, teachers, bookkeepers, administrative staff; a few graduated from higher education and about one-fourth are retired. Unlike in rural areas where elderly churchgoers are overrepresented (Sibireva 2009a), the urban churches in which I worked attract mostly middle-aged and younger active members and occasional visitors. I also noticed that, among the daily visitors, there is an equal number of women and men. This is a noticeable difference in comparison with the observations of higher female attendance reported by most sociological studies. This is also a noticeable difference in comparison with the late Soviet times, in terms of both gender and age. The Soviet surveillance of church attendance made it easier for elderly women to go to church and more difficult for men and younger women who were in priority enrolled as members of the Communist Party or of its branch for youth, the Komsomol.

Plate 3. Offerings of eggs for Easter.

The second largest church, Saint George the Warrior, is located within a five-minute walk from Trinity. Though it rivals Trinity in historical importance and claims an equal number of parishioners, Saint George the Warrior has only three priests and one deacon who are employed full-time. The church's reconstruction has figured prominently in the construction of local identity in the early post-Soviet period. Even people who never go to church or are openly opposed to religion, know and respect the church's recent achievements (see chapter 3). Originally opened in 1914, the church was closed in the early 1930s after the priests refused to collaborate with the Soviet state. It reopened in 1991 and remained under reconstruction for more than ten years. Like Trinity, the parish today counts some 500–600 parishioners. An impressive number of people attend the church for important religious feasts, including people who otherwise do not go to church, or only do so occasionally. But the casual daily visitors are far fewer than at Trinity. Saint George the Warrior is not as centrally located, and it is open only a few hours per day on a few days of the week. As I detail in the following chapters, Saint George the Warrior has taken on the identity of a 'true' religious community in opposition to Trinity in many ways.

The smallest parish, Saint Michael the Archangel, is located in a distant neighbourhood which was a separate village until the early Soviet period. This parish had around 200 regulars. It is open only on Sundays and for some important feasts, and therefore I collected less material there.

In the overall life of the city, Trinity and Saint George are recognized as making an important contribution. Their relative identities, roles, and importance are, however, agreed upon by people of all levels of religiosity and practice. Some of the reasons for these locally shared and taken-for-granted distinctions between the churches need to be located in their general orientations, and in encompassing legal and canonical positions. Hereafter, I provide basic information about the circumstances that made economic inequality between individual churches become an instituted norm. By presenting this situation from the outset, I aim to spotlight the background against which street-level Orthodoxy has unfolded before I address the street-level itself more extensively in the rest of this book.

The Instituted Rule of an Unequal Church

The number of parishes in Russia has grown dramatically since 1991. The importance of local churches is still growing in urban and rural Russia. This process finds no precedent in Russian history. In 1914, the number of parishes was estimated at 40,000. There were fewer than 500 in the first years of the Second World War (Bremer 2013: 88).[20] By 1988, there were fewer than 7,000 parishes on the territory of the whole Soviet Union. This same year saw the celebration of the Millennium of Christianity (also referred to as the Millennium of the Baptism of Rus'), which marked the beginning of the so-called Orthodox rebirth, even though openly pro-Orthodox policies were launched only in the early 1990s, following the collapse of the Soviet Union.

In the span of two decades, Russia nearly regained the number of parishes recorded prior to the revolution. According to an official Church report, there were 35,496 parishes by the beginning of 2015.[21] A new impulse was given to church construction directly from the top by Patriarch Alexii II (1990–2008), and especially by his successor Kirill. During a meeting of the hierarchs of the ROC, held in February 2015, Patriarch Kirill emphasized that one of the most central tasks of the Church was to build new churches and to contribute to a more dynamic parish life, with the integration of new members as a key mission.[22] The magnitude of the phenomenon and the continuing encouragement from above are incontestable. But equally incontestable is the fact that the post-Soviet Orthodox resurgence has taken place against the background of officially instituted economic inequality for the parishes. Market success and the availability of influential connections have become absolutely instrumental to the material well-being of every single parish, thus making inter-parish differentiation a normal feature of the ROC.

Political Choices

Since the early 1990s, the ROC has developed a complex economy at the parish level. Commerce in goods and rituals has been flourishing. TV channels and other media advertise requests for contributions to church (re-)construction and wealthy entrepreneurs make large donations with a political intent (Köllner 2011). Politics have played a prominent role in this process of resurgence (Bourdeaux 1995; Agadjanian and Rousselet 2005; Knox 2005), even though the agendas of the ROC and the state do not coincide (Richters 2013) and, legally, the Church has remained divided from the state

---

[20] In 1943, by the end of the darkest period of Stalinist purges against the clergy, all monastic and educational institutions were closed and 'only 500 out of the 50,000 churches in the country were utilized' (Bremer 2013: 29).

[21] See Patriarch Kirill's report: http://www.patriarchia.ru/db/text/3979067.html, accessed on 24 February 2015.

[22] Meeting of the Archbishops on 2 February 2015. http://www.patriarchia.ru/db/text/3977933.html, accessed on 20 June 2017.

since 1918.[23] Presidents Putin (2000–08, 2012– present) and Medvedev (2008–12) did much to facilitate 'the rebirth of Orthodoxy', not least regarding the church economy. A key aspect of state policy is treating church money as a donation (*pozhertvovanie*) free from income tax, including all income from goods and rituals for religious use, which comprises virtually everything. The ROC has become the largest real estate owner in the Russian Federation since the Law on the Transfer to the Religious Organizations of Property of Religious Significance under State or Municipal Ownership came into force on 3 December 2010.[24]

But these supportive policies have by no means resulted in an overall church prosperity. To the contrary, stunning inequalities are found especially at the parish level. Key to the post-Soviet disparities among the parishes is the rule according to which every parish is an economic unit that must provide for itself. Unequal access to resources from trade, paid-for rituals and services, donations from supporters, and good connections to influential political and economic leaders engender deep economic divisions. The hierarchs have not supported models for a top-down redistribution of resources; their commitment of material support to local parishes is limited to the provision of basic liturgical materials. Moreover, the legal separation between Church and State, established since 1918, means that the state does not directly contribute to the financial solvency of the ROC. The adoption of tithing as a solution that would allow parishes to guarantee that they could provide salaries and meet other basic needs of their clergy is largely considered unrealistic.[25]

Historical Legacies

This situation of almost complete reliance on church trade, paid-for services, and donations is not entirely new. In pre-Soviet times, in addition to payments and emoluments, the land allocated to every parish guaranteed clergymen's families a baseline of subsistence. For centuries, the unequal material circumstances between Russia's parishes were considered a serious problem by the state and by Church hierarchs. Especially in the eighteenth and nineteenth centuries, clerical poverty and the problematic upkeep of

---

[23] An opinion poll of the Levada Center for the study of public opinion revealed a prevalent view that the strong relationship between Church and State is desirable and necessary. http://www.levada.ru/11-10-2012/rossiyane-o-religii-i-tserkvi, accessed on 20 June 2017.

[24] http://www.rg.ru/2010/12/03/tserkovnoedobro-dok.html, accessed on 20 June 2017.

[25] Similar claims belong to a romantic view of a desirable return to largely imagined pre-Soviet conditions. Vsevolod Chaplin, a former high-rank church official, supported the idea of collecting the tithe. http://www.gazeta.ru/social/news/2012/05/05/n_2328409.shtml, accessed on 20 June 2017.

church buildings were at the centre of several reforms. In 1765, for example, the state intervened by fixing the tariffs for rituals, with the objective of avoiding additional emoluments from parishioners (Freeze 1983: 54–56). During the nineteenth century, in spite of numerous debates among state and Church officials, attempted reforms related to the introduction of state subsidies, stable salaries instead of the customary gratitudes, and the reduction of the number of parishes gave less than the expected results (Freeze 1983: 65–101; Chulos 2003; Shevzov 2004; Bremer 2013: 78). Various regulations were issued. A reform introduced by the Holy Synod in 1864 stipulated that a parish council (*prikhodskoe popechitel'stvo*) had to be created in every parish across the canonical territory of the ROC to address clerical poverty, among other issues. In many localities, this reform was met with resistance by villagers who wished to continue using their customary ways of provisioning for the church and the clergy (Chulos 2003: 56–57). In other rural settings, most of the collected funds went to church renovation and upkeep (Young 1996). A new disposition was introduced in 1905 imposing a new reform whereby 'an array of grass-roots organizations of the faithful' (ibid. 56) had to take care of all material aspects; this new disposition did not solve the fundamental problem of clerical and overall parish poverty. In spite of the numerous attempts to address this issue, most often only meagre salaries were allocated to the priests by the diocesan authority. These salaries were then supplemented with money and goods in kind by the parish community, and with small contributions from the state.[26] Generally, most rural priests did agricultural work in order to provide for themselves and their families (Freeze 1983: 52–101; Bremer 2013: 78). Overall, on the eve of the Bolshevik Revolution, the economy of the ROC's parishes was best defined in terms of the 'kaleidoscopic diversity' (Freeze 1983: 51), characteristic of earlier times as well.[27] During the Bolshevik Revolution, a church council was held in 1917–18 that, among other reforms, entirely revised the Statute of the Parish. The parish was given full autonomy from the secular state authority. The council negotiated for financial support from the Soviet state, but failed to achieve it. As a result, the resources of the Church in general, and that of the parishes in particular, became legally independent from the state budget and at the same time the Church gained organizational independence. These dispositions have remained unchanged in post-Soviet Russia (Agadjanian 2011: 17–18).

---

[26] This combination of various kinds of income did not prevent some parish priests from facing dire economic circumstances, typically in poorer areas (Freeze 1983).

[27] About why this situation was unique in comparison with Western Christian churches, see Freeze (1983: 62–65).

Self-Provisioning Parishes

Material inequalities have remained a steady characteristic of the post-Soviet parishes. The novelty of parish inequalities in the post-Soviet period stems from the relative absence of regulations by Church or state. During the period when I conducted fieldwork, there were yet no regulations that would guarantee a basic income for parish clergymen or for the sustenance of their churches.[28] It is only recently that the idea of controlling the material conditions of the parish clergy and church workers has received official support from the top hierarchs of the Church. In 2013, the Council of Archbishops adopted a statement about the material and social support to be provided to 'servants of the sacred', church servants, workers in the religious organizations affiliated with the Russian Orthodox Church, and members of their families. Their statement recommends creating commissions at the level of the eparchy to identify problems and find solutions. For example, the commission should find ways of providing support to clergy and church workers living under the state-defined subsistence minimum, and guarantee income to the family members of clergymen and church workers who are deceased or temporarily unable to serve. The document also formulates an expectation that the parish rectors should prevent substantial differences from arising between the salaries of parish priests, and that the rectors should provide adequate official payment for other positions, such as parish bookkeepers and choir directors, taking levels of education into account. The priests heading a deanery should report to the eparchy about the payments provided to their clergy and workers.[29] These dispositions, however, do not imply that the Church hierarchy has taken any further control over the kinds and levels of various material resources available to a parish or over the overall parish incomes; neither are there guidelines for preventing clerical and church workers from entering poverty in the first place. Other Church regulations stipulate that it is the parish members who are obliged to provide for their clerics and for the upkeep of their church.[30] Still, there is no official parish affiliation; lay parish membership takes place only on a voluntary basis. There are no registers of church members (see also Agadjanian 2011: 27–28).[31]

---

[28] The clergy is entitled to a minimal old-age pension, provided by the state to everyone who has reached retirement age. During my fieldwork, I found that in Saint Petersburg Region, the parish usually adds an extra pension, the size of which varies from one parish to another.

[29] http://www.patriarchia.ru/db/text/2775729.html, accessed on 12 August 2017.

[30] This 'obligation' of the laity is specified in point 3.33 of the Statute of the Parish. http://www.patriarchia.ru/db/text/133141.html, accessed on 5 April 2017.

[31] http://www.patriarchia.ru/db/text/133141.html, accessed on 5 April 2017.

As I mentioned in the introduction, in pre-Soviet times, parish membership was defined on the territorial principle. All births, marriages, and deaths of 'Russian Orthodox' individuals (as defined by the state) were recorded in the parish that coincided with their place of residence. Such individuals were considered as members of their local parish, whether or not they attended church with any regularity or sincerity. The Statute of the Parish adopted in 2000 no longer relies on a territorial principle. But it also introduces no other way of recording membership. The absence of formal criteria for membership makes the Statute's expectation of members' support for their parish churches and clergy merely declarative. Control over the real contributions made by lay 'parish members', a particularly elusive category, is now practically impossible. Under such conditions, parishes must rely on church commerce and the ability to attract wealthy supporters as the absolute prerequisites to their material well-being.

In the post-Soviet ROC, material resources move from the bottom to the top. In addition to its own provisioning, every parish (*prikhod*), through the intermediary of the deanery (*blagochinie*), hands over part of its income from commerce and donations to the eparchy, or diocese (*eparkhia*), which in turn is directly accountable to the Patriarch and the Holy Synod. The diocesan bishop defines the tax that each parish pays through the deanery. After important amendments of the Statute of the Russian Orthodox Church in 2008 and later in 2011 under Patriarch Kirill's ruling, the tax burden on the parishes has increased significantly. This new situation derives directly from the Patriarch's attempt to strengthen his own and the Holy Synod's power over the two lower levels of the Church (the eparchies and the parishes), as well as over the monasteries, educational institutions, and all other canonical units.[32] This parallels the political trend to 'strengthen the vertical of power' initiated by President Putin (Rousselet 2013b: 17–20). The reformed Statute of the Parish has put more power in the hands of the parish priest, especially the rector (*nastoiatel'*), at the expense of the parish lay council and the founders of the community, and has simultaneously accentuated the power of the bishop to control and intervene in parish and deanery life. The latter developments mean that if more power and control are exercised from the upper hierarchy upon the parish, in contrast, resources irremediably move from the lowest territorial level to the top.

---

[32] https://mospat.ru/en/documents/ustav/xiv/, https://mospat.ru/en/documents/ustav/xiii/, and https://mospat.ru/en/documents/ustav/xviii/, accessed on 20 June 2017.

Plate 4. The popular forms of Orthodox pilgrimage most often respond to a quest for divine grace and offer affordable recreational outings.

Geographical location plays a significant role for the relative well-being of the parishes. It is not unusual to see young enthusiastic priests, who just graduated from the seminary, leave the big urban centre where they were trained in order to join a modest parish in a remote locality. It is not unusual either to see them, a couple of years later, exhausted from the lack of resources for their parish and from hard living conditions for themselves and their families (often with children born in the meantime), searching for opportunities to go back to a big city with more prosperous parishes. Trying to keep up with the law of the market, small churches in remote places strive to establish themselves as pilgrimage destinations. Usually, they advertise a 'holy spring', a local saint, a well-known *starets* (spiritual counsellor or elder, who is not necessarily ordained), or simply the beauty of the surrounding landscape. Some are relatively successful in attracting visitors, others much less so.

Plate 5. Pilgrims waiting their turn to bathe in a holy spring nearby Pskov.

The instituted model of self-sustained parishes and the absence of levelling mechanisms have spurred controversies within the Church. Clergymen who disapprove of it have claimed that this mode of economic provisioning encourages priests to approach the parish as a 'franchise' under the label of the Russian Orthodox Church. Their concern becomes a business-oriented one instead of a spiritual one, as they seek ways to provide for themselves and for the bishops above them, these priests claimed.[33]

Stratified Orthodoxy

Besides marked inter-parish differentiation in the post-Soviet ROC, socio-economic inequalities characteristic of Russian society have translated clearly into distinctive uses of Orthodoxy. Part of the top clergy caters for the economic and political elite. Wealthy businessmen have their 'private' confessors to whom they make donations; top political leaders have their own spiritual advisors. The companies organizing pilgrimages offer another example of stratification. Cheap pilgrimages, massively advertised and typically using old buses as transport, which – I can confirm based on my

---

[33] See http://www.portal-credo.ru/site/?act=news&id=116006, accessed on 20 June 2017.

own experience – often break on the road, offer simultaneously a connection to the divine and 'economy class tourism' (Kormina 2012: 218–19, 37 ff.). They have little in common with the expensive pilgrimages taken by pious well-to-do people to prestigious destinations, including abroad.[34] Even some saints 'specialize'. Jeanne Kormina and Sergey Shtyrkov (2011) have shown that among the faithful who worship Saint Xenia of Petersburg, women, especially singles, elderly, and needy are overrepresented. In all these respects and probably many others, one's position in society determines one's access to specific church services, activities, and goods. And yet, the relationship between Russia's citizens and their religious life at the parish and street level should not be reduced by viewing it only through the prism of socio-economic and gender inequalities.

In the following chapters, I attempt to maintain a sense of the complexity of 'religious life' while examining several arenas of disparity that are constitutive to the life of ordinary parishes. In the following chapters, I use the case of Ozerovo to address several topics: early post-Soviet church reconstruction and further inter-parish differentiation; the church economy; the role of laywomen as parish school workers; the relation of priests to beggars; and informal grassroots charities.

---

[34] Mount Atos in Greece and Bari in Italy (where the relics of Saint Nicolas of Myra are kept), are among the prestigious destinations. See also Kormina (2012: 212).

Chapter 3
Rebuilding the Church: A Key Moment in the Shaping of Street-Level Orthodoxy

An overall reinvigoration of church life was one of the expressions of the 'rebirth of Orthodoxy' (*vozrozhdenie pravoslavia*) during the early post-Soviet period. In a large number of cases, this reinvigoration began with the reconstruction of old churches and the erection of new ones. Socio-economic differentiation marked this process from the very beginning. On one side, there were spontaneous initiatives of church (re-)building by local enthusiasts who had only scant resources at their disposal (Kormina and Shtyrkov 2015: 37–41). On the other side, churches were rapidly erected thanks to generous donations made by businessmen, often with a political intent (Köllner 2012). These two contrasting models of church construction were given distinct moral assessments. Churches built with money donated by rich businessmen were said to be 'built with gold', while churches built with benevolent volunteer labour were 'built with tears' (Köllner 2011). Another form of distinction in status also marked this period of resurgence. Older churches that had operated continually under Soviet rule consolidated their established local position. The newly opened and reopened churches, however, struggled to sustain themselves. In the case of Saint George the Warrior, discussed below, such economic difficulties were seen as the continuation of the material hardship encountered during rebuilding. These dire circumstances, rather than being perceived as petty parochial concerns, had a strong impact on the formation of groups of committed churchgoers, and were met with great empathy at the local level.

The stunning mushrooming of Orthodox churches in the early post-Soviet period and the programmatic initiatives of the Patriarchate of Moscow since 2015 to establish churches 'within walking distance' (*v shagavoi dostupnosti*) in Russia's cities and towns[35], can be approached as

---

[35] The plan for massive church construction initiated by top leaders of the ROC in 2015 has sparked controversies. Civil protests have risen around the goals of Programme 200 to erect 200 new churches in Moscow. See http://www.portal-credo.ru/site/?act=news&id=112120,

the most recent developments in a centuries-long turbulent history of church construction. Indeed, since the beginnings of Christianization in Russia during the tenth century, church construction has been a central issue. The way to new constructions was often difficult and even controversial. For instance, in the nineteenth century, the parish 'temple of God' (*khram bozhii*) was seen as the sacred centre of communal spiritual life in rural areas. Initiatives to build churches often came from the peasant laity, but to secure permissions they had to advance to the Church authority the reasons why they 'needed' a church and explain how they planned to provide basic income to sustain their parish clergy (Shevzov 2004: 59–62). Church construction was rarely a simple endeavour. As Chris Chulos wrote about the late nineteenth-century peasant communities in Voronezh Province: 'For all but the largest and wealthiest villages, the erection of a new parish church required blood, sweat, and tears of fund-raising activities, debates about the use of communal resources, and years of perseverance' (Chulos 2003: 62). In contrast, some landlords built churches for the peasants as a gift to the village. Sometimes the villagers refused to use these churches for various reasons, and instead struggled to erect their own temple (ibid. 63).

Even though the pre-Soviet tensions around church construction partly resonate with the contemporary controversial atmosphere, the process of church construction in post-1991 Russia bears some genuinely new features. In this chapter, I depict the unprecedented way in which, in Ozerovo, national dynamics of postsocialist market capitalism, deepening social differentiation, and an overall post-atheist expansion of the ROC have combined to shape the making of local Orthodoxy. This combination of processes also contributed to the formation of core groups of parishioners and had a crucial outreach beyond the circles of churchgoers. It also defined the terms of the relationship between neighbouring churches.

In short, church (re)construction is not merely the outcome of revival. It is, instead, one of the most lively expressions of personal and collective engagement with Orthodoxy. Construction itself is an important phenomenon in the shaping of street-level Orthodoxy.

Accordingly, this chapter presents an ethnography of the rebuilding of Saint George the Warrior. Firstly, I describe how devotion to the common endeavour of reconstruction served as a vehicle through which participants

---

accessed on 21 June 2017. In other large cities too, local dwellers opposed church construction. About the controversies of church construction in Saint Petersburg, see http://www.portal-credo.ru/site/?act=news&id=112153, accessed on 21 June 2017. Most protests have occurred in instances when the projected church constructions are to be on the territory of public parks and urban green areas. In some cases, there were violent clashes between pro-Orthodox paramilitary groups and protesting citizens. In several cases, the army was sent to protect the construction.

'discovered' Orthodoxy and through which the parish community emerged. Started in the mid-1990s, reconstruction became key to the shaping of an ascetic parish identity. The asceticism of the community at the Church of Saint George the Warrior elicited sympathy beyond church circles too, and the church's reconstruction is now among the stories told by Ozerovo's inhabitants about their city. Quite unintentionally, the church's reconstruction has been transformed into a marker of local identity and a part of memory.

An Enthusiastic Church Rebuilding

In numerous cases of post-Soviet church (re)construction, the main motivation for restoring religious materiality was and continues to be the desire to give life to something that is seen as genuinely Russian (Kormina and Shtyrkov 2015). A similar motivation is found in Ozerovo too, as Orthodoxy is largely perceived as a common heritage. But here I wish to underline another aspect. After the demise of the Soviet state, inter-parish disparities have resonated continuously with other disparities in the complex, rapidly changing Russian society. In the atmosphere surrounding a stunning outburst of economic inequality, parish insiders and outsiders who committed to rebuilding Saint George the Warrior shared a sense that moral elevation results from achievements realized with meagre material resources. The common value assigned to ascetic experiences has contributed to the fluidity of categories distinguishing churchgoers from non-churchgoers. The value is held by those who view themselves as parishioners and by those who, during reconstruction, 'simply came to work … directly from the street', as a former worker recalled. Acquisitiveness, as a counterpoint to asceticism, also defined the reconstruction process and contributes to the continuing ambivalence of inter-parish relations in Ozerovo to this day (chapter 4).

In 2006–07, most of the assiduous churchgoers at Saint George the Warrior had technical professions. There were manual workers and engineers, but also accountants, medical staff, and teachers.[36] These vocational groups were also the most affected by the economic collapse of the 1990s. Accordingly, the Church of Saint George the Warrior could be described as a middle-range urban parish.

The church has a unique history for Ozerovo, and is proud of it. The content of several booklets documenting its history are even available on the parish's web page. Sometime before the 1917 Revolution, the land on which

---

[36] This matches findings about the sociology of churchgoers in the 1990s by Kääriainen and Furman (2000).

the church is built had been donated by a rich merchant and his wife to establish an urban representation (*podvor'e*) of a convent located some 35 kilometres outside the city. When the same couple later won money in a lottery, they gave a significant part of it for the construction of a big church. The construction of the Church of Saint George the Warrior ended in 1914; the building was then consecrated and opened.

The church was closed in the 1930s and turned into a salt warehouse. For more than five decades, churchgoers told me, the salt attacked the wall paintings from inside, slowly and destructively. In 1990, the building was given back to the ROC. It reopened officially in 1991, thanks to a group of twenty persons who led its reconstruction.[37] A priest was appointed by the Church, but he showed little commitment to the reconstruction. Today, the reconstruction itself is described as difficult and uncertain: a long battle against a shortage of money and to recruit benevolent workers. The renovation lasted nearly ten years, and some of the participants were still the most important people in the parish. Some had started going to church at the beginning of perestroika, but many of them said they became engaged with Orthodoxy only during the reconstruction.

It was the *starosta*, then working as a school teacher, who initiated and coordinated the rebuilding.[38] His grandfather had been a clergyman, and he himself was already a practising Orthodox. Faith and the continuation of his family tradition were the basic motivations for him to engage in the reconstruction, he said.[39] When the reconstruction was coming to its end, he was given the honour and privilege of painting the altar.

The *starosta*'s wife, about thirty years old in the beginning of the 1990s, cooked a lunch every day for those who came to work. When, in 2006, she told me about her cooking, she stressed several times that money was scarce. As she could not afford to buy products, she cooked vegetables and simple foodstuffs that some of the workers brought from home. As elsewhere in Russia, experiences of exorbitant monetary inflation that culminated in 1998, unemployment, and a general feeling of dispossession coincided with the widening desire to revive Orthodoxy. An emphasis on frugality often reappeared in the ways in which the members of the core

---

[37] During perestroika, the state allowed churches to be reopened if a group of twenty persons declared itself the civil initiator of the reopening. Such a group was called colloquially *dvadtsatka* (lit. a twenty).

[38] *Starosta* refers literally to a 'church elder'. In this case and elsewhere in this book, it is an everyday term of reference for the head of the parish lay council.

[39] Under Soviet rule and during perestroika reforms the head of the lay parish council became the real leader of the parish, although officially there was a rector who must be a member of the clergy. In some cases, the position of head of the lay council was occupied by people almost not acquainted with religion. This was not the case of the parish that I present here.

community at the Church of Saint George the Warrior, former benevolent workers, presented themselves. When I was invited to share meals with them, I was always warned that they had only simple food to offer. In general, the core group of parishioners consistently insisted on the lack of material resources, on their capability of managing without much money, and on their hard physical work.

'We Were Building with Our Hands'

During reconstruction, manual labourers and people with technical skills were highly appreciated. Women participated too. One of them was Nina. She was around fifty-five years old when I first met her in 2006. In the late 1990s, she worked elsewhere for a salary and participated actively in the rebuilding at the same time. A friend of hers had brought her to the construction site. She made acquaintance with the benevolent workers whom she liked because they showed themselves to be friendly and very committed to their work. This was the main reason why she decided to help them. She said: 'In 1999 I used to come simply like this, not as a parishioner. I came to work'. After reconstruction, she said she sometimes wanted to hear the choir singing: 'I used to come simply and stand listening to all of them singing together, and I was standing'. After some time, Nina approached a female member of the choir and asked if she might join the choir herself. The choir director, a man in his thirties at that time, found Nina to be a promising singer and invited her to join. For Nina, this was the turning point after which she started considering herself as a real parishioner. She insisted that she became 'a real parishioner in 2000'.

During reconstruction, Nina left her home every day at five o'clock in the morning. She went first to her salaried work as a construction worker. At the end of the workday, she took the bus to the construction site and worked as a mason until late at night. Other former workers who subsequently became parishioners spoke of Nina's life as having been the most difficult among them at the time. She was a full-time worker in a construction company and a single mother of a young daughter. She accepted the hard working conditions imposed by her employer because she was afraid of losing her job – many companies went bankrupt overnight. Working for the renovation of the church made her happy in this difficult moment, she said. She knew almost nothing about God, the saints, or faith, but was nonetheless one of the most committed members of the informal team. When I first arrived in Ozerovo, about six years after the end of the reconstruction, Nina's life was completely devoted to the church. Nina's case was a typical one for members of the core parish community of Saint George the Warrior. Many of the benevolent workers did not know much about Orthodoxy and felt attracted by the spirit of community and the common goal (for a comparison with the meanings of volunteers' physical work in post-Soviet monasteries, see Dubovka 2015). This group and the work it pursued proved particularly appealing in a period when the Soviet social frames of belonging, such as the work collective, Communist Party sub-organizations, as well as cultural and sport clubs, were being eroded or were disappearing altogether. Often, joining the group of workers happened in moments of personal hardship. Some workers remained in the parish community; others left before the end of the reconstruction or once it was completed without having ever become in-churched.

Nina and others voiced their physical connection to the church with the phrase, 'We were building with our hands' (*my stroili svoimi rukami*). Handwork was associated with strong physical effort, even suffering, and it was highly valued. A couple of men who had renovated the roof repeatedly told me (and themselves) that their painstaking and risky task was a continuous confirmation of their devotion to the common goal. Normally, roofing should have been undertaken by professionals with suitable technical equipment, but the lack of money in those years prevented the *starosta* from making such a contract. Instead, the volunteer workers had waged the risks. The collective effort, perhaps more than the achievement itself, created solidarity among the volunteer workers and enhanced their identification with the church. This, however, did not mean that all of them remained part of the core community. One of the young volunteer roofers left Ozerovo to become a successful lawyer in Saint Petersburg. When I met him he was in his forties. Although he was rarely in town (and on those occasions he went to light candles in Trinity Church), he also came back from time to time to visit his former benevolent colleagues from Saint George the Warrior. Drinking tea with them, he would tell and retell how he climbed, with no rope or equipment, up to the roof to fix it. These narratives made evident his pride in a challenging, morally valuable achievement, associated with a sense of material deprivation. He also told me that the rebuilding was the first occasion for him to read the Gospels. This is when he read the Bible for the first time – 'the synodal translation', he specified.[40]

A Community with Two Cores

About ten people from the first generation of parishioner-workers at the Church of Saint George the Warrior were still active when I arrived in

---

[40] The 'synodal translation' was first published in 1876. It has become the standard and most widespread version of the Bible in Russia, but this does not dilute its authoritative status as the most comprehensive version – to which my informant referred.

Ozerovo. They were evenly divided along gender, and had a relatively uniform profile: not younger than forty, most of these individuals had almost no family or they had problems in their family relations; they usually had gone through a big disaster (accident, illness, family tragedy, sudden poverty); and came from a modest social background. Most had graduated from technical education, and some even had higher education.

While a community formed spontaneously around the church during reconstruction, it changed shape afterwards. Faith, solidarity, and mutual support of all kinds brought some of the workers into a closer community; other former workers left to follow different trajectories. Those who remained in the 'core' often lent money to each other and helped each other in all kinds of practical matters. They sang in the choir and took care of the church. Participation in the choir too served to deepen the sense of community. The *starosta* presented the choir director to me as 'creating a collective'. The former rebuilders sometimes too referred to themselves as a collective.[41] They had lunch together with the priests and other church workers every Sunday in the so-called lower temple of the church.[42] Those who were not officially employed elsewhere and did not have family obligations spent almost all their time in the lower temple. Every night somebody slept there in order to look after (*storozhit'*) the church, and this obligation gave them another reason to become strongly related to their church. At Trinity, an electronic alarm had been installed to spare parishioners from the overnight service. But the key parishioners of Saint George the Warrior claimed their parish had no money for such devices. Indeed, some were proud to emphasize that they were able to manage without such sophisticated equipment, by offering instead their physical presence.

Diversification of the members' sociological profile and complication of the informal structure of the parish characterized Saint George the Warrior in the 2000s. While the integration of some new members directly connoted ideas of material limitation, the arrival of others did not. After the end of the reconstruction in the early 2000s, the group of benevolent workers-parishioners included new members: younger people in need, some of whom were offered support (visits at the hospital when family was not

---

[41] The Russian term *kollektiv* became rooted in everyday speech during the Soviet period above all as a reference to a group of fellow workers; its members were expected to show abnegation and devotion to the goals of the socialist collective. Long after the collapse of the regime, *kollektiv* has remained a positive term for community of belonging beyond kin relations. On Soviet and post-Soviet notions of *kollektiv*, see Kharkhordin (1999) and Vladimirova (2006: 120–26).

[42] The basement is not simply a basement, but a 'lower temple' (*nizhnii khram*), a smaller church located under the big public church.

able to come, material support, foodstuffs). In several cases, receiving support and becoming a believer were explicitly linked. For instance, I met a young woman who received moral support and small amounts of money and food from the church's core community when she lost her job, a couple of years before I met her. The woman lived with her mother. The mother had no income either at the time, but she was a close acquaintance of one of the parishioners. Thanks to this acquaintance, the young woman started going to the church; she was received warmly there and became progressively more religious. By the time I met her, the young woman had found work again (as a guide for pilgrims at one of the most important monasteries in north-western Russia), but remained part of the community. We met one day when she was paying a visit to her former helpers. They had immediately invited her into the lower temple – a clear sign that they recognized her devotion to the community.

If this young woman, brought into the church's core community by former rebuilders, more or less matched their own profile, a very different new generation also joined the core of the parish after the end of the reconstruction. This second core was comprised of individuals who were distinct from those integrated by the former workers. They introduced more social diversity into the church's core. The members of this second core were less present than the former rebuilders in the church's everyday life. Managerial and practical tasks, as well as door-keeping functions were exclusively taken over by the older core group. The new parish activists concentrated on more publicly visible activities. They were extremely committed Orthodox believers who started engaging with Orthodoxy mainly through readings. Unlike the older core members, they occupied rather well-paid jobs and many had a family life. Most were in their thirties and forties. Many had a professional career in large enterprises, or had established their own businesses. They observed a rather strict Orthodox dress code, such as wearing a long skirt for women, and rules of piety presented as traditional in the 2000s, such as frequent communion and weekly confession (Sibireva 2009b). They did not, however, exhibit signs of wealth and were reluctant to speak openly of donations they made to the church, even with their co-parishioners. There was no competition between these two cores because they occupied very different positions in the parish.[43] The new parish activists were not 'rebuilders' but 'further developers'. For example, in the winter of 2007, they organized the first Christmas party for children in the lower temple. The older generation had never undertaken similar initiatives,

---

[43] This informal two-core structure, determined by two different generations – those who re-established the parish in the 1990s and those who joined it later – seems typical for reconstructed churches in rural areas too (Sergazina 2006).

but it was well received by parents and grandparents, many of whom volunteered to help; and it even drew teachers from Trinity's religious school.

The older core had acted in response to immediate needs of urgent renovation and its members spontaneously became deeply related to each other, including in their practical lives. This is how most of them discovered Orthodoxy. Conversely, the younger ones rather tried to make their ideal of Orthodox community a reality. They were introducing new forms of parish life, proving more innovative without being present in the church on a daily basis. They reinvented parish life in deliberate and intentional ways. There was a lot of sympathy between the two cores. The new group did not erase the prominence of the rebuilders as the symbolic kernel of the parish and continued to spread the story of reconstruction as central to the church's history and identity. In this way, the second core upheld a story of imposed limitations, chosen renunciation, victimhood, and physical effort.

The Moral Worth of Material Limitation

As a founding event, reconstruction informed a positive collective identity of material restraint and abnegation. Although this identity was not claimed by all regular churchgoers as constitutive of their own personal identity, most of them could tell the shared story of rebuilding, and some did link their own personal sense of self-esteem to the narrative. Even those who visited both the Church of Saint George the Warrior and Trinity Church drew on the collective narrative of the first church's reconstruction. One might have expected the ascetic identity of Saint George the Warrior to fade away as new generations of better-off parishioners arrived, and as general social values evolved to celebrate economic success and power. In fact, this did not happen. Distinctive discourses and behaviours upheld the reproduction of ascetic communal identity.

In fact, the story of the reconstruction of the Church of Saint George the Warrior spread throughout Ozerovo. It was common to hear the story told by local people who had never entered the church, and even by people who were obviously unsympathetic towards religion. Personal atheism did not prevent respect for the rebuilders' achievement. Throughout the city, the reconstruction of Saint George the Warrior became part of collective local identity, well beyond the parameters of religious affiliation. If Orthodox devotion does not provide a satisfactory explanation to the widely shared identification and esteem, then what can explain them?

I argue that the case of the rebuilt church shows firstly that asceticism of a non-religious origin was taken up and became key in the shaping of a religious community. Because this asceticism was already present in the secular community, the church's story was taken up subsequently by the broader community as its own.

The rejection of material comfort and acquisitiveness for the sake of spiritual elevation is usually rendered as asceticism. Historical evidence indicates that religious asceticism has been highly controversial and much criticized, including by adherents (Freiberger 2006). Recent critical studies of religious asceticism stress the bewildering plurality of its actual forms and functions (Wimbush and Valantasis 2002). Sometimes, asceticism is not accompanied by claims of religious transcendence.[44] The ascetic practices and discourses associated with the reconstruction of the Church of Saint George the Warrior were of this last type. They were not accompanied by claims to religious transcendence, nor by soteriological claims.

In Ozerovo, the moral value of asceticism is deeply entrenched in broader cultural understandings of what is good and worthy. As such, asceticism unites those who belong to the community of the Christian faithful, but it also provides a bridge between the Church and wider community. The wider community values the reconstruction because it proceeded through hard work and under conditions of material shortage. In the case of the rebuilt church, we see two additional implications. The first is that the ascetic practices of reconstruction drew volunteers from the wider community, many with little previous religious engagement, into a new religious community. The second implication is that the bridge between the Church of Saint George the Warrior and the wider community has remained open after reconstruction. The narrative that constitutes the church's identity finds resonance far beyond the parish activists. In particular, the church reconstruction elicits sympathy and identification among local inhabitants, whether or not they are sympathetic to the ROC or to Orthodoxy per se. In these two ways, the shared sense of moral elevation attained in spite of material depravation has produced a wide identification with Saint George the Warrior regardless of religiosity. Such wide identification in turn reasserts the high degree of porosity between the local church and its secular environment. It is the continuous resonance of ideological and pragmatic Soviet legacies with the sudden and complex experiences of post-Soviet economic distress that have largely shaped the development of this ascetic parish identity.

---

[44] Fenella Cannell has argued that there is a transcendental-Christian bias in anthropological studies of Christianity, religion, gift, and ritual. Anthropologists, she claimed, have unreflectively postulated transcendence and this postulate has inflected scholarly analysis towards the consistent reproduction of what she terms the 'ascetic stereotype' (Cannell 2005, 2006, 2007). Thus, Cannell implies that asceticism is always related to transcendence.

The shared sympathy of local inhabitants for the ascetic character of the rebuilding of the Church of Saint George the Warrior is intriguing in the sense that it emerged in a period when upward social mobility was strongly desired by everyone. The dual valuation of abnegation and of material betterment might appear contradictory. Yet, it is not so in light of the Russian Orthodox tradition, nor is it a rupture from Soviet precedents. For example, in her study of post-Soviet religious pilgrimages, Naletova (2010) reported that pilgrims who prefer to walk on foot (instead of taking comfortable modern transportation) to reach distant Orthodox shrines exemplify the values of self-limitation, poverty, humility, and non-resistance through their bodily attitudes. For such pilgrims, walking revives the kenotic tradition of Russian Orthodoxy; they passively accept suffering in imitation of the 'self-emptying' Christ. It is important to note that the pilgrims who choose to walk are a minority of post-Soviet pilgrims. Most take the more comfortable transportation. Thus, the practices of pilgrimage evidence both values: for asceticism and for comfort.

This dual valuation, with deliberate suffering constituting a nevertheless minority practice, parallels a historical tendency. Russian Orthodox theology has cultivated a longstanding emphasis on asceticism and self-restraint as means of spiritual elevation (Fedotov 1966; Florovsky 1983 [1937]; Meyendorff 1995 [1960]; Pelikan 2003 [1974]). Nevertheless, asceticism has been expressed as radical renunciation only in a few cases. Radical renunciation, for example, is exemplified by the Orthodox figures of the holy fool and the monk hermit (Fedotov 1966: 316–43; Pryzhov 1996). It is rarely described as a condition that should be pursued by ordinary believers, or indeed, even by priests. Moreover, a variety of practices and views of asceticism thrived. In the Middle Ages, for example, the increased attraction for monastic life (and the expansion of the monastic economy) spurred disputes about whether monks should engage socially or shun the world. Both sides emphasized the asceticism of monastic life, but for the former asceticism meant helping the needy and ill, while for the latter it connoted withdrawal in a contemplative life devoted to prayer (Kenworthy 2008: 28–30).

Similarly, Russian literary works from the Middle Ages until the first three decades of the twentieth century are populated with idiosyncratic ascetic heroes (Morris 1993). The particular forms of asceticism that appeared in literature followed cycles of waxing and waning, drawing on Christian (and later Communist) inspiration. At the end of the nineteenth and the very beginning of the twentieth century, for example, popular literature was infused with representations of the moral superiority that accompanied asceticism, and with religious motifs of suffering and piety. Popular novels of this period presented heroes and heroines who achieved fame and wealth as a reward for long and passive suffering. Brooks explained this moralistic bias with reference to the religious tradition of kenoticism (Brooks 1985: 288–89). But just as Naletova (2010) noted that walking pilgrims constitute a minority, Brooks specified that ascetic literary heroes rarely exhibited monastic ideals. The heroes were virtuous because they suffered; not because they pursued virtue. Later, Soviet dissident novels represented characters whose Orthodox asceticism was in fact a form of resistance to state-administrated violence (Kobets 1998).

As in literary oeuvres, in reality, twentieth-century Russian ascetic motifs and aspirations, official and actual, were complex and multi-layered. The early post-revolutionary Soviet ideology promoted ideals of material restraint as part of an effort oriented toward the collective construction of a radiant transcendent future. The Soviet political, economic, and teleological framework was very different from the Orthodox theistic spirit. That is, Soviet and early post-Soviet individual and collective understandings of accumulation and consumption continuously contested the idea that personal material accumulation could go together with moral elevation. Nonetheless, the possibility of marrying materiality with morality remained in that some forms of consumption, especially the ones controlled and advertised by the state, were perceived as 'cultured'. Western-style consumption was considered to lack a moral basis, but 'cultured' consumption was the moral imperative of Soviet citizens (Boym 1994; Humphrey 2002; Patico 2002, 2005). Religious connotations were not always completely left out; for instance, during perestroika, popular laments often represented material deprivation not merely as a source of moral worth, but also as a path to sanctity (Ries 1997: 126–60). At the same time, practical experiences and ideas under Soviet rule encouraged various forms of acquisitiveness, alongside the emphasis on the moral worth of material limitation. Even in the revolutionary period, certain material refinement was recommended along with 'everyday asceticism' (Gurova 2016). Already in Stalin's times, which were characterized by harsh deprivation, middle-class petty-bourgeois values of consumption were promoted by the state (Dunham 1990). From model department stores created under Stalin (Hessler 2000) to luxury goods appreciated as presents in the 1980s, much of what was worthy, good, and desirable was also expensive (Patico 2002).

In post-Soviet capitalism, one finds tensions reminiscent of previous decades, as the moral desirability of wealth has continued to leave room for ambivalent moral tenets (Patico 2005, 2009). The idea that material limitation, whether chosen or imposed by external forces, is connected to spiritual perfection is still at work in various forms, including in Orthodox groups. In this respect, 'Orthodox' and 'Soviet' cannot be set up in opposition, for traditional religious morals and Soviet teachings are neither mutually exclusive nor simply cumulative (e.g. Luehrmann 2005, 2011; Paxson 2005; Wanner 2007; Steinberg and Wanner 2008; Pelkmans 2009; Rogers 2009). Among Orthodox adherents and beyond their milieu, the two strands are combined in various, creative ways. This shared cultural valuation of ascetic tenets, stemming from different historical and moral frames of references, explains why the determination to reconstruct the Church of Saint George the Warrior under the conditions of material hardship has elicited sympathy and participation among Ozerovo's inhabitants and has durably marked local identity and memory.

Chapter 4
Inter-Parish Differentiation

The past hardship of the Church of Saint George the Warrior became a milestone in its relationship with Ozerovo's central church, Trinity Church. On the one hand, it can be said that the two churches have good relations. The clerics are on good terms, and there are some fruitful collaborations (such as Christmas parties for children organized by teachers from Trinity's religious school). On the other hand, however, it can be said that the relations between the parishes are antagonistic. This antagonism had emerged by the time of reconstruction. It had to do with the financial inequalities between the two churches and their uneven access to influential connections.

In this chapter, I describe how churchgoers and local residents define the differences between the two churches, and how they actively produce some of these differences. I further depict the emergence and consolidation of distinct loci of spirituality in each church. Trinity Church boasts the relics of a new martyr saint, while Saint George the Warrior has an outstanding head priest. Though the story about the material difficulties that emerged during the church's reconstruction is still narrated in Ozerovo, the new line of division between the two churches has become more meaningful. Each parish has taken to cultivating its own distinctive connection to the divine.

Hidden Transcripts

The re-establishment of the Church of Saint George the Warrior directly affected its relationship with Trinity Church. From the outset, there had been a localized and partly masked rivalry between the two churches. Saint George the Warrior had limited financial resources but its parishioners provided enthusiastic labour in its activities; a comparison to the Trinity Church with its political and economic clout (but weaker sense of community) seemed almost inevitable. Certainly such a contrast played into the scripts of religious belief and belonging, and comparisons found their way into gossip throughout the city.

There was more to it, however. For the active members of Saint George the Warrior, the self-reification of their identity was a way to engage in expressions of a perceived inequality. Various forms of 'transcripts' (Scott 1990) indicate that what was at first glance a parochial differentiation found in fact much wider resonance. Besides the relatively standardized narrative about the reconstruction, I encountered scattered discourse encompassing remarks and short comments. There was even evidence that St. George's core community had excluded two young parishioners who were at odds with the group's desired sociological portrait. These scattered remarks and rejections took their meaning in a general atmosphere of semi-concealed and semi-claimed differentiation between the two churches.

Two Churches

Trinity Church had always been Ozerovo's most prominent church. It remained open almost continuously during Soviet times. In the post-Soviet period, it has maintained strong relations with the local authorities and benefits from donations made by the city's new businessmen. Its existence is taken for granted. In comparison, the Church of Saint George the Warrior was a relatively peripheral one and it had been undergoing a long and uncertain reconstruction. Some of the devoted parishioners of Saint George the Warrior, as well as non-churchgoers, saw it as suffering relative to Trinity. It is not clear whether this sense was improved or worsened by the structural relations between the two churches: Trinity's rector is head of the deanery to which Saint George the Warrior belongs.

Trinity Church is open every day, almost the whole day. Saint George the Warrior is open only four days per week, and then only for a few hours.

Trinity has a professional choir. Its director, a young lady, trained as a professional choir director. All the members are paid for their singing.[45] Saint George the Warrior has a choir, but at the time of my fieldwork it was hardly of 'professional' quality. The parishioners of Saint George the Warrior did not seem to mind: they described participation in the choir as an expression of devotion to the community and to Orthodoxy. But it did matter in the balance of relations because Trinity's choir director was proud to say that she worked with trained singers.

Trinity Church had five full-time employed priests by 2007. In addition, there were around 40 part-time employees. Saint George the Warrior had only three priests and one deacon who were employed full-time. Their salaries were lower than those of their counterparts. About five people received money for cleaning, selling in the church shop, and bookkeeping.

---

[45] On the important role of choir singing in Russian Orthodoxy, see Engelhardt (2014).

Trinity Church offers 'expensive' services and items. Saint George the Warrior is said to be 'cheaper' (see chapter 5). Indeed, 'poorer' believers sometimes make an effort to visit the Church of Saint George the Warrior, even though it is not centrally located.

Making Meaning from Difference

Comparisons such as those listed above were rarely made to be neutral. For example, the wife of the head of the lay parish council of Saint George the Warrior was also its unofficial bookkeeper. She was one of the informants who commented on the different prices offered for services at the two churches. But this is how she did it: Trinity Church, she reminded me, is situated very close to the market place. Then, she mimicked a person carrying heavy packages: 'the people who go there have bags full of commodities'. Then, to conclude the comparison, she explained that those who visited Saint George the Warrior were poor. They 'could not shop' as much as those who visited Trinity Church. The comparison pulls together disparate facts: some of those entering Trinity Church laden with bags are hardly wealthy; they stop in to the church because it is convenient to do so. Yet the bookkeeper's distinction is no less true. Most of those who come to Saint George the Warrior cannot afford to fill their bags with all kinds of desirable goods.

On another occasion, the librarian[46] of Saint George the Warrior was showing the churches of Ozerovo to a small group of Ukrainian Orthodox women who were visiting the city on their trip to shrines throughout Saint Petersburg Region. The librarian had invited me along because he thought I might benefit from the guided tour. After having spent some time in the Trinity Church, looking at its interior and praying before the icons, the librarian-improvised-guide urged the group of visitors to 'leave this place before they ask us for some money for looking at their icons'. No one could miss his accusation of the church's greediness because visitors are never charged for looking at icons in an Orthodox church. At the same time, the comment was meaningless for the tour group; they were complete outsiders who had no idea of the local divisions. At that moment, I was alone able to understand the allusion. The librarian did what other active members of this parish did all the time as part of their 'infrapolitics' of powerlessness (Scott

---

[46] There is a two-storey building next to the church with several rooms that are used as a workshop, a small meeting room, a larger room where catechism courses for adults take place. A small library is improvised in another room. It is used mostly by the active parishioners and the people who attend the courses.

1985). He asserted, mostly for himself, the values supported by his community by criticizing Trinity Church of acquisitiveness.

Rejection and Exclusion

Many unfriendly but 'harmless' commentaries built up the differences between Trinity and Saint George the Warrior as parishes. Sometimes, individuals who did not fit the desired image were rejected by other parishioners. Such rejections served the construction of strong communal identities (at least at Saint George the Warrior), but they also contributed to the antagonism between the two churches.

Among my informants there was a young Orthodox couple. The woman was in her early thirties. She took care of the couple's four children, and described herself – unusually – as a housewife (*domokhoziaika*). Russian women rarely claim such a title because they prefer to define themselves above all by referring to their work outside the home. This woman, however, insisted on her primary occupation as a housewife because this was an important aspect of her commitment to an Orthodox family model. In reality, her situation was quite exceptional compared to women in any of the groups formed around the church (see chapter 6). Her husband was a successful lawyer in nearby Saint Petersburg, and she drew pride from taking good care of her children and home, and not being obliged to do salaried work.

One might expect that such a family would be welcome in any church. They were a model Orthodox family, devoted, and well-off. They wanted to contribute, and by the time I met them had made large donations to Trinity's religious school and smaller ones to the church. In 2006, their donation had amounted to 9,000 US dollars.

By the time I met them, the couple was strongly involved with Trinity Church, but they had prior connections to Saint George the Warrior. The couple had been married there. At the very end of the 1990s, the woman had gone occasionally to the newly reopened church, and sometimes the couple attended Sunday services. Then, at one service, the wife heard someone whispering behind her: 'Look, New Russians came here'. She was offended. Being called a 'New Russian' was disparaging by anyone's standard; it meant that one had money but no 'class', that one's wealth was ill-gained and improperly displayed. As Caroline Humphrey wrote of New Russians, 'Theirs is regarded as unjust consumption, the outcome of some unfair magic, outside the huge struggle to move upward in the power game of Russian society' (2002: 62).

Also by 2006–07, popular critique was no longer conveyed as much by the term 'New Russian' as it was by 'oligarchs', but my informant still smarted from the earlier attack. The young woman refused to return to Saint

George the Warrior; and she declared that there were 'crazy people' there. Indeed, the family would have been unwelcome still in the church's new climate.

In the years preceding my fieldwork, some better-off parishioners had become active in Saint George the Warrior. The older community had become more tolerant of moneymaking people, provided they did not display their capacity for conspicuous consumption or exhibit a provocative demeanour.

My informants, the lawyer and the housewife, could not have fit in. They often invited to their large apartment the women who headed Trinity's religious school and other prominent parishioners (mostly intellectuals and successful businessmen). The couple was hospitable and generous. They offered their guests fine French cognac and excellent food, accompanied by the discreet sounds of classical Black American jazz. The atmosphere was warm and friendly. The occasions were expensive, surely, but they were not marked by the lavish feasting or gross conspicuousness attached to the image of the coarse-mannered New Russians. This family's consumption is refined and explicitly gentle; they see it as marking Orthodox hospitality, albeit of an upper-class variety.

Socializing among parishioners of Saint George the Warrior, in contrast, required an emphasis on scarcity. The most active parishioners and clergymen of the church's community met in the afternoons (not evenings). They drank tea and ate simple and cheap foodstuffs. They were deliberately unpretentious.

Poor, but Pious

When I began fieldwork, some six years had passed since the end of reconstruction at the Church of Saint George the Warrior. Nevertheless, renovation works were still a permanent topic, and not only as part of the founding narrative already documented. Many things did need frequent fixing, and the meagre resources available to the church were an issue of perennial discussion. Some committed parishioners had attracted donations from businessmen. These donations had made a notable impact, but church workers and active parishioners still often spoke of their church as a poor one.

The usual churchgoers at Saint George the Warrior's, they said, were poor people, little old ladies (*starushki*). Sometimes, an informant would simply look in the direction of one of the beggars hanging around the church and say to me: 'This is how they are, our parishioners'. This portrait could by no means apply to all churchgoers, and especially not to the new active members of the second core (see chapter 3). Nevertheless, scarcity, lower prices, and lack of material resources were constantly stressed. These were overtly or elusively depicted as the genuine characteristics of the parish.

Many individuals associated with Trinity Church were known – even at Saint George the Warrior – for their asceticism, but this did not shake the overall image of the two churches' distinctions. Clerics and some other people associated with the central church had a reputation for voluntarily renouncing material ease. For example, one priest was known for his chosen poverty; he refused to accept personal donations from churchgoers despite the fact that he had three children and that his wife did not earn any money.

Trinity remained known as the wealthier and more powerful church. Other events confirmed the church's dominant position. For example, a valuable icon that was exhibited there officially belonged to Saint George the Warrior. According to employees at Saint George the Warrior, Trinity's rector had promised to return the icon, but had never done so. These and yet other stories supported the active parishioners' self-image as victims. Yet their complaints about the church's material limits and lack of influential relationships, coincided with an implicit claim to spiritual superiority.

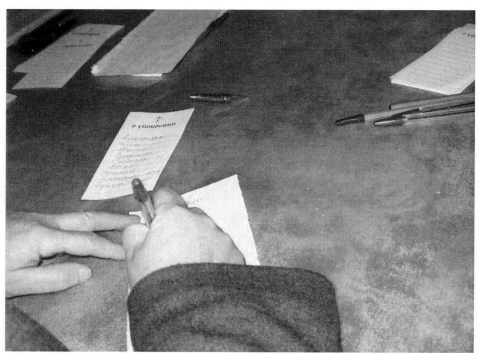

Plate 6. Ordering prayers for the living and dead is one of the most widespread and accessible post-Soviet religious practices.

Cultivating Distinct Connections to the Divine: A Priest with 'Strong Prayer'

My neighbour from Ozerovo, a man in his seventies who used to work as a teacher, had no sympathy for the ROC. Yet he too recounted the standard narrative of the reconstruction of the Church of Saint George the Warrior. He spoke of the builders' hardship; he had seen them working at the construction site of what was until 1990 the half-ruined, full-of-dirt building of the former salt warehouse. My neighbour expressed respect for this achievement and praised the team. His opinion was the same as all local inhabitants; I heard the same story from those who were strictly observant of church rules, casual droppers-in, or removed from all religious practice. And like everyone else, my neighbour could not talk about Saint George the Warrior without a comparison to Trinity Church. He commented on the rector of Trinity Church: 'This priest is, you know, this one is not ... . The other one is a real one'. The other one, the 'real one', was the rector of Saint George the Warrior. My neighbour explained further: the head of Trinity was a manager and a politician; the head of Saint George the Warrior was entirely devoted to spiritual matters.

As with other elements in the comparison of the two churches, the reported differences between the rectors are not transparent. On the one hand, many people do approach Trinity's rector for mundane matters and spiritual advice. For many, he does fill the 'real' functions of a priest. On the other hand, the rector of Saint George the Warrior has earned his reputation. He is a wise old man, deeply devoted to priestly service, endowed with 'strong prayer' (*sil'naia molitva*), and an outstanding ability to deliver spiritual guidance. Yet the strong contrast between one as 'real' and the other as 'only' a manager and politician takes as its evidence a recent development: Trinity has valuable icons, and in 2007 it acquired the relics of a recently canonized saint. The two churches now cultivate distinct connections to the divine. Differences between the priests are brought to the fore in this process of cultivation.

The rector at the Church of Saint George the Warrior has played a key role in shaping the image of his parish. The spiritual virtue associated with this church directly derives from the limits of material ease and the voluntary anti-acquisitive behaviours of its active parishioners. The rector, however, has not acted alone in developing either his own career or the shape of his church and its mission.

The rector of Saint George the Warrior, whom I call Father Ioann, used to serve as a priest in Trinity Church. He left in order to serve in Saint George the Warrior in the very beginning of the 1990s. Father Ioann is famous in Ozerovo. He is considered to be endowed with great skills as a spiritual counsellor, and to offer local inhabitants a privileged way to spirituality. He is said to fulfil all his work 'with kindness'. His role is reminiscent for many of the role played by spiritual elders (*startsy* and *dukhovniki*) in the Russian Orthodox tradition, and especially since the nineteenth century (Paert 2010). The tradition of the elders, most of whom are priests and monks, has been actively revived – or rather reinvented – in the post-Soviet period, since the Soviet period broke most of the pre-Soviet tradition.

In several of our conversations, Father Ioann insisted on the image of poverty and renouncement of his church. He told me that all the money for his parish comes from the donations of its 'poor parishioners'. Father Ioann said that he too had given all he had to this church. At home he had only 'some valuable books and a few little icons'. The limited parish resources motivated his choice of personal poverty and conscious renunciation, in the name of the church.

Plate 7. Unpretentious Christmas supper.

Father Ioann was sincere, but his sincerity required crafting, and it had consequences for the development of his church's profile.

At the age of 60, Father Ioann was invited in 1991, by the lay members of the rebuilders' committee of Saint George the Warrior, to head the new parish. He arrived at the very beginning of the reconstruction process. Another rector had been appointed 'from above' (i.e. by the Church hierarchy) a few months earlier, but had been defrocked shortly afterwards in an unmentionable scandal. Only a couple of persons mentioned this fact; those who knew about the incident were particularly reluctant to talk. For everyone else, Father Ioann has been the spiritual guide of the parish from its beginning, and no competitor has ever appeared.

It was the lay parish elder, a school teacher, who had proposed inviting Father Ioann to the church. Father Ioann was already well known in Ozerovo. He had served as a deacon in Trinity Church since 1963, and he had been a rector between 1986 and 1990. The wife of the parish elder (who herself serves as the bookkeeper) told me the story. 'Knowing that a very good priest (*ochen' khoroshii batiushka*) serves in Trinity Church, we invited him to become our leader. This is how it happened'. As the uncontested spiritual leader of the Church of Saint George the Warrior, Father Ioann's reputation stretches far beyond the circles of his parishioners. He is usually described as gentle, kind (*miagkii*), modest, and always available to respond to everybody's worries and questions. A middle-aged woman member of the choir at the Church of Saint George the Warrior described him in the following way:

> In Father Ioann even his eyes are bright. When I saw him for the first time ... he has these eyes! You look at his eyes and he looks at you and you feel that he is there only for you. There is this feeling that his smile, his kindness, it is all for you. This really makes you feel comfortable. I can hardly explain how he makes you feel good and attracts you. And he has such a strong prayer!

In the beginning of the 1990s, this woman used to go to Trinity Church. When she first entered the Church of Saint George the Warrior, she said she felt 'like in a monastery'. The church was still undergoing basic renovation, with boxes and construction materials everywhere inside; beautification was not yet under way. The church looked unattractive, she said, unlike the usually richly decorated Orthodox churches. Nevertheless, she felt 'warmth in [her] soul'. From that moment, she began to go to the Church of Saint George the Warrior. Eventually, she joined the church community and began singing in the choir. 'The people here are real believers, not career-makers'. Once again, her comment suggested a comparison with the image of Trinity Church.

Like other people, this woman volunteered evidence of Father Ioann's strength as a priest. She told me that she had been heavily addicted to tobacco. Smoking is considered a vice in Orthodox milieus, and far worse than moderate alcohol drinking. She had been trying hard to give up smoking for a long time. Once, right before leaving for a weekend to the countryside with her husband and children, she decided to address Father Ioann for advice. She confessed to him that she felt weak despite her strong desire to give up smoking. Father Ioann simply expressed understanding and told her to go to the countryside and enjoy the weekend rest. She was surprised by his response. She had expected to be summoned to pray intensively or to apply some other spiritual exercise. Several hours later, when she arrived at her remote summerhouse (*dacha*) in the countryside, she realized that she had forgotten her cigarettes. The closest store was almost 50 kilometres away. Unwilling to take the bad roads leading to the closest shop, she did not smoke during the weekend; in fact she felt no need to smoke. This happy incident, she told me, could be nothing but a direct outcome of Father Ioann's spiritual power.

This was one of many personal testimonies to Father Ioann's power that I heard in Ozerovo. Providing spiritual advice in response to mundane needs and anxieties is a significant part of Father Ioann's daily workload. Everyone knows this. What is less known across town – but well known to the most assiduous churchgoers at Saint George the Warrior – is that the lay parish elder has played a crucial role in enabling Father Ioann to perform these spiritual tasks. Indeed, the *starosta* has had a major role in developing his spiritual career. It was the *starosta* who proposed inviting this priest as a rector. Since Father Ioann's arrival, the *starosta* has taken upon himself the task of freeing the priest from any practical or administrative obligations pertaining to church management. Father Ioann, of course, 'decides' many issues, but I witnessed conversations between the two men when the parish elder presented the rector with a specific practical issue that needed a solution, proposed a solution, and offered to take care of the problem. In addition, the parish elder 'filtered' access to Father Ioann, vetting casual visitors who tried to approach the famous priest. The two men were satisfied with their informal allocation of tasks.

Witnessing the degree to which the *starosta* shapes Father Ioann's daily schedule, practical decisions, and availability to the 'right kind' of supplicants, one might wonder how far his influence over the priest stretches. Both men shared a common fascination in delivering conservative views about correct behaviour, women's dress, and especially conspiracy theories. Their views were not quite the same. The *starosta* was openly anti-Semitic, but Father Ioann was not. The *starosta* also detests hidden enemies whom he suspects of preparing an assault against the community of Saint George the Warrior and against Orthodox Russia in general. Was it coincidence that their concerns were so similar? Had one influenced the other? Perhaps it was the *starosta* who had created a priest according to his own desires. At the very least, he had attracted one to build a church and a community which he, the *starosta*, found 'real'.

It is worth noting that Father Ioann could be a controversial figure. He is overtly opposed to the use of tax-payer identification numbers (INN) in Russia, a position supported in particularly conservative milieus.[47] He expresses contempt for the 'godless'. Yet to this day, none of Father Ioann's positions have done any harm to his image of a person possessing great wisdom, spiritual power, or gentleness.

And, a New Martyr Saint [48]

In the long history of Russian Orthodoxy, people have believed that saints brought divine grace to their spiritual quests and mundane lives (Greene 2010). Orthodox sainthood gained renewed vibrancy after 1988. The year 1988 marked the celebration of the Millennium of Christianity in Russia. A series of saints were canonized on traditional grounds in conjunction with this observance. Then, from 1989, the soon to be post-Soviet Orthodox Church started a massive campaign to canonize saints known as 'New Martyrs and Confessors' (*novomucheniki i ispovedniki*).[49] This category comprises individuals who stood for their faith in the face of Soviet anti-

---

[47] Since the 1990s, fears about invisible powers and unclean forces that could take control of simple people's lives crystallized around the introduction of tax-payer identification numbers at the national level, but also around bar codes and electronic microchips that allow the recording of personal data. These fears spread particularly in Orthodox milieus, including among the clergy. Resistance to the use of these bureaucratic devices created a series of problems at the levels of state and local administration. The hierarchs of the Church issued several official statements in which they reaffirmed the need for the state to collect and process personal data. But they stressed also the potential threats and the need for the state to make available alternative technologies of data recording. The Church interprets the right to refuse the use of tax-payer identification numbers, bar codes, and other coding devices as one of the freedoms guaranteed to individuals by the Constitution. For a recent example of a Church statement, see http://www.patriarchia.ru/db/text/2775107.html, accessed on 22 June 2017.

[48] The historical data presented in this section draw on data collected by the secretary of the Diocesan committee on canonization and made available on the well-maintained parish website of Trinity Church. I also draw on booklets authored by *kraevedy* (self-trained local historians). I do not provide the list of these sources in order to protect the anonymity of the town and that of the parishes. Ethnographic data about the local reception of the saint and developments since 2006 are based on my own fieldwork and follow-up phone conversations.

[49] According to Semenko-Basin (2010), these categories of sainthood were introduced in 1918 after the first Orthodox priest had been shot by the Bolsheviks (Semenko-Basin 2010: 49–53, cited in Christensen 2015: 54).

religious repression (Christensen 2015). The new 'martyrs' fell victim to violent death directly caused by the Soviet regime, while the 'confessors' suffered from Soviet persecution but died from natural death.

In 1988, the ROC counted approximately 300 saints from within its jurisdiction (Christensen 2015: 8; 50–51). The number of new martyrs and confessors quickly outstripped the old saints, as the canonization process intensified. In the year 2000, the Council of Archbishops canonized 860 new martyrs and confessors. By 2015, the ROC had canonized 1,776 new saints.

Clearly, the fall of the Soviet regime authorized this unprecedented wave of canonizations that Karin Christensen has called a 'religious work of memory' (ibid. 34). Jeanne Kormina has argued that all Russian Orthodox canonizations are political acts (see also Freeze 1996). But the post-Soviet situation has a specific feature; the new saints' 'hagiographies and cults are part of the process of making Soviet history usable in the post-Soviet context' (Kormina 2013: 410).

The political goals to be achieved by canonization are of two kinds. On the one hand, canonization recognizes as saints those who were victims of Soviet state violence. On the other hand, canonization also incorporates those who had a relatively typical Soviet life, such as Saint Matrona of Moscow (Kormina 2013). The first type of canonization, now by far more spectacular, is in the most obvious way 'an exercise of power' by the Church against a state (Christensen 2015). It would seem to proclaim the inevitable victory of Orthodoxy over Soviet ideology, providing a history of the regime's eventual collapse.

Yet both types of canonization reflect also on the politics between two Russian Orthodox Churches: the canonization of new martyrs and confessors was laid down as a precondition to the reunification of the ROC (Patriarchate of Moscow) with the Russian Orthodox Church Outside of Russia (ROCOR). ROCOR, also called the Russian Orthodox Church Abroad (ROCA) was created by anti-communist Russian émigrés in the United States.[50] ROCOR initiated the canonization of Soviet martyrs earlier – in 1981. Long under discussion, the Eucharistic unity of ROCOR and ROC was finally proclaimed in 2007. In practice, their structures have not been merged and they have maintained their previous autonomy.

This canonization is in fact a way to integrate, in the most convenient possible way, the Soviet past into the present. The post-Soviet state has been marked by very limited political efforts to examine Soviet repressions and crimes. Christensen (2015), for example, has argued that the preference of ROC's top leaders to canonize people killed under Stalin's regime is a way

---

[50] ROCOR's formation was precipitated by a split from the ROC after Metropolitan Sergius (Starogorodskii) proclaimed allegiance to the Soviet authorities in 1927.

to condemn the distant Soviet past.[51] The less violent, more common types of anti-religious repression of late Soviet times are left un-commemorated and unexamined (Christensen 2015: 109–11). The Church's politics of memory thus parallel the state's politics of memory, which are – on the whole – uncritical.

Finally, canonization reflects controversies within the ROC. That is, the top leaders and members of the lower levels of Church hierarchy disagree about the canonization criteria (Christensen 2015).

The processes unfolding around these canonizations are extremely complex because the new saints are useful in many national-level projects of remembering and forgetting. At the same time, the career of a single saint, while reflecting some of these intricacies, can also exacerbate other tensions and contribute to locally specific achievements, which, in turn, connect local Orthodoxy back to the broader challenges.

Saint Lidia of Ozerovo[52]

The canonization of Saint Lidia of Ozerovo has become part of local identity and Orthodoxy. Saint Lidia links local Orthodoxy to large-scale processes within the ROC, but the developments of new martyrdom in Ozerovo also give a locally specific twist to the Church's national-level politics. By pursuing with determination the canonization of new saints, the Church is marking Russia's territory with its renewed presence and potency. In turn, Ozerovo's new saint marks the city's place in the new Orthodox topography.

Throughout Russia, the possession of a local saint has always been considered a mark of the locale's overall piety. A saint's relics have always been seen above all as providing a privileged connection to the divine by more or less observant Orthodox. Now, people from Ozerovo and pilgrims to Ozerovo can address the local saint for assistance in an impressively large range of issues. Finally, veneration means economic betterment for the church housing the relics. This, of course, is a central concern for contemporary parishes suffering, as they do, from chronic underfunding. Saint Lidia's canonization was smooth and easy. So too was her popular appropriation. Yet her appearance marks inter-parish tensions that connect contemporary disparities to the Soviet past. I will attend to each of these aspects below.

An impressive ceremony was held in spring 2007, with a cross procession (*krestnyi khod*) in which more than a thousand people, as

---

[51] The perpetrators are not necessarily condemned. Apocryphal Orthodox icons of Stalin continue to circulate throughout Russia.

[52] I have replaced the real name of the saint by a pseudonym.

reported by local media, walked through the city's main streets. The people followed all local clergymen belonging to the ROC, several hierarchs from Saint Petersburg, and the heads of the local political authorities. The relics of Saint Lidia of Ozerovo, the first saint to bear the name of the city, were brought to Trinity Church. A year before, a diocesan committee on canonization had recognized Lidia as an 'all-people revered martyr' (*vsenarodnaia prepodobnomuchenitsa*).[53] Her remains had been exhumed three days before the 2007 ceremony with consent from the heads of the Church and the city authorities of Saint Petersburg, where she had been buried. The removal of Saint Lidia's remains was the outcome of the strong commitment of Trinity Church's rector. He had worked relentlessly towards this achievement.

Plate 8. The crowd accompanying Saint Lidia's relics to the church.

Shortly before the ceremony, I asked the rector if the committee had conducted forensic investigations to verify whether the remains were really those of Lidia. Her grave, located in a cemetery in Saint Petersburg, had been venerated for several years. In 2006, I had visited the site and noticed

---

[53] Lidia had already been sainted by ROCOR.

that the big wooden Orthodox cross engraved with her name was brand new. If the cross was new because it had been placed recently, it might mean that the identity of the buried person was uncertain. Were they sure the grave was Lidia's? The rector confessed that there were no archives that clearly attested the grave's identity. He continued, 'There was no scientific testing of the remains. But there has been popular veneration for a long time. This means that the body is hers'. Indeed, his answer is consistent from the perspective of the Church. The Orthodox Church claims that it institutionally recognizes saints but does not make them. Thus, the Church follows popular cults in identifying saints.[54] After a pause, the rector continued, 'Well, when we exhumed the remains, we saw her deformed bones'. During her lifetime, Lidia had suffered from a painful disease which had deformed her entire skeleton. The answer to my question about the scientific evidence was that, probably, these were Lidia's remains. But I want to point out that this physical evidence was less valuable in her identification than was an existing popular veneration at the gravesite. From the outset, the Church's desire to canonize new saints should only follow the paths of existing local cults.

In fact, the new canonization rarely follows such paths. The availability of Saint Lidia's relics makes her a relatively unusual new martyr. The existence of relics makes her closer to the traditional type of saints because the remains of many of the new martyr saints cannot be found, buried as they were in mass graves. In contrast to Lidia, most new saints therefore 'lack the materiality that is so crucial for popular veneration' (Kormina 2013: 412). Lidia's relics give her more appeal within popular Orthodoxy. Unlike the immense majority of new saints, Lidia was made 'from below' as well as 'from above'.

The Powerful Workings of Improvisational Ease

The unprecedentedly large-scale, strong institutionalization and routinization of the process of canonization of new martyrs are novel policies in the Church. But there is some continuity too. The frequency of institutional recognitions has always fluctuated in history. Political reasons have been of crucial importance.

For instance, at the turn of the twentieth century, the deep crisis in the tsar's political authority motivated the Church to undertake an increased number of canonizations. About a dozen new saints were recognized in a

---

[54] Robert Greene has explained the ROC's position thusly: the Church 'giv[es] sanction to the veneration on earth of men and women to whom God ha[s] already granted glory in heaven' (Greene 2010: 74).

period of twenty years (Freeze 1996; Greene 2010: 74–75); four had been canonized in the preceding two centuries (Greene 2010: 14).

As I have indicated above, the surge in post-Soviet canonizations can be linked to both unprecedented Church policies to promote religious resurgence and the political positioning of the Church in relation to secular authorities. But national politics – whether of Church or State – tell us only part of the story. At the very local level, clerics and worshipers work towards the establishment of the cult of a given saint. Local people (and local churches) keep alive a saint's cult and make the saint relevant to their daily lives (Kormina 2011, 2013).

At the local level, any given saint accomplishes two central functions. A saint operates as a channel through which the local inhabitants can demand divine grace to solve a range of issues – from the most elevated spiritual questions to the most down-to-earth anxieties, pains, and problems. A saint also brings in much-appreciated economic resources to those who house and host him. Indeed, shortly after the relics of Saint Lidia were transferred to Trinity Church, buses of pilgrims – destined for prominent shrines in and around Saint Petersburg – began to push several dozens of kilometres off their normal itineraries through the Russian countryside to reach Ozerovo. The relics of Saint Lidia, covered with a cloth and put in a fine wooden chest (*raka*) with a glass top, are now positioned to the right of the central altar. Booklets with the prayers in praise of the saint (*akafist*) and a presentation of her life (*zhitie*), as well as icons in different sizes, are sold at the stall inside the church. For Trinity Church, these new sources of income are a welcome addition (see chapter 5).

Since the first days after the transfer of Saint Lidia's relics to Trinity Church, hundreds of local inhabitants have come to venerate her. Their reasons are many. For some, whose comments I overheard, she is comparable to Saint Xenia of Petersburg. Also called Xenia the Blessed, this saint is the most widely worshiped female saint in the region. Like Xenia, the less-widely venerated Lidia is said to bring consolation (*uteshenie*). Saint Xenia is mostly known for bringing solace to suffering women and to those struck by family problems and material hardship (Kormina and Shtyrkov 2011). Lidia, however, has no such narrow specialization. She is, in this way, an adaptable saint – useful and accessible to all locals.

After her relics were installed and exposed for worship, many came to place flowers on the floor in front of the chest containing the relics. This practice signalled the inauguration of veneration far beyond the milieus of the observant faithful. During the first weeks, the quantity of flowers was impressive; on the weekends, it became difficult to get access to the chest. Most people want to kiss the glass top covering the relics and to pray at the chest itself. Some want to kneel, others want to stand. These unexpected offerings imposed an adjustment in practical church management. A new task of periodically removing flowers had to be assigned. Women who are otherwise invisible components of the official structure and function of church activities (see chapter 6), circulated among the visitors, removing the flowers.

A couple of months after the relics had been set in place, I was visiting the church. I was accompanied by a young woman who worked for the parish school. She was a medical nurse by profession. I had been sneezing and scratching my eyes for several weeks already, due to a pollen allergy. My acquaintance told me that I should 'press my head and my upper chest against the relics' (*prislonit'sia k moshchakh*) in order to be healed. This gesture had become quite typical; many of the worshipers had started doing it: first kissing, then laying gently the upper part of their body on the chest's glass top for a few seconds. My acquaintance explained further, the power of Orthodoxy in healing pollen allergy had already been attested. She herself had witnessed how a woman suffering from strong hay fever a couple of years earlier had been healed immediately after a nun had prayed for her. Analogically, she expected Saint Lidia to heal my allergy.

Robert Greene wrote, 'the improvisational ease with which the faithful adapted a centuries-old set of ritual practices to meet the exigencies of everyday life at the turn of the twentieth century reveals the degree to which Russian Orthodoxy was able to incorporate innovation into practice and remain culturally relevant in an age of supposed "secularization"' (Greene 2010: 14). At the turn of the twenty-first century, Russians exhibit this same 'improvisational ease' with regard to Orthodox beliefs and practices. As a saint, Lidia has been rapidly integrated into the life of Ozerovo's inhabitants, while at the same time attracting worshipers from afar. She can solve, it would seem, almost any problem.

From Troubled Past to New Disparities

That the process of Saint Lidia's canonization was taken over by the clergy of Trinity Church and that her relics were transferred to that church did not go unquestioned in Ozerovo. Trinity Church had suffered from Soviet repression by far less than the Church of Saint George the Warrior. During her lifetime, too, Lidia had associated with the Church of Saint George the Warrior – not Trinity. A few active members of Saint George the Warrior made note of these ironies and the unfairness in the allocation of her relics. 'Now', said one, 'she is with those whom she had always opposed'. But such observations were not made public beyond the circle of the most committed parishioners, in particular those who had initiated the reconstruction of the church and who knew its history before its closing in the late 1930s.

Nevertheless, street-level Orthodoxy was untroubled by – and apparently unaware of – the idiosyncrasies in Lidia's restitution by the post-Soviet Church. Nor did clergy from the Church of Saint George the Warrior blame colleagues from Trinity Church for claiming the saint. Nor did Ozerovo's inhabitants give much attention to the troubled past that could have been recalled alongside Lidia's exhumation. The effervescence around the recognition of the city's own saint has overwhelmed all of these other possible discourses. However, the scattered trails of such alternate commentaries are important. They hint at connections between the experience of violent Soviet repression in the 1930s, post-Soviet competition over the canonization of new martyrs, and inter-parish disparities. These I tell below.

In February 1932, when the Stalinist regime launched bloody attacks against the 'black clergy' (monks and nuns), Lidia was a nun living in Ozerovo. She was affiliated with the urban representation (*podvor'e*) of a distant convent. The Church of Saint George the Warrior, as mentioned in chapter 3, belonged to this monastic institution, and the priest rector was Lidia's spiritual guide. Both Lidia and her spiritual counsellor openly opposed the anti-religious campaigns, declaring that they were ready to give their lives but not their faith. Lidia was then already known for her gifts of consolation and perspicacity. Ordinary local people, as well as members and relatives of the so-called *byvshye* (the 'former people' who had served the imperial regime) such as clergymen, officials and military, used to address her with demands for spiritual advice and protection. Matushka Lidia[55], as most booklets and websites have referred to her since canonization, was soon accused of anti-Soviet propaganda and the spread of religious obscurantism. Most monks and nuns arrested in the region, along with their family members, were fated to deportation or death. Although unable to move her body due to disease, Lidia was imprisoned in Saint Petersburg while the authorities decided her fate. During this short incarceration, she declared herself outright a 'true Orthodox' and 'unlike Metropolitan Sergius', she refused to collaborate with the Soviet state.[56] The authorities

---

[55] Literally meaning 'little mother', *matushka* is used to address nuns and the wives of priests.

[56] In 1927, Metropolitan Sergius (Starogorodskii) issued an encyclical letter in the name of the Church whereby the hierarchs of the Orthodox Church declared allegiance to the Soviet state (available at: http://www.gumer.info/bogoslov_Buks/ortodox/Article/Dekl_Ser.php, accessed 17 August 2017). A proponent of the wide oppositional movement was Iossif (Petrov), Metropolitan of Saint Petersburg, whom Lidia followed. In 1943, under Stalin, Sergius was elected Patriarch. His predecessor, Patriarch Tikhon, elected in 1917, was the

decided to deport her, but before their decision was enacted she died in detention.[57]

In the same period, the Church of Saint George the Warrior was closed, and its building used for other purposes, until the eve of the collapse of the Soviet Union. In contrast, Trinity Church, first opened in 1852, remained open almost continuously. It was closed during the war between 1938 and 1941, during which parts of the building were damaged. Under Stalin, too, religious paraphernalia was removed from the church and at least two priests were killed by the regime. Yet soon after the war, the church was renovated, and became again the central church in Ozerovo. Its history of resistance was brief: some faithful who continued to oppose Patriarch Sergius (Starogorodskii) into the 1940s gathered there; they were eventually arrested and some were killed. After this brief episode, the parish had no further troubles with the Soviet authorities, and maintained a prominent place into the post-Soviet period.

The canonization of Saint Lidia of Ozerovo has opened new horizons for Trinity. By the end of 2015, the rector, in his role as head of the deanery, formed a committee charged with 'the inquiry and the spread of knowledge about the feat of new martyrs and confessors [...], as well as about all devotees of piety (*podvizhniki blagochestia*)[58] whose memory is surrounded by the prayer veneration of the faithful people'. He appealed in a call published on the parish website to all local inhabitants 'in possession of whatsoever information about sufferers for the faith (*stradal'tsy za veru*) ... letters, diary notes, photographs, related to the church life of our district and to particular persons' to inform the canonization committee. Thus beyond celebrating Lidia's canonization, Trinity Church has turned its attention to canonizing new saints generally. The Church of Saint George the Warrior has not taken a similar initiative.

It is interesting in this turn of events to notice that the facts of the past have not been silenced forcefully. Those who know that the Church of Saint

---

first to assume this office after the position's suppression by Peter the Great, who had replaced it with a Holy Synod.

[57] Saint Lidia is relatively untypical among the new saints for yet another reason in addition to those mentioned above. She died in 1932, but most of the new martyrs were victims of the Great Terror of 1937–38. This period saw mass executions – for example, 20,000 'enemies of the people' were killed at the Butovo Polygon near Moscow (Rousselet 2007, 2011; Christensen 2015). Many of these 'enemies' were executed because of their religious commitment: there were 940 Orthodox clergymen, monks, nuns, and church workers (*tserkovnosluzhiteli*), along with their family members and other faithful laypeople. Faithful of other denominations were killed too (Rousselet 2007: 56). Massive canonization of the martyrs and confessors killed at Butovo started in 2000.

[58] *Podvizhniki blagochestia* also translates as 'ascetics of piety' (see Christensen 2015: 77).

George the Warrior had opposed the Soviet regime and that many associated with it – like Lidia – were punished, may say so publicly. They may also remind themselves and others that Trinity collaborated with regime. And some do. But for the most part, these memories have been rendered simply unattractive, and irrelevant in the overall excitement that everyone shares in Saint Lidia's sanctification and the public display of her relics. Yet Trinity's power to claim and possess Ozerovo's saint is important to note. It reveals that old local political and religious divisions have been reintegrated in the new conditions of a disparities-ridden Orthodoxy.

The multi-layered dichotomy between these two churches in Ozerovo is not necessarily found in every locality. This case concentrates divisions along several lines: the different fates experienced by each church under Soviet rule; post-Soviet material disparities; an unequal possibility to claim the relics of a new saint; and different visions of religious identity (asceticism versus prosperity). Their distinct connections to the divine do not form a general pattern of inter-parish differentiation that one should expect to find elsewhere; no similar configuration and causality should necessarily be sought for the ROC in general. Nonetheless, this case illustrates how dynamics of community and divisions intermingle giving the neighbourly relations between two churches complex meanings, some of which resonate beyond the walls of the churches, while others stay confined to core communities.

Chapter 5
The Economy of Street-Level Orthodoxy: Struggling over Moral Values, Power, and Equity

Common practice within the church economy deserves attention for at least two reasons. First, it is instrumental to the material sustenance of each individual church. Second, by participating in the church economy, that is, through engagement with religion, different people express views about spiritual worth, moral values, desirable justice, perceived suffering and disparities, as well as about power in its political, economic, and moral dimensions. Material sustenance and spiritual-moral views are deeply entangled. Thus by looking at the economic aspects of street-level Orthodoxy, we gain insight into the social worlds and moral views of ordinary Orthodox people. The church economy embraces many as soon as they walk into the church. It is common for people to come into the church 'directly from the street' to light a candle or buy a booklet, even if they have little other interaction with the church in their daily or annual lives. Others come into the church to order prayers, pay for a ritual (or get it for free), or donate money. All of these incursions into the church economy are largely independent of familiarity with canonical knowledge or 'correct' belief.

Since the early period of post-Soviet liberalization of religious practice, the economy of the ROC has been one of the most controversial issues in Russia, spurring debate within and without the organization: Can the Church act as a profit-seeking enterprise? Is the sale of religious goods and rituals acceptable? Or should the Church rely on unsolicited, benevolent gifts alone? It is important to understand why these questions have become so central in post-Soviet society. Are they a mere revival of an old controversy? Or is there something specifically post-Soviet that can explain the emotional intensity with which they have appeared after the fall of the Soviet regime?

While addressing these questions, I stress the impressive diversity of meanings and messages found within the church economy, which both draw on and go beyond notions of the marketable and the non-marketable. In doing so, I try to uncover the multiple ways in which the current rules and practices of the church economy are embedded into people's lives.

Anthropological studies of different Christian denominations show that religious economies depend on history, belief, cultural meaning, as well as the relevant framework in which religious economies operate (Obadia and Wood 2011). Variations are found at the level of the small community (e.g. Gregory 1980)[59], larger denomination (e.g. Kiernan 1988)[60], and global level (e.g. Coleman 2000, 2004, 2006).[61] Strict reciprocity, famously phrased by Marcel Mauss as the 'triple obligation' to give, to receive, and to return (1950 [1924]); 'pure gifts' defined by Jonathan Parry (1986) as an expression of a quest for transcendence present in the world religions, ideally done in secrecy and without expectation of a worldly return[62]; and standard commerce – are three extreme types out of a plethora of transactions within Christian economies. Instead of attempting a classification of the different transactions found in the ROC, I draw inspiration from the above studies to show that participation in the church economy aims to reach out to the wider frame of Russian society by creatively referring to ideas of self-interest and selflessness. Through the technicalities of price-setting,

---

[59] Gregory (1980) has demonstrated how clans in Papua New Guinea turn the occasion to donate to a Protestant church into traditional competitive gifting. Gifts to a Christian church follow an indigenous logic of emulation so that giving to the church ends up placing the most generous clans at the top of the local hierarchy. This also results in more material wealth being accumulated by the local church.

[60] The South African Zulu Zionists studied by Kiernan (1988) deploy three forms of money gifts – offerings, collections, and tithes. The first two express the relationship between the individual and the congregation, the third the interdependence between the congregation and the headquarters of the church.

[61] Swedish Prosperity Christians, whose congregation is part of the complex economy of the global neo-Protestant Faith Movement, see their transactions as a spiritually motivated sacrifice, notwithstanding the internal diversity of the movement's economy. The money given is conceived of as having the power to return to its original giver with increment through global spiritual channels. Coleman (2011) argues that the common 'theoretical trope' of sacrifice unites the two anthropological ways of dealing with global Prosperity's economy, one that treats this neo-Pentecostal strain as a reaction to global processes, another one that refuses to see it merely as a 'response to' and rather conceives it as a 'more complex model of co-constitution' between the 'religious' and 'economic' dimensions (Coleman 2011: 33).

[62] The expression 'pure gift' has a long and controversial history in anthropology which began with Malinowski's own contradictory positions. In his most famous monograph on the Trobriand Islanders, Malinowski labelled as 'pure' or 'free' gifts those that were made from husband to wife and from parents to children (1984 [1922]: 176–77). Later, challenging the stereotype of 'primitive communism' which pervaded Western debates at that time, he declared his own analytical category of pure gifts to have been 'a mistake' (1926: 40). He then subsumed the large variety of differently motivated transactions depicted in great detail in his earlier book under a single characteristic: 'reciprocity as the basis of social structure' (ibid. 46).

gifting, and bookkeeping, people engage notions of gift and commerce, and mobilize visions of their differential moral valence, in order to address social stratification in Russian society, to communicate about the public image and power of the ROC, and to express ethics of equity and honesty.

In other words, I claim that with the post-Soviet Orthodox resurgence the church economy has become a controversial arena for making statements about politics and morality in Russian society. It is an arena in which different participants restate, reassess, or call into question politics and morality. The plurality of views expressed and the occasional discrepancy between official Church positions and parish-level views and practices do not preclude perceptions of relatedness between the people and the organization or between different members of society. Instead, the practical workings of the church economy testify to multiple views about how differences unite.

Below I provide a brief overview of the economy of the ROC at the parish level. I claim that atheist Soviet and post-Soviet views have shaped ideas about religious sacrificial gifting and church commerce and increased expectations that the Church should act selflessly. I demonstrate too that the practicalities of parish life unsettle notions that sacrificial gifting reflects a higher morality than does commerce. I then demonstrate how action (and reflection) within the parish economy addresses major political and moral themes, such as the perception of disrupted social equity and the ROC's authority.

Inside Church Commerce

Each ROC parish is a self-funding economic unit, which makes commerce an important source of income (see chapter 2). Each parish hands over part of its income to the eparchy, which is directly accountable to the Patriarch and the Holy Synod, but receives no money from it.[63] Each parish pays fees for water, electricity, local services, and renovation and construction works. Each also buys merchandise for its shop from ROC suppliers and pro-

---

[63] See the Statute of the Russian Orthodox Church, chapter xx, 'Property and Assets', §26. All real estate property, goods, donations, financial assets held by parishes, monasteries, brotherhoods and sisterhoods, educational institutions and other canonical units, belong to the ROC. https://mospat.ru/en/documents/ustav/xviii/, accessed on 23 June 2017. The Statute (chapter xvi, §5) specifies that the parish is formally obliged to 'allocate through the Diocese the funds for general church needs in the amount established by the Holy Synod and for the needs of the Diocese – in the manner and amount established by the bodies of the Diocesan Authority'. English version available at https://mospat.ru/en/documents/ustav/xiv/, accessed on 23 June 2017.

ducers.[64] The higher the number of visitors, priests, and church workers, the higher the turnover and expenditure of each parish. Sizable income disparities among the parishes are reflected in the priests' salaries. Officially, it is the responsibility of the parishioners – a particularly elusive category (see chapters 1 and 2) – to provide material support for their clergy.[65] No funding is secured from either the Church hierarchy or from the state.[66] Although donations from businessmen and support from the local authorities are important sources of income, the sale of religious items and services is vital.[67] The bookkeeper at Trinity Church told me that half of its income came from sales, while the other half came from donations collected during the services (*na kruzhku*) and from boxes placed in the church. Therefore, how a church sets the prices for rituals and goods is of utmost importance for its continued functioning.[68]

It is in the parish churches where most occasional visitors and active parishioners experience the church economy. Therefore, I focus on this level, particularly on parish clergy and church workers who are daily involved in this economy. Church workers belong to what can be defined in Russia's urban settings as belonging to the middle and lower-middle class. In my field site they were predominantly middle-age former and current teaching staff (see Patico 2005), factory workers, technical and medical staff (see Rivkin-Fish 2005), administration employees, and pensioners (see Caldwell 2004, 2007).

I was told that the practices I witnessed beginning in 2006 greatly differed from those in the early 1990s. That is, in the early 1990s, no written prices for rituals were displayed in the church shop. Visitors needed to ask

---

[64] Most items sold in Ozerovo's churches came from the factory Sofrino. Sofrino is run by the Moscow Patriarchate. It is the leading manufacturer of Russian Orthodox religious paraphernalia in Russia and caters to all kinds of customers. The factory produces a large range of items: from heavy church furniture and decoration to tiny necklaces and crosses, and from hand-painted magnificent icons to cheap printouts.

[65] Since 2013, the eparchy is expected to support parish clergy and lay employees who live below the subsistence minimum (see chapter 2).

[66] The Statute of the ROC stipulates this obligation of the parishioners in chapter XVI, §33: https://mospat.ru/en/documents/ustav/xiv/, accessed on 23 June 2017.

[67] Contributions from entrepreneurs are central to certain expenses, such as church construction. Köllner reported donations as large as 300,000 euros donated by two separate entrepreneurs to build a church in the city of Vladimir in 2007 (Köllner 2012: 124).

[68] The most frequently listed rituals are: baptism; marriage; funeral service at the cemetery or in the church; including a person's name in the prayers said at the altar for periods of forty days, six months, or twelve months; a single inclusion of the name of a live or deceased person in different kinds of prayers; individual prayer for a living or deceased person; the blessing with water of apartments, houses, offices, cars; photography and video recording of a ceremony.

the price. There were not many things to buy from the shop: only candles and a few crosses. Shops then really matched their name, *svechnoi iashchik* (lit. candle box).

Plate 9. Some church stalls offer hundreds of items for sale.

It was in the beginning of the 2000s, I was told, that the interior of many churches had to be changed to accommodate the growing shops and expanding commerce. The church shops are increasingly called *lavka* (shop). They now offer hundreds of objects, including books and pamphlets, candles in four or five different sizes, oils, DVDs, and a large range of icons. Trade has become an essential part of the churches' activity. The demand for services has also expanded. Many people get baptized; religious funerals have become a norm; people commonly order prayers for their kin and acquaintances by writing their names on slips of paper (*zapiski*). All these services require payment.

Trade in religious goods and services is not new in the ROC. But earlier, the circle of customers was smaller. Prices were known within the community. Recently, as church attendance expanded, prices have been displayed to save staff time from explaining the various costs. In an unprecedented way, in the early 2000s, church trade accomplished its own 'bureaucratic revolution' (Hart 2000: 204–6), that of 'fixed and open pricing' (Carrier 1995: 80–83). Yet the revolution has remained incomplete and the 'fixed and open pricing' often serves as a point of reference that is subverted in practice.

The different levels of prices applied in each church have proven a major source of differentiation within the post-Soviet ROC. In everyday talk, people compare the churches by this criterion. For example, in Ozerovo, people ranked informally but quite consensually the churches according to the prices they used. Trinity Church was considered the most expensive. Saint George the Warrior, the city's second largest parish, was considered cheaper. The third church in which I conducted research, named after Archangel Michael, was the smallest and cheapest of the three. It was held normal that prices for candles and rituals there were lower than elsewhere; it was located in a remote neighbourhood and offered only a few items for sale. Officially, there was no strong competition between the churches through shop sales and prices. They catered to geographically – and to some extent socially – distinct groups. Yet it was not unusual for occasional churchgoers to consider the prices and the location of a church when they needed religious goods or services.

Plate 10. Other shops propose fewer items.

The ROC has always sought income and church economy has always been controversial. Before the 1917 Revolution neither the parishes nor the monasteries lived from gifts alone. Their economy was shaped by fluctuating state support, donations, and a wide range of economic activities. These centred on farming and craft production (especially in the monasteries), as well as on trade in religious items and rituals, on emoluments, donations, clerics' and believers' labour. Thyrêt described this mix of activities in the seventeenth century as 'monastic entrepreneurialism' (2010: 499). Certainly the economic condition of parishes and monasteries varied widely (Freeze 1983: 51–101; Bogdanov 1995: 66–69; Rozov 2003: 39–40, passim; Shevzov 2004: 54–94; Bernshtam 2005: 134–47; Nazarov 2006). Records from the eighteenth and nineteenth centuries indicate that prices for rituals also varied according to region and the economic situation of parishioners (Bernshtam 2005: 134–47).[69] Some prices were agreed upon by the priest and community, others were fixed by the state (Bernshtam 2005: 141). The state intervened sometimes to limit the frequency of collections (*sbory vo vremia obkhodov*) in poor areas. Generally, rural parishes were known for the dire economic circumstances of their clergy; at the same time, it often occurred that peasants accused their priests of extracting high fees (Chulos 2003: 56–61).

Under Soviet rule, the churches (Orthodox and others) were confined to a modest and mostly silent existence. Their economies shrank dramatically. The clergy of the ROC depended upon its own resources; the state did not provide them with a salary or other income. Accusations of greed and unfair gain characterized Soviet anti-clerical propaganda, although most of the clergy led miserable lives.[70] Anti-clerical voices, in particular those attacking church commerce, have remained strong in society after the

---

[69] Detailed lists of prices exist for the most frequent services in the Moscow Region and in the Ukrainian Eparchy (Bernshtam 2005: 140). It is clear that within the Ukrainian Eparchy, higher prices were applied in the wealthier agricultural lands than in poorer regions. See also Nazarov (2006: 194–95).

[70] The issue of the churches' wealth was used for both atheistic propaganda and control over the clergy. Without drawing excessive generalizations about other churches, it is worth mentioning that in 1964 the Pskovo-Pechorskii monastery (located in Ozerovo's neighbouring oblast' of Pskov) was obliged by the authorities to give people receipts attesting to the amounts received by the clerics for services rendered. This bureaucratic innovation aimed at achieving higher transparency, and had the effect of making the anti-clerical critiques even more aggressive. The amounts listed on the receipt were claimed to be 'too high'. In response, the monastery took down the posted prices for candles, arguing that people could give what they wanted without any obligation imposed by a written price. Interestingly, people gave more than the stated price had been. The research on the Pskovo-Pechorskii monastery in the 1960s was carried out by Jeanne Kormina. She generously shared her findings with me. See Kormina (2008) on the parishes in the region of Pskov after the Second World War.

fall of socialism, even as many Russians started engaging with Orthodoxy. Clerical self-criticism has also risen. These moral evaluations of the church economy are deeply connected to Soviet popular morality and to encompassing post-Soviet circumstances.

The Differential Moral Valence of Gift and Commerce

Patriarch Alexii II, head of the ROC from 1990–2008[71], addressed the clergy in an official speech in January 2005.[72] He appealed for the pricelists (*tsenniki*) for rituals to be removed and extended this to the prices for the candles. He often expressed this position. The former patriarch called the usage of pricelists 'a vicious practice' and 'trade in grace' (*torgovlia blagodat'iu*). He urged the clergy 'to reflect on this in order to rescue the Church from criticism'. Public criticism has often emphasized the Church's commercial activities and anti-clerical voices regularly demand for the Church to be recognized officially as a business corporation.[73] 'The sale of spirituality' (*prodazha dukhovnosti*) was a popular phrase in public debate.

Some clerics and laypeople supported Patriarch Alexii's views. For instance, during my fieldwork, a young parish priest expressed disagreement with the practice of determining prices for rituals. He said, 'I personally do not agree with prices in the churches. I understand there should be donations, but fixing some fee for a mystery – this is highly suspicious, because nowhere in the Scriptures is it said that this should be fixed. To the contrary, the Lord cast out the merchants from the temple. [I say] yes to donations, but voluntary donations'.

According to state law, payments for goods and services proffered by the Church are 'donations' because the Church is not a commercial enterprise. But, as this priest noted, when prices are fixed and posted, they cannot be considered 'voluntary'. In one of our numerous conversations on the material situation of the parishes he told me, 'Our system is very sick now'. In the past, he said, the Church had really lived only from donations;

---

[71] On 5 December 2008 Patriarch Alexii II died. Patriarch Kirill was enthroned on 1 February 2009.

[72] 'Otkazat'sia ot ustanovlenia platy za treby v khramakh prizval patriarkh Aleskii' (Patriarch Alexii appealed to renounce fixing payments for clerical services in the churches). http://www.pravoslavie.ru/news/050117133025, accessed on 23 June 2017.

[73] An organization for the defence of consumer rights has started a legal procedure against the Moscow Cathedral of Christ the Saviour, claiming that this church must obey the laws on commerce, in particular by using fixed and open pricing, guaranteeing the quality of the merchandise, and paying the income tax. http://www.portal-credo.ru/site/?act=news&id=105839&topic=333, accessed on 23 June 2017. This church, one of the most famous and rich in Moscow, is placed directly under the Patriarch's authority.

there had been nothing like present-day church commerce, which had become a shameful necessity.

The priest had graduated from seminary only a few years earlier. I found it interesting that he should be the one priest among my informants who endlessly recounted how pious and assiduous in prayer Russia's pre-revolutionary peasants had been. An important aspect of their piety, he said, was their gifting practices. The idea of a high morality and various romantic views about pre-revolutionary Orthodoxy are typically found in the thriving popular post-Soviet Orthodox literature. Representations of donations that alone sustained the Church pertain to such views.[74] They tend to exacerbate a dichotomy between commerce (as epitomized in posted prices) and 'voluntary donations'.

Plate 11. A box destined to receive prayer orders and money gifts.

---

[74] An influential Orthodox deacon imagines the absence of church commerce in old times: 'There was almost no money (especially in the village). People brought in the church a little part of what they cultivated and made themselves. They did not buy candles in the church, but brought them from their home. They did not buy a small bottle of oil for their home icon lamps, but from home they brought oil made with their own hands. They did not buy host from the church but brought for the church their own homemade bread or flour' (Kuraev 2006: 233).

In fact, the unprecedented magnitude of church commerce in the post-Soviet era is not the consequence of an effacement of moral boundaries. Neither is commerce in religious goods and services a new practice – even though posted price is a technical innovation. To the contrary, the evidence is that there has been a resilient and yet fluctuating ideology that opposes self-interest to selflessness. The assessment of the Church's place within this ideology has varied over time. It is clear that the political and economic transformations in post-Soviet Russia have had a major impact on the prominence and intensity of this ideology in public discourse. But what is it about the post-Soviet era that has prompted the strengthening of a moral expectation that the Church will express disinterest in financial affairs?

An ideology of self-denial and renouncement for the sake of spiritual elevation is considered a cornerstone on the path towards salvation in Orthodoxy, with selfless and anonymous almsgiving being among the highest religious acts (e.g. Fedotov 1966: 80). Orthodox theologians trace this ascetic pattern back to the early Church Fathers. The same ideology underpins the perception of a differential moral valence of gift and commerce. The idea that gift is morally and spiritually superior to commerce is obvious in the words uttered by both Patriarch and young priest (see also Gregory 1982; Parry 1986; Carrier 1995). But the wide sympathy for such positions in highly secular Russia, where many firmly stick to their atheist education, can hardly be explained as the simple resurgence of old religious morals. Clerical self-criticism and lay disapproval of the search for profit has occurred in a situation of systemic transformation from planned to market economy. The economic and social conditions were met for this critical discourse to find a poignant resonance among the wide masses of those who painfully experienced the new conditions. The Soviet regime succeeded in dramatically reducing religious knowledge among its citizens; most Russians hardly new anything about Orthodox theology. Yet, Soviet moral teachings assiduously insisted on selflessness and, for various purposes, mobilized harsh criticism of profit-seeking commerce. Thus, partly, the vibrancy of the dichotomy between gift and commerce in the frame of the church economy derives from the religious notion of pure, unreciprocated giving as an expression of selflessness and a way to transcendence (Parry 1986). But this dichotomy owes its popularity to the fact that the religious pattern meets a popular ideology of disinterestedness. Patriarch Alexii II criticized trade in rituals and candles not because it could hinder spiritual efficacy, but 'to rescue the Church from criticism' meaning criticism within Russian society.

Studies on late Soviet and early post-Soviet Russia show that popular thought was infused with the idea that selfless action is an expression of higher morality.[75] Authors researching late Soviet and early post-Soviet Russia have noted that, while informal activities aimed at making a profit were far from unusual, they were simultaneously accompanied by resentment and likely to be labelled *spekuliatsia*. 'Buying low and selling high' was further identified by the Soviet state as an extreme form of illegality and self-interest (Humphrey 2002: 58–61; Humphrey and Mandel 2002). In post-Soviet Russia, Orthodox priests still refer to this Soviet notion to condemn businesses that are preoccupied with buying low and (re)selling high (Köllner 2013: 47–48). Widespread relationships of trust that provided access to scarce goods and generally inaccessible services, called *blat*, conveyed a plethora of thoughts and deliberations about the balance and tensions between freely offered favours and reciprocal ones. 'Small favours, altruistically given and received as "help" or "friendly support" are inherent in *blat*', wrote Ledeneva (1998: 61). People saw these acts of altruism as mutually beneficial.

Dale Pesmen (2000) demonstrated that the beginnings of the Russian market economy in the early 1990s simultaneously exacerbated and reconciled notions of altruistic gift and profit. Enrichment and profit were culturally framed in opposition to the cultural notion of soul (*dusha*). Thus illegal transactions were followed by 'soulful' socialization, such as drinking together, in order to protect relationships from the threat of selfishness (Pesmen 1995: 74; 2000: 170–71). That there could be such a wide gap between the widely-held and absolute moral dichotomy of self-interest (bad) and 'gratuitous giving' (good) and the bewildering diversity of transactional practices reflected, according to Pesmen, 'different moments of consciousness' (2000: 135).

The medical system provides another good example of the clash of values in this period of transformation. For instance, in the 1990s, physicians hardly survived on their tiny state salaries. Nonetheless, those trained in the Soviet system 'treated the exchange of money as "dirty", as a sign that one's professional commitment to helping all patients was compromised' (Rivkin-Fish 2005: 182). Taking money directly from the patients in addition to one's salary was still 'morally wrong' (ibid. 189). Slowly, however, economic success and wealth came to represent a fair reward for one's work and skills (Patico 2005, 2009). Among medical doctors, 'taking money for services gradually gained legitimacy', first as a 'necessary evil' and later as an appropriate monetary compensation for medical services. Eventually, pricelists were displayed in hospitals and clinics (Rivkin-Fish 2005: 182–206). Paying for medical services came to be interpreted as a sign of the

---

[75] On moral discourses on wealth in post-Soviet Ukraine see Wanner (2005).

patient's commitment to care for his or her own health (Rivkin-Fish 2005, 2009).

While religious practice was not extensively researched in the early 1990s, sociologist Natalia Dinello (1998) interviewed 61 bankers trying to assess if they were closer to an ideal-typical Western money-making *Homo economicus*, or to an equally ideal-typical *Homo orthodox*. She defined the characteristics of the latter drawing on Russian literary and theological works mostly from the late nineteenth and early twentieth centuries. The primary importance of collective over individual interests, anti-commercialism, anti-materialism, and affectivity were among the qualities attributed to *Homo orthodox*. Surprisingly enough, only one of her informants, a woman with long-term experience from Soviet banking, supported these values. The overwhelming majority of the others, young motivated bankers, clearly endorsed the profit-seeking and individualism of *Homo economicus*. Dinello reported the view of her anomalous informant, 'her vision of success did not include money as a component', and then conveyed the woman's own words: 'Money satisfies certain needs, but success is when one is needed by other people' (Dinello 1998: 55). Moral incentives, the woman had further explained, superseded monetary ones as her motivation for work. Dinello's interviews do not comment on the actual practices of her informants, but they nevertheless reinforce the impression of a late-Soviet mind-set and its progressive transformation, documented by the above scholars for other professional fields.

The vivid rhetoric against the Church's self-interest and money-making that I found in public discourse in the mid-2000s points to moral tensions that were exacerbated by nearly two decades of profound social upheaval. This rhetoric was a Soviet one, intensified by the post-Soviet experience. Jonathan Parry (1986) argued that early Christianity provided an ideology of unsolicited and unreciprocated gifting, but that it flourished as a central Christian ideology because specific economic and political conditions allowed it to flourish. The post-Soviet example shows that the transmission of this ideology has now gone in the opposite direction, from the secular to the religious sphere. In the absence of religious engagement for most of the population over some seven decades, the dichotomy of self-interest and selflessness must be seen as reflecting secular Soviet values. It is these values that have been drawn upon to reassess the church economy.

Below I depict how people draw on the ideological partitioning of selflessness and self-interest as they act within the church economy. They use the markers of standard commerce and gifting to communicate on a large range of issues that matter beyond the church walls.

Malleable Pricing and the Ethics of Equity

Church commerce is sometimes transformed into an instrument of equity. For church workers, rhetorical and practical manipulations of pricing become ethical instruments used to express who one is, to act in favour of social equity, to acknowledge social relationships, and hence to address central concerns in Russian society. There has been an enduring aggravation of poverty and social exclusion since the reforms launched in the 1990s (Manning and Tikhonova 2004).[76] Its acuteness has spurred criticism of social debasement. These are Russia's social disruptions that parish staff members have in mind when they use pricing as an ethical instrument.

Indeed, I came across an individual case where the church visitors were explicitly offered the possibility to give less than the usual price, or to not pay at all. In the shop of a tiny church located on the ground floor of the local hospital and belonging to the parish of Trinity Church, there were several boxes of candles. Most had prices indicated. But in front of one box containing small thin candles, there was no price, only an inscription announcing 'candles for the poor' (*svechi dlia maloimushcheikh*).[77] One could take a candle for free, or give as much money as one wished, explained the woman who worked in the church shop. She had set up the boxes in agreement with the priest. The idea behind the system was that visitors who considered themselves able to pay the requested amount could buy candles from the box with a price label. Those who considered themselves not well-off could take the small candles and decide whether and how much money they wanted to leave. The box with 'candles for the poor' was a charitable gesture to visitors of modest income. The shopkeeper reported that it was mainly elderly living on meagre pensions who availed themselves of the 'candles for the poor'. It is interesting that when visitors were left to make an assessment of their own financial circumstances, most chose not to self-identify as 'poor'. As in the earlier example of a Soviet-era price-removal at Pskovo-Pechorskii monastery (see also Kormina 2008), most objections to posted prices would seem to have relatively little to do with the profit-margins of religious goods and services or with the financial capacity of people to pay for them.

---

[76] Coupled with this phenomenon are cultural perceptions of the relative normalcy of class distinction (Rivkin-Fish 2009; see also Patico 2005, 2009).

[77] *Beden* and *nishchii* are the more commonly used words for 'poor', while *maloimushchii* appears most frequently in the context of public social services and in other administrative domains with the intent of referring more neutrally to one's 'means'.

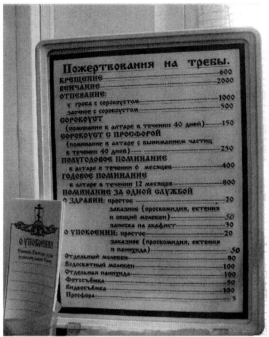
Plate 12. A price list.

Beyond the overall moral framework of self-interest and selflessness, the pricelists do worry at people's concerns for social equity and, relatedly, class belonging. The pensioners who take the 'candles for the poor' do have heavily restricted incomes, but they also accept the label of being 'poor'. Younger people do not accept such a label, regardless of their income. To be young and poor grates against shared social values, but to be old and poor is morally acceptable (and perhaps even superior to being old and rich).

In actuality, even in churches with pricelists it is not mandatory to pay the stated price. This is Church policy and common knowledge. Some churches – although none of those is Ozerovo – mention this flexibility in a sentence at the bottom of the pricelist. Yet no one negotiates prices if there is a list. The pricelists for rituals in all local churches had a sober but authoritative outlook; they were very readable and easily noticeable, usually placed near the church shop. They were taken as presenting a would-be customer with only one option: to pay as much as the label says (Hart 2000: 204–06).

Priests themselves insisted that they would never refuse to perform a baptism or a funeral (*otpevanie*) for free if they were requested to do so. Some of them even initiated free services: I witnessed one such free funeral. The death was a particularly sad one. There were two siblings, a teenage girl and her younger brother, who begged at the entrance of Saint George the Warrior. One evening in the middle of the winter, a third sibling – an elder brother – got drunk, fell on the street, and froze to death. Though most of the church workers and priests disapproved of the young beggars who were often drunk and impolite, the priests took it upon themselves to offer a free funeral service. This was not simply charity offered to a family of limited or no means. Parish priests are rarely sympathetic to young (drunken) beggars. In this case, they were moved to offer a free service by religious and social concerns, but also because they felt a certain social relationship – however critical and disapproving – to this marginal family.

Transactions in churches are often impersonal, as in consumer markets. Then, the fixed prices hold. Nonetheless, church pricing is far from having achieved 'the institutionalization of impersonality' characteristic of retail sale that first took root in ninetieth-century Britain and the United States (Carrier 1995: 13). Different practices on the ground are rather reminiscent of what Janet Roitman described in Cameroon: 'Price, as a practice, is a way of discussing a social relation' (Roitman 2003: 221). Sometimes, the impersonal and discretionary status of authoritatively displayed prices is subverted through inventive manipulations. Transactions are made negotiable in relation to social status (as exemplified by the 'candles for the poor') or to acknowledge a relationship (as shown by the gifted funeral service). By playing on the multiple avatars of the gift-commerce complex some church workers transform pricing or sidestep it for the ethical purpose of making religious practice accessible to the needy.

Organizational Image and Power

Some practices in the lived economy of the churches concentrate on claiming high spirituality as a way of improving the ROC's image. Yet other practices assert the connection of the Church to political power. Indeed, the ROC's image and power are encoded in the subtext of parish economic life. In particular, insiders of parish life communicate over the power and image of the Church. The public duel in images of the Church as a calculating entrepreneur or as a spiritual recipient of donations has been among the most controversial issues in Russia since the 1990s (Mitrokhin 2004). The actors of the parish economy participate in this debate by using inventive techniques to reinforce, blur, or break down the distinction between commerce and gift. Through rhetoric and tricks of price display, clergymen, and church workers use their power to set a price, but also to disguise it. The price makes a public statement about a particular church vis-à-vis others, and about the Church's role in society more generally.

The ROC's religious moral economy is closely entwined with its politically buttressed legitimacy. The non-profit legal categorization of the ROC by the state is critical. The legal view of Church income as 'donations' intrudes into practical assessments as people conflate and distance notions of gifting and commerce. This moral economy uses the privilege of state support, that is, the privilege of power. The ROC too bargains on its official 'non-commercial' status. It assumes high public legitimacy for its own commercial activities by disguising them in contrast to competitors in the marketplace for religious goods. In larger cities and outside monasteries, for example, street sellers proffer candles and other goods. But the churches incite visitors to avoid buying from such vendors, redefining the payment of a higher price in the church as 'sacrifice'.[78] One announcement I saw on the door of a churchyard in Saint Petersburg read:

> Dear brothers and sisters in Christ,
> NO BLESSING IS GIVEN (IT IS NOT ALLOWED) to bring and to light candles acquired outside our parish! Always remember that the candle symbolizes not only an ardent prayer, but the candle, above all, represents your Christian sacrifice for the maintenance of the temples of God.

The text was signed by the two priests of the parish. Here, the encouragement to contribute to church income is justified in terms of need – 'for the maintenance of the temples of God'. Religious sacrifice and standard payment are not separate categories; the payment for candles is, from the point of view of these priests, a sacrifice which 'above all' helps the church to live. Much like in Fair Trade, standard commerce is made to support a higher purpose (Carrier and Luetchford 2012). The ideological vitality of sacrificial gifting is deeply intertwined with pragmatic economic concerns. Moreover, by displaying the announcement on the entrance of the churchyard from where all passers-by could read it, the priests publicly claimed higher authority for their parish over other parishes and street vendors. In addition, while articulating a public message merging together 'Christian sacrifice' and the sale of candles, the priests asserted the ROC's organizational power in the subtext, restating and taking advantage of the semantic potency of the ROC.

If political power is encoded in the subtext of pervasive announcements demanding support for church building (or simply to buy candles), spirituality is encoded in the subtext of some techniques of pricing.

---

[78] The Church has recently adopted a rule according to which 'The church use of candles and other church items purchased or produced outside the Church shall not be allowed'. Statute of the ROC, chapter xx 'Property and Assets', §40, https://mospat.ru/en/documents/ustav/xviii/, accessed on 23 June 2017.

Church shops use some techniques of pricing to indicate that freely decided gifts stand as an ideal, but that commerce is a practical norm. Such techniques of veiling fixed pricing mobilize the widely shared view that commerce and gift have different moral valences, and that gifts are a sign of high spirituality. Pricing techniques are not simply interested or disinterested actions; nor do they aim simply at either profit or spirituality. They convey messages about image and power.

In 2008, I came across a creative way of disguising posted prices. As mentioned above, former Patriarch Alexii II overtly opposed the use of pricelists. Yet even the recently rebuilt and high-rank Moscow Cathedral of Christ the Saviour, of which the Patriarch himself is head, had to balance its need for income against its image with regard to pricing. A solution was devised that let continue a standard trade in candles without marking prices. Candles of different size were presented in separate boxes and each box was given a number – N. 10, N. 25, N. 35. Ostensibly, the number referred to the size of the candle, but in fact it was understood that it indicated the price in roubles. The people patiently waited their turn, without questioning the numbers. To each person who had selected candles, the shop worker announced the total sum to pay, and the buyer kindly handed over the money. Everyone seemed to understand and accept the system. The church respected the Patriarch's will to eliminate standard trade in candles, but exacted fixed prices. Similarly, there was no list of prices displayed for rituals. When my Russian friend inquired at the church shop: 'How much do you charge for baptism?', the shop worker readily replied: 'One thousand roubles' (a common price in middle-range urban churches at the time).

Was the Patriarch aware of the price-disguising in the church he headed? Perhaps. But it does not really matter. This church distinguished itself from the great majority of churches in the country by avoiding overt displays of price. At stake was an attempt to polish the public image of the Church by exhibiting a non-commercial façade to the visitors' gaze.

Often, committed Orthodox see gift where outsiders would see commerce. Several among my informants claimed that payment or gift was a matter of interpretation. Devout churchgoers, for example, claimed that prices simply specified the amount of an otherwise religiously-motivated donation. It was practical to treat a price as fixed, but the money handed over can be seen as a voluntary donation.

This distinction does not arise entirely of its own accord. Adults undergoing conversion receive this perspective as part of their teaching. I learned this when I attended a talk given in the poorly furnished room of the parish school for adults at the Church of Saint George the Warrior. On that particular evening, there were five adults in attendance: two women in their late thirties, two elderly women, and one man in his forties. All appeared to belong to what can be defined as the low or lower-middle class. The man leading the course was considered a particularly knowledgeable Orthodox. After the usual prayer and a short reading of the Gospel, he announced the topic of this meeting: What does it mean to give money in a church? He explained that the candles in the church were not there for commerce (*torgovlia*), but to allow the visitors to make a donation (*pozhertvovanie*). 'It is written "5 roubles" there', he explained. 'The real price of the candle is 50 kopeks. So when one gives money, it is a donation. But one can also give 50 roubles, though "5 roubles" is the written price. That is what a donation is'.

The public nodded. The speaker expressed a usual position defended by parish workers: to give money for a ritual purpose (here in order to acquire a candle) means to make a donation to the church. That evening, the lecturer justified this in two ways. Firstly, the difference between the production cost of the candle and the written price must be seen as the amount of the donation. Secondly, the money given is not bound by the written price; one is free to give more. 'The state understands this', he added. 'Of course, one cannot put a cash register in a church'. Thus he explained, by allusion, why the state considers money paid into churches for goods and services to constitute 'donations' rather than 'commerce'. The alternative is simply unthinkable. In this way, he used the state-enforced category of donation to emphasize the existing perception of a differential moral valence between the 'gift' of a donation and commerce. His invocation of the cash register as incongruous also explained away the need for fiscal accountability in churches.

This was a powerful teaching. The speaker drew a firm line between trade and donation; and he made them belong to different worlds. Profit bureaucratically-recorded by cash registers had nothing to do with the Church. Money in the Church could only be understood in terms of spiritually-elevated donations that cannot (ought not) be captured by the futile devices of bookkeeping. For him, the donation instilled spirituality into the organization and, in a circular way, the religious frame meant that the transactions were donations and not commercial payments. His interpretation and the actual politics of pricing and disguise of price stress the higher value of gifting over commerce. Yet, some practices may turn upside down this differential moral valence of gift and commerce.

When Gifts Undermine Honesty

During the first two decades of post-Soviet transformation the notion of honesty (*chestnost'*) has encapsulated much of the lively public debate about conflicting values, not least in relation to church donations and trade. The notion of honesty is indexed too with reference to the ROC's economy, alongside ethics of equity and a struggle for ROC's image and power. Since the 1990s, there has been a widespread view of the Church as a 'mafia' living off the contributions of 'poor people' (e.g. Ries 2002: 308–09). This view was part of a wider discourse; Russians bemoaned the pervasiveness of dishonesty and moral corruption, expressing a bitter sense of being part of a country of 'ubiquitous cynicism' (ibid. 277). Insiders of the parish economy echo this criticism to some extent, as indicated by continued questioning of, if not aversion to, commercial practices within the church. In general, insiders too prefer 'gifts' because they convey honesty and a higher morality. However, parish bookkeeping turns on its head the usual differential moral valences and in some cases, it is unsolicited 'voluntary' donations that seemed to undermine honesty within the church; money earned through sales allowed for true accounts.

As noted at the beginning of this chapter, each parish contributes a portion of its income to the eparchy. When I inquired how the eparchy defined the amount due, I learned that it relied on the quarterly reports submitted by each parish. The fee, I was told, is relatively low and should present no burden for a parish. Yet there is no standard percentage or amount specified in advance by the hierarchy; each eparchy decides how much each parish should contribute every quarter, after perusing their reports. On the one hand, the amount could be adjusted by bookkeeping. On the other hand, it was never clear how recording more or less income, and more or fewer donations, would affect the parish's required contribution. The bookkeepers among my informants drew my attention to ways in which a commitment to fairness clashed with the occasional opaque uses of money gifts in their parish.

Usually in Orthodox parishes the amounts of money earned through commerce and donations, or any indication of their turnover, are never publicly announced. The overwhelming majority of churchgoers are given neither figures nor approximations. This practice stands in sharp contrast with the public announcements of collected money in other denominations, and particularly in charismatic churches (Kiernan 1988; Coleman 2004: 431, 2006: 178). However, informants gave me some hints. One priest, who was open to discussing money gifts, told me not to believe that the two wooden donation boxes of his church were largely empty. 'Sometimes', he said, 'there is lots of money inside. I do not know who donated it. Some people do not want anyone to know that they gave'. Yet even this priest would not mention any numbers. I could never get the slightest approximation about how much money represented the type of Russian Orthodox gift that most closely reproduces the ideal pure gift: unsolicited, unreciprocated, and done in secrecy (Parry 1986).

My attempts to come up with figures about the daily or monthly income of the studied churches proved equally unsuccessful, despite the fact that among my close acquaintances there were parish bookkeepers and shop workers. Partly, the difficulty stems from the bookkeepers' and priests' very limited openness in discussing this matter. It is simply an unvoiced norm that one does not speak of such matters. Partly, no one knows how much money comes in. Bookkeepers collect figures about the income from the cash desk of the shop, usually kept by female church employees, and from the priests. But not all the income is reflected in their reports. Priests do not always report donations made directly to them, or the full sums that they removed from the donation boxes. In parishes with several priests, the problems of tracing such figures are compounded.

My informants included four women who worked as parish bookkeepers. They were all in their forties and activists of the parish for which they worked. All of them had another professional occupation too, within the parish or elsewhere. All were devout believers with solid knowledge of the canon. All of them emphasized in our conversations that they tried to do their work correctly. The periods during which they had to prepare the quarterly reports for the eparchy, they said, were the most stressful time for them. They wanted to deliver true accounts.

One of them was considered by her fellow parishioners to be kind, observant of the rules, and very fair. It was she who wrote quarterly reports to the eparchy. Yet she had no way to know how much money the church had really received. I learned this by inquiring after a donation that I had made of 10,000 roubles (approximately 260 euros in 2007). I had given the donation to the parish priest. A few months later, I decided to ask the bookkeeper to deliver a certificate for this donation which I could show later to my academic employer. I was right to ask her: she was responsible for issuing such certificates. But she was very surprised by my request. 'I did not know that there was such a donation', she said. Then I asked her how precisely she was informed about the income of the church. It came out that the shop workers reported to her regularly with great accuracy on the income from goods and rituals sold on fixed prices. 'But whatever is given to the priests, I cannot know', she said, 'what I write in the quarterly report is what they report to me'.

Another bookkeeper confided to me a similar experience. As devout Orthodox women, the bookkeepers generally avoided being judgmental, especially about priests. Expressing disagreement publicly is unthinkable. Rather, in a friendly, empathic company, they would laconically utter their tormenting thoughts, their moral suffering caught between the conflicting obligations to obey the priest and to behave honestly. Gifts posed dilemmas to them because they were likely to infringe transparency and encroach on accurate bookkeeping. Unreported monetary donations were an obstacle to honest accounts. In contrast, trade with displayed prices allowed for clear accounts thanks to the records kept at the church shop.

For bookkeepers, fixed posted prices exercised a discipline not only upon customers, but also upon the shop staff who reported sales. Conversely, money gifts could open the door to fiscal misconduct, and this troubled the bookkeepers' cherished sense of honesty. Though money gifts might seem to follow the high ideal of religious sacrifice on the part of the observant faithful, they enable misconduct by the Church. In contrast, the practices of commerce help to inflect the moral balance of parish practices in favour of honest behaviour.

Conclusion

The deep transformation of Russia's political and economic order since 1991 and the simultaneous promotion of the ROC resulted in swelling both commerce and gifting practices within the Orthodox churches. If criticism of the ROC's economy has always been present, the post-Soviet circumstances have given it a new impulse. Concentrated on the moral legitimacy of profit-oriented action, the debates have mobilized notions of self-interest and selflessness. Commerce and harsh criticism of it have thrived simultaneously within and without the Church. Russians' painful experience of an overall systemic transformation since 1991 has intensified the critical discourses levelled at church economy. Being aware of this pervasive criticism and, more widely, of popular notions of interested and selfless action, parish priests and workers apply multiple practical arrangements in their everyday economic practice. In particular, they creatively use the markers of trade and gifting to point to national policies and society-wide processes: the strong organizational power and controversial image of the Church, social stratification, notions of equity and honesty. This non-economistic use of the church economy means not only that cultural and social factors have a decisive impact on this specific economy. It also means that the practices and thoughts associated with the church economy always cross the Church's organizational boundaries. The most common forms of participation in street-level Orthodox economy encapsulate a variety of links between Church practice and thought, national politics, the deeds of powerholders, and Russia's unequal society.

Chapter 6
Women in Orthodox Schooling: Living an Ordinary Life and Making Society Better

Laywomen form the large majority of the workers in Orthodox parish education. At odds with the high level of female participation is the fact that women find almost no recognition in the official hierarchy of the Church. Only in monasticism do women hold an officially recognized position. Outside of this narrow path, the Church is determined to uphold the exclusionary criterion of masculinity as a fundamental prerequisite to formal participation in its structures.[79] In practice, there is a complex informal female hierarchy with discreet types of participation in different sectors and levels of society (e.g. national-level media and publications, local or national cult of saints, schooling), some of which is geographically specific. Ozerovo's parishes evidence some of this complex in the sphere of parish education. A closer examination of laywomen's activities in the ROC and its organizational margins brings answers to the following questions: Who are these women? Why and in what precise ways do they engage in work for the Church? How does their involvement help shape the relationship between the ROC and society?

Focusing more specifically on the sphere of Orthodox parish education, I have found that some of the most salient and common gender disparities, as well as widely shared aspirations, shape women's involvement in parish education. Post-Soviet parish schooling presents a unique combination of pivotal female participation with specifically female economic disadvantages, structural ambivalences, and spiritual projects. In parish schools, women suffer from the same structural disadvantages as elsewhere on the job market. Here too, age is a disadvantage in acquiring

---

[79] The wife of a parish priest (*matushka*) is granted a half-official status. Western Orthodox theologians have argued in favour of women's ordination (see Karras 2008 for a well-argued example, including an extensive overview of the theological literature), but in Russia, the issue hardly appears in public debates. Among the personnel of Orthodox schools, clergy, and activists, I never heard anyone even vaguely suggest that women should be ordained.

work, women's salaries are lower than men's, and their payments are more often 'undeclared' which means that they pay no tax, but also receive no benefits. Nevertheless, women choose to work in this sector, patiently shaping it because they see it as a morally higher, cultured enclave amidst society's rude and often brutal relationships. They see spreading the faith as a way to reach out to the youngest generations, to teach amiable social relationships, and to thus improve society. These objectives matter to them no less than do more soteriological motivations.

Thus, the women who work in parish education bring into the everyday life of the post-Soviet Church the sociological characteristics and moral-spiritual quest of an average 'woman on the street'. Many of them claim only loose belonging to the Church as an ecclesiastical organization. But their contributions are pivotal. It is through these women that Orthodox education is provided to youth. These women are important actors in the effervescent domain of street-level Orthodoxy.

My focus on women's participation in Orthodox education, especially in its 'lowest' levels of organization, is emblematic of women's contributions to the Church more generally. Women have played a prominent role in the consolidation of post-Soviet Orthodoxy in a variety of ways. Sociological surveys regularly document higher rates of church attendance for women than for men (a pattern documented also in Soviet times). In addition, in the post-Soviet Church as in the long history of Russian Orthodoxy, women have forged specific relations to the divine (see for example Meehan 1993; Thyrêt 2001; Weaver 2011b). Moreover, women's participation is particularly high in areas that have been crucial to the ROC's post-Soviet resurgence. Female saints are among the most popular ones in Russia, and it is women who most often venerate them: Saint Xenia of Petersburg (Kormina and Shtyrkov 2011) and Saint Matrona of Moscow (Kormina 2013) bear particular mention.[80] Women have been active in the establishment of sisterhoods (Medvedeva 2015) and the revival of monasticism, as well as in the development of the now thriving Orthodox media (Kizenko 2013).

In her analysis of post-Soviet Orthodox print and online media, Nadieszda Kizenko (2013) has claimed that the leading role played by women has contributed to the expression of different opinions. Post-Soviet Orthodoxy is now demonstrably multivocal. While still inherently patriarchal, the Church has become more 'feminized'. But feminization has also taken place beyond the circles of the national Orthodox elite noted by Kizenko. At the local level, women working in the parish and Sunday

---

[80] The veneration by women of a particular saint is a religious pattern also found in Roman Catholicism (Orsi 1996).

schools[81] also form an elite whose didactic authority is acknowledged by priests and within the milieus of secular education (Ładykowska and Tocheva 2013). Moreover, the authority of such women extends beyond their 'classroom' presence. They are the direct interlocutors of the parents' and grandparents' whose children they teach with the potential to shift relations and perspectives in family life and upbringing. As women too, they have the reputation for being more available and approachable than the parish priests in Ozerovo. Local residents who are relatively unfamiliar with canonical rules address them – instead of the priests – with questions about correct practice. On numerous occasions I witnessed how such women were approached spontaneously: in the school, at church, in the churchyard, on the street. Through such ordinary interaction, their advice has a wide reach into the otherwise casually observant population.

Even women who are less prominent than the most 'elite' teachers and directors are critical to the everyday operation of Orthodox schooling. They have eagerly assumed their new roles, at the heart of the spread of Orthodoxy, even as they remain on the margin of the ecclesiastical organization. I turn now to a consideration of these women.

The Bottom of the 'Hierarchy': Little Old Ladies

In Ozerovo's parishes, very low-paid jobs are reserved for elderly women. Some of these women are employed occasionally, some on a permanent basis; some legally, others illegally. Whether stable income or occasional payment, the monies paid to elderly women are likely to be for doorkeeping, helping in the church, or cleaning during important celebrations. The small payments are a welcome addition to the women's tiny pensions. They are unable to get a better job or rate of pay elsewhere, so these women (who are often committed believers) feel comfortable in their roles at church. These roles too are ascribed to them by society with an unvoiced agreement.

---

[81] The specificities of parish and Sunday schools are provided with more extensive ethnographic notes where they are critical.

Plate 13. A church cleaner.

Elderly women most often work as cleaners (*uborchitsi*). Dressed in long wide clothes with a headscarf carefully knotted under the chin, they endlessly come and go inside the church, clean here and there, collect what is left from the burned candles, and remove wax from the floor. They are stereotyped sometimes as grumpy sanctimonious grannies. But these old women may be far from the stubborn Orthodox zealots that they are imagined as being. For example, through the intermediary of a friend, one of the elderly women who comes to clean at Trinity's (especially during important celebrations when the influx of visitors challenges the work capacity of the usual cleaners) belongs to a small Pentecostal congregation.

The cleaner's religious belonging to both churches was ambiguous. She explained that she had joined the Pentecostal congregation in part because she had received material support from them. She made little out of her membership there, and nobody in the Orthodox church where she cleaned knew about her other commitments. The work at the Orthodox church was important: meagre, but nonetheless an important supplement to her old-age pension. No one had asked about her motivations to clean in the church, nor about her spiritual state: her old age, gender, and outward appearance were enough. Nor was she concerned that working for the

Orthodox church might be in any way disingenuous; nor that there were any contradictions between her associations with both Orthodox and Pentecostals. Being an old woman gave her unquestionable rights, roles, and privileges within the religious sphere.

Plate 14. A cleaning lady of a parish school.

When not stereotyped as grumpy zealots, elderly female church workers are affectionately referred to as 'little grannies' or 'little old ladies' (*babushki*, *starushki*). Their image became inextricably linked to that of the Church under Soviet rule, mostly because it was admitted that elderly female members of society could, to some extent, depart from the general expectation to profess atheism. Their nearly paradigmatic role continued in the post-Soviet Church. Immediately after the liberalization of religious practice, it was the 'little old ladies' who assumed the informal office of teachers of correct behaviour. Even today, an occasional visitor entering a church is more likely to see – and perhaps be addressed by – several such women before glimpsing a priest.

However, an important transformation has occurred as the post-Soviet period has progressed. The 'little old ladies' have lost ground as informal guides to the Church and appropriate behaviour with the expansion of priestly guidance, Sunday classes, Orthodox schooling, and Orthodox print and online publishing. Said to have been severe and authoritative in the 1990s, elderly female church cleaners have become more self-effacing in the 2000s. Many have withdrawn to perform only the technical tasks for which they are hired.

Women at the Middle and Top

On the more prestigious side, middle-level service, bureaucratic, and commercial jobs in local churches are reserved for middle-aged women. For example, the job of church stall seller is most often granted an official salary.[82] In some places, the church shop is run by the priest's wife, but not in Ozerovo. In Ozerovo, the priests' wives are removed from the churches' everyday operation, although they are known to the churchgoers and local residents.

In Ozerovo, the middle-aged women employed in the church shops, or in other bureaucratic or bookkeeping tasks, are considered pious and trustworthy. Most of them have vocational training as bookkeepers or secretaries, and prior work experience in the private sector. Among my closest field acquaintances, there were four parish bookkeepers (chapter 5). All four women held degrees from higher educational institutions, and two of them continued to work in the private sector alongside their parish jobs.

In general, the top of the informal female hierarchy in parish education is occupied by Orthodox teachers, with the heads of the Sunday school occupying the top of the top. The prestigious positions of catechist, parish school leader, pilgrimage organizer, or head of the parish newspaper are usually assumed by women with university degrees. It is possible, as I encountered in several cases in the parishes of Ozerovo and its surroundings, that one woman holds several of these jobs.

At the top of the hierarchy, age is no longer the most significant element in a female worker's moral claim to work in a church setting. Instead, a woman's level of secular education is determinant of her authority vis-à-vis the (male) Church hierarchy. This is particularly clear in the case of women catechists who teach in the Sunday schools and/or classes for adults. These women are ascribed with unprecedented credit and didactic authority by clergy and laity alike (Ładykowska and Tocheva 2013). But their authority is founded in their professionalism; priests and laity recognize

---

[82] Those who work in the shop are called *svechnitsi*, referring to the small beeswax candles they proffer.

these women's educational and organizational expertise.[83] Frequently, the same women act as the actual managing directors of the Sunday schools, although priests are the official heads, and they may well have other jobs in organization and management.

Work at the Top

In Ozerovo, each of the three parishes offers Orthodox classes. The Church of Saint George the Warrior offers only classes for adults in the evening twice per week. The Trinity Orthodox School has classes for children on the weekend and during the week, as well as classes for adults one evening per week. The school of the Church of Saint Michael the Archangel offers only Sunday classes for children and is closed on working days. The largest parish school where I conducted research, that belonging to Trinity Church, is run entirely by women, though the official director remains the parish rector, as in the other cases.[84] Only the school of the Trinity parish has an active male teacher: the priest who is the school's spiritual guide (*dukhovnik*). He teaches catechism on an irregular basis and participates in important events organized by the school.

In all cases, there are anomalies between official positions, actual duties, and public perception. For example, the woman who acts as the head of the Trinity parish school is always called 'the Sunday school director', but her official position is only 'deputy director'. In turn, the woman who functions as a deputy director is a former journalist and officially employed to take care of the parish newspaper.[85] Just as the rector is the official director of the Sunday school, he is also the official editor of the newspaper.

---

[83] In the second half of the nineteenth century, young women who were trained in diocesan schools (mostly daughters of the clergy but not only) became teachers in the network of parish schools that was expanding by then (Wagner 2007: 133). There is no continuity between women's participation in parish schools in the late imperial period and the post-Soviet situation.

[84] The Trinity parish school hosts some 50 children at its weekend Sunday school classes. In addition three classes from a secular state school study in the building during the week. The arrangement, made with the agreement of the parents and local administration, is meant to enhance the pupils' knowledge of Orthodoxy while at the same time offering them more attentive pedagogical control, better skills in English and in other subjects considered as prerequisites to a successful professional career. The students are accompanied by their teachers from the secular school.

[85] An important change occurred in 2010, when the woman who acted as the actual head of the school left, followed by part of the personnel, to begin establishing a private Orthodox school in Ozerovo where she assumed office as a director. The informal deputy director took the role of head of the school, where she still works to this day.

Though professionalism is important for female Orthodox teaching cadre, not all teachers are as qualified as others. For example, 13 women worked directly for the Trinity parish school in 2006–07, with insignificant changes of staff in the following years.[86] Of these, four had initially trained as secular teachers, and five had graduated from a three-year course in Orthodox pedagogy in Saint Petersburg. All were between their thirties and mid-fifties. Only three of the thirteen actual employees were employed officially by the parish: the director, the deputy director who acted also as the head of the parish newspaper, and one of the teachers. The others delivered work as 'volunteers', but considered their small but regular payments as an undeclared salary.

There is no statistical data about the level of women's salaries and their general conditions of employment in the parishes. Nonetheless, direct observation and interviews show that their economic reward is meagre and hardly commensurate with their pivotal contributions (Ładykowska and Tocheva 2013). In Ozerovo, most of these women combine two or more jobs in order to make a living. Their work in the parish is often already a combination of several jobs, as indicated above, and they have additional work in state schools, as medical staff, or as secretaries or other kinds of employee in private companies. Orthodox education at the parish level thus reproduces the striking discrepancy characteristic of employment in Russia between high female participation and low payment.

Orthodox education also reproduces the ambivalent legacies of female participation in Soviet education. On the one hand, education in general – a strongly feminized profession – still holds high symbolic status as it did in Soviet times. On the other hand, however, the Soviet period also saw the payment of low salaries to women and their disproportionate allocation to lower professional positions. Despite the fact that official Soviet discourses emphasized women's emancipation, state policies were far from emancipatory from the end of the Second World War until the collapse of the USSR (Lapidus 1978; McMahon 1994; Engel 2004). In practice not only did women grapple with the double burden of paid work and reproductive work (childrearing and housekeeping), they also occupied the most poorly paid jobs. Teachers constituted the largest of the professional (and university credentialed) clusters with a high proportion of women (Lapidus 1978: 143, passim, 172, 185–87). Yet wages in education gradually decreased in comparison to the national average (ibid. 190–91). Beyond the sphere of education, the Gorbachev reform period and the post-Soviet changes brought

---

[86] The staff changed partly after the departure of the head of the school in 2010 (see above).

hardship and the feminization of poverty (Pilkington 1996). This trend has continued in the Putin-Medvedev era:

> Although there is no noticeable gender gap in employment rates in Russia, the gender pay gap remains very high; on average, women are paid 64 per cent of the pay of men for their work. This gap is related to relatively high levels of gender segregation in Russia's labour market, where women traditionally dominate in lower-paid public sectors; for example, the number of women working in the healthcare sector is almost four times higher than the number of men and in education there are more than five times more female than male employees. [...] women and men are paid differently even when they do exactly the same work. Moreover, women in the Russian labour market face the problem of the 'glass ceiling'; only 20 per cent of companies have female top managers, while 29 per cent of firms have female participation in ownership (Oxfam 2014: 21).

The ambivalences of the structural and symbolic position of women as professionals in the sphere of education have been reproduced in the Church. Parish religious education replicates the professional credit given to women as educators and school workers in the secular world, and couples it with the usual structural disadvantages (Ładykowska and Tocheva 2013). Thus, the case of laywomen engaged in Orthodox schooling evidences a structural isomorphism between Russia's general employment market and the situation inside the Church. But even with the disadvantages they experience as women in the workplace, female catechists build up substantial social authority and draw a sense of moral privilege from their participation in Orthodox education. Workers with lower education who take care of the less prestigious tasks in parish schooling draw similar 'benefits'.

Below the Teachers

It is women too who take over lower tasks in the informal hierarchy. These tasks include cleaning and cooking, taking care of the school's library, helping to organize outings for the pupils, and shopping for the school. These tasks also comprise teaching technical subjects that involve manual work. All of these tasks are most often taken over by women without formal training as pedagogues. The prestigious subjects, such as catechism, the rules of observance as described in the so-called Law of God (*Zakon Bozhii*), Church Slavonic, singing, and the history of the Church, are reserved for women with a degree in pedagogy.

Plate 15. A parish school library.

While lower tasks are essential to the good functioning of parish schooling, the women who assume them have so far fallen out of the scope of scholarly research, including large-scale surveys and ethnography. I suppose that one of the reasons for this lack of attention is precisely the non-prestigious status and the technical character of the work they provide. The other reason lies, I think, in their structurally undefined participation in relation to two critical groups: official church employees and active parishioners. The women occupying lower positions are not 'employees' in a strict sense. They are considered benevolent workers (*dobrovol'tsy*); the payments they receive as compensation do not offset this image. Additionally, these women are not necessarily active parishioners. The frequency of the participation of some of them, for instance in confession and communion, is by far inferior to the informally agreed post-Soviet norm: strictly observant persons confess and take communion on a weekly basis. On the other hand, some are quite observant, albeit in unexpected combinations.

One such worker is Valentina. Valentina works for the Sunday school of Trinity Church, but considers herself as a parishioner of the Church of Saint George the Warrior. Yet, Valentina's spiritual needs are not fulfilled by either church. She has chosen as her spiritual father a priest who heads an

Orthodox settlement in southern Russia. Valentina's triple affiliation stands completely at odds with the category that Jeanne Kormina (2012) describes as 'the structural Orthodox', an active and strictly observant member of one parish community. Valentina's fellow parish school workers, and Valentina herself, consider her a pious Orthodox who follows the right path.

Valentina: The Challenges of Low-Paid Jobs and the Normalcy of Single Motherhood

There are at least two sociological characteristics that, taken together, single out women in relation to men in Russia. The first one is the pervasiveness of lower salaries for women for all sectors and levels of employment, often coupled with the practice of multiple jobs. The second one is the normalcy of single motherhood from sociological and subjective points of view during the Soviet period and after (Utrata 2015). The massive participation of laywomen in Orthodox parish schooling has made these characteristics an intrinsic part of the functioning of the post-Soviet Church and an important aspect of the post-Soviet mutual embedding of Church and society. Working single mothers and their aspirations fly in the face of a conservative image of the Orthodox woman promoted by clergy and some of the Orthodox media (Kizenko 2013). In conservative images, a strictly observant woman should be the mother of a large family; she should not work outside the home; and her husband should be the only breadwinner. In fact, in Ozerovo, there are young couples who try to make this conservative ideal a reality. Among my informants, there were five young families who attempt to enact this familial model of Orthodox perfection. But this is a tiny minority. No such profile of Orthodox piety is to be found among women engaged in Orthodox schooling in Ozerovo. Some of these women share the Orthodox ideal. They explain their situation of single motherhood as a practical option.

Valentina, invisible in so many ways, is seen by everyone who enters the Sunday school at Trinity Church. Everybody in Ozerovo knows this school. It is the largest Sunday school in the city. The school building stands some metres away from the churchyard. It was inaugurated in 1901 as a parish school, but was then taken from the church by the Soviet state. During the Soviet period the school building was used for various purposes, including as a House of Pioneers, the Communist Party's section for schoolchildren. It was given back to Trinity Church immediately after the demise of the Soviet regime and re-established as a religious school. People who had attended educational and leisure activities as Pioneers in the late Soviet period told me that the building and the internal rooms had not changed much since that time, excepting perhaps the new windows and refreshed wall painting.

The entranceway too of this building is well known, especially because from the entrance, a five-metre high wall-painting welcomes visitors. It depicts Saints Cyril and Methodius, the Byzantine brothers, monks, and theologians who created the basis of what later became the Cyrillic alphabet.

In the entranceway there are also benches where pupils, parents, and other visitors are expected to take off their shoes and put slippers during the months between October and May. During these months, the ground outside is damp and people's shoes are clumped with dirt and mud. The floor between the main door and the benches needs constant cleaning. In winter time and on rainy days, it is Valentina who tirelessly washes the floor with a large mop. A tiny fifty-year-old woman, she is the cleaning lady of the school. Whoever enters the school on the weekend is likely to meet her.

On weekdays, Valentina works for the local police in a declared administrative job. But her salary is inadequate; as a complement, she earns money from making toys at home in the evening for a small local enterprise. Her thirteen-year-old son Kolia helps her. Valentina's unofficial salary as a cleaner in the Sunday school on the weekend provides her with another additional income. Valentina is a single mother. She is far from being an exception; nearly half of the school workers are single mothers who have two, or even three, jobs. Some half of the pupils' mothers, too, are single mothers with multiple jobs and incomes.

Single mothers like Valentina, who turn to the Church through work or by sending their children to Sunday school, gain in their sense of self. It matters little that as 'Soviet' women they neither participated in religious activities nor sought to model their personal lives on Orthodox gender ideals. Moreover, the trajectory of single motherhood in Soviet and post-Soviet times is so common, that they experience no condemnation. Finally, the Soviet part of one's life does not conflict with the post-Soviet religious commitment. On the contrary, the conscious turn to the Church and religion is positively integrated into a personal narrative. In Valentina's words, work and secular education stand out as particularly valuable components of her Soviet life. Her self-awareness as an Orthodox faithful harmoniously integrates these aspects of her Soviet trajectory (see also Tocheva 2014).

Valentina was born in 1956 and has always lived in Ozerovo. When she graduated from high school in the early 1970s, her mother took her to one of the largest factories in Ozerovo and arranged a job for her, so that Valentina could work during the day as a factory worker on the conveyor belt and follow evening courses in order to receive a higher degree.

Valentina appreciates her mother's decision to incite her to go beyond secondary education: 'When you have only secondary education, you know, there is a saying: "Ten classes and then a corridor". This means that you go to school a bit and then everything is over'. When Valentina graduated from college (*tekhnikum*) with a degree in economics, she stayed in the same factory. But then she worked as an economist and later as a norm-setting engineer (*inzhener-normirovshchik*). All in all, she spent 20 years of her life there:

> I loved my factory very much. It was a good factory, with many young people, a promising (*perspektivnyi*) factory. You know, our system was very politicized. So this is also how I talked myself. There was lots of talk about unemployment [elsewhere]. Then I said this: 'Everything can happen in the course of life, but I will never lose my job. Our factory stood, is standing and will continue to stand (*nash zavod stoial, stoit i budet stoiat'*)'. I said this because this factory firmly stood on its own two feet, so to say. And what do you think happened? A few years after my prophetic words, perestroika came [ironic smile]. Everything collapsed. It is not that I found myself in the street. No. But there was simply nothing to do in the factory, no more production. Can you understand this? This is when I decided to leave. Because production ended.

Valentina talked about her past on her own initiative; I had not asked her questions about her life under socialism. Fifteen years after the demise of the Soviet state, Valentina's self-irony about her own misconception about the eternal life of the Soviet system is understandable. Her words express people's awareness of having been part of a country where, as Alexei Yurchak (2006) writes, 'Everything was forever, until it was no more'. Besides self-irony, it is worth noting Valentina's deep conviction that her real professional career ended when her factory stopped producing goods, at the moment when 'Everything collapsed'. She occupied different administrative jobs afterwards. The one she had at the police at the time of our interviews in 2006 and 2007 was a good one, she said. But she never spoke of the police office with the deeply emotional tone which she used when she spoke of the factory.

Valentina's salary does not suffice, even when she supplements this income with the payment for her weekend side-job (*podrabotka*) of cleaning the Sunday school and money earned from making toys at home in the evening. Again, she contrasted this money shortage to Soviet times when she could afford going to theatre, travelling, sitting in coffee shops, making barbecues with friends. Nevertheless, she said, it was difficult to find good shoes, to dress elegantly. Such goods were simply unavailable. Valentina draws a typical, widespread picture of the material situation in Soviet times. Her presentation of the difficulties to receive adequate payment on the post-Soviet job market is also fairly typical.[87] But her narrative becomes by far less conventional when she turns to her personal experience from the post-Soviet situation of money shortage. Precisely when the market opened up, and consumption desires and acquisitiveness went skyrocketing, she says, material things stopped being so important for her: 'Now, thank God, I have a different relationship to this "cult of material things" (*veshchizm*). There is what there is, thank God. Can you understand that my worldview changed? I became a believing person and I changed a lot'.

Valentina felt awareness of the importance of God in the beginning of the 1990s. Although baptized in her early childhood, an event from which she has no memories, she did not practise or even talk about religion before the early 1990s; neither was her mother a practising Orthodox. How then, had she turned to religion? It was not out of desperation: Valentina had repeatedly tried to have a child, and after several miscarriages, she had almost lost hope. She divorced her first husband in the 1980s. Then, in 1990, she met Kolia's future father. She got pregnant in 1993. Surprised that this time her pregnancy was going well, she felt that she should 'entirely rely on God'.

> V: I was worried because of the previous miscarriages. I had thoughts of doubt. But I chased them away. I trusted only God. I thought: 'He is the Lord. Whatever He decides, I will accept it'.
> Q: So at that time you were already a believing person?
> V: Well, I was not exactly a believer, but apparently there was something in me because I had never denied the existence of God. I knew that there is God, but I did not address him. But if you do not address God, He does not support you in your life, don't you think? It is necessary for the person to have some desire to begin with. In reality, I had the faith, very strong faith. So I decided that I let it be the way God wants.

In Valentina's words, her strong faith was her first step towards God. In fact, she distinguishes between two phases. During the first one, she had strong faith, but did not really address God. Then, the event she had hoped for during many years finally happened: she got pregnant, and it was this event that led her to 'come to the Lord' (*prishla k Gospodu*). Her christening was a necessary prerequisite that had taken place in her childhood:

---

[87] The points raised by Valentina about Russia largely resonate with the situation of gendered experiences of postsocialist transformation in Central and Eastern Europe (see, for example, Gal and Kligman 2000).

It came out that I was baptized, thanks God. I was lucky. But this is only after Kolia's birth that I came to God. And my mother too. This happened when Kolia was born. In the very beginning I came to God when I started thinking: 'How shall I keep my son away from this world, from the craziness which is happening now in this world?' This was simply a complete lack of spirituality. And I did not want that. I started to think that in his life there must be something more elevated, holy, something for which a human being should strive instead of living with these bodily pleasures. I started to think and came to God. And then, unnoticeably, my mother ... too. Well, she went her own way. We did not go to church together.

Valentina's first step was to start reading what she calls 'spiritual literature'. She began with books written by 'Western priests and foreign spiritual persons'. Prior to that, she had developed interests in astrology and alternative healing. However, while Kolia was still a toddler, she felt that something held her back from these kinds of spirituality. She felt attracted to God 'from inside'. Valentina's feeling of responsibility for raising and educating her child incited her to join Trinity's Sunday school. When Kolia was four, she took him to the director of the Sunday school, a woman well known across Ozerovo for her kindness and good knowledge of Orthodoxy. The director initially declined Valentina's request because the school lacked teachers for very young children. Valentina insisted, arguing that Kolia would turn five very soon and that she wanted him to receive a good moral education. Then the director accepted, and even took the initiative to create a small group of preschool-aged children. The new group was put in the hands of an experienced Sunday school teacher; this woman too was well known, and would later establish the Sunday school at the parish of Saint Michael the Archangel (the smallest one in Ozerovo). For seven years, these children, accompanied by their mothers, attended the Sunday classes. At the age of 12, Kolia asked to stop attending. Valentina agreed, but continued her own relation with the church: the school director perceived that Valentina was faced with a serious shortage of money, and offered her the informal job as a cleaning lady. Valentina was working for the second year there when I met her.

Over the years, Valentina had turned to reading Orthodox literature for guidance in the upbringing of her son. Some five years prior to our meeting, she had come across several books authored by a priest specializing in family matters. She was deeply impressed by the first book she read: 'I thank God for this book'. The priest was also the founder of an Orthodox settlement in southern Russia, and Valentina had three times travelled there to meet him, eventually taking him as her spiritual father. For each of the three summers before we met, Valentina and Kolia had spent three weeks living and working in the community. The trips had necessitated substantial planning: the settlement was 1,700 kilometres away and the train tickets were expensive for her. The year we met, Valentina faced a shortage of money and the need to renovate her apartment, and was prevented from planning a new trip.

Valentina's path to the Church was entwined with single motherhood. And indeed, motherhood shapes the choices she makes with regard to spiritual practice. Valentina considers herself as a parishioner of the Church of Saint George the Warrior. She holds in high esteem Father Ioann, the parish rector; he is famous in Ozerovo for his asceticism, kindness, and wisdom. 'Of course', she says, 'I address Father Ioann for advice'. 'But', she continues, 'my spiritual father is Father Antonii [in southern Russia]'. It is important for her to get her most practical advice and spiritual guidance from a priest specialized in family issues.

It is important to note that Valentina did not enter the Church in a state of repentance. Single motherhood did not leave her feeling shame or disgrace. Single motherhood, if not preferred, is certainly socially accepted. It may be chosen, like the path to the Church, as a way to care for a child and to improve family life.

Kolia's father left Valentina approximately at the time when she gave birth to Kolia. She does not consider this departure as a traumatic experience. Her mother had raised her alone too. Her father had left from home when she was three and she did not remember him. She had no memories of her maternal grandfather either. In Russian families, fathers have long been often absent – whether divorced, still married, or never married. Single mothers therefore do not think of their experience as abnormal; many were themselves raised by a single mother, and usually a helpful grandmother (Utrata 2015). Women rarely experience men's absence as a reason for material hardship. They do not expect men to shoulder the burden of family care, and my informants described material shortage as deriving from their own low salaries, rather than the lack of a man's salary. To the contrary, as Jennifer Utrata demonstrated, drinking and/or unfaithful men are most often considered a burden for the family.

Valentina, like so many mothers, worked and cared for her child with the generous support of her own mother. She once told me that she would have appreciated having a man at home – he could help renovate the apartment, as she felt herself unable to do some of the works. But then her thoughts turned to the other aspects of having a man at home. A good friend, she said, had a husband at home, but the only two things that matter to him are his work and drinking. Neither wife nor children concern him. 'There is nothing else in his life', Valentina said. 'What should I do with a man like this?'

In her interviews with single mothers, Jennifer Utrata (2015) found few who were interested in having a husband. In variance with Utrata's informants, the Orthodox single mothers whom I met do contemplate the possibility of living with a partner, ideally a husband who is also the father of their children. But making this ideal come true, as Valentina said, is unthinkable if the man does not take care of the children, thinks that his life is boring, and finds solace in alcohol. In Valentina's words, it is impossible to realize the ideal of the loving married couple who takes good care of their children without the love of God:

> There are such families in our temple [the Church of Saint George the Warrior] and in the Orthodox community [i.e. the one run by her spiritual father in southern Russia]. They have children. In their communication with each other there is such peace, such quiet. They are not rich. [...] And I see how they relate to each other and I think: 'My Lord, how good is this!' [...] When the love of God is inside the person, this is so beautiful. They may have some disagreements, but nevertheless this is a real family, an Orthodox one. I look at them and I think to myself: 'My Lord, what a beauty, how charming, in what a wonderful world their children get educated!' This is the world of the family. Do you understand that for me this is stunning?

Valentina's appreciation of the importance of the love of God has a much wider implication that goes beyond family relationships. In hers and the school workers' understanding, the love of God is a precondition to making social relationships warmer and more humanistic.

Tamara: Practising Orthodoxy 'Out of Love'

Tamara, an elegant and thin lady in her mid-fifties, works as a secretary. She is a very good friend of the school director. A few years prior to my arrival, she had brought her five-year-old grandson to the Sunday school. Since then, she has occasionally taught Sunday classes herself, in particular manual works for girls and boys.

Tamara too is a single woman. A few years before she brought her grandson to the Sunday school, she had divorced from her husband. The former couple continued to live together in the same apartment because neither could afford to buy or rent separate accommodation. Tamara's divorce was a long time in the making, entwined as it was with her path to God. Tamara had 'come to God' (*prishla k Bogu*) in the early post-Soviet period, and had attentively conducted her own religious upbringing through reading and priestly guidance. Like Valentina, she is not a structural parishioner; no one sees her as an assiduous churchgoer, neither does she claim to be such a person.

Like the other regular and occasional workers of the Sunday school, Tamara has nothing of the severe outlook that zealot novices often exhibit. She does not cross herself endlessly and does not fear committing a sin every time she says or does something. Nor does she conform to the Church's most conservative expectations of an 'observant woman': she does not dress in dark clothes, her skirts do not reach the ground (they come only past her knees), and she wears no headscarf outside of church. Tamara's relation to religious matters is undemonstrative, but infused with quiet self-confidence. She is kind, attentive, and considerate in her relations with pupils and the adults in her midst.

Tamara's colleagues have very similar attitudes. This is important to note because their shared style creates the relaxed atmosphere considered typical for this school. Here, children are free to run around, shout, and play in lively and joyful ways. The school webpage announces the main mission: 'Our task is to create an atmosphere of love and mutual understanding in the school'. Disagreements emerge sometimes in the course of the everyday, but they always get solved. Everybody is convinced that mutual understanding and peaceful resolutions are by far preferable to major clashes. This attitude is not grounded in simple pragmatics; it derives from a moral-spiritual stance that pertains to a specific understanding that the love of God transforms social relationships and society as a whole.

Once in a conversation with a couple of other school employees, standing in the corridor mid-way between the director's office and the canteen, Tamara bemoaned the fact that many people had started practising religion because they are afraid of God's punishment. She advanced that other people would do it for political reasons, and yet others in order to show off. 'But who does it out of love?' Her question elicited agreement: Yes, people should practise religion out of love for each other and, above all, out of love for God. Helping spread Christian love is a way of making society better.

Among these women, Christian love is a value of utmost importance for the making of a better society. Official Russian Orthodox teaching holds – as do many other patriarchal religions – that faithful women should demonstrate their love through humility, obedience, patience, and docility (Wagner 2007). Such teachings have the effect of making humility, obedience, patience, and docility the highest virtues for women (Klassen 2001; Mahmood 2001, 2005; Kościańska 2009). Yet the women I worked with reversed the order. Or rather, they combined a teachers' emphasis on professionalism in the area of upbringing (*vospitanie*), with the virtues of love, empathy, and goodness to create another value hierarchy. (Accordingly too they do not find it important to dress themselves into a stance of self-effacement). These women conceive of their work as an active contribution to making society better. They spread Christian love, they teach it, or they assist in its teaching, by accomplishing even the most 'trivial' or menial tasks. Valentina's ceaseless floor washing is out of love, and enables love to be taught.

Coming to Love

In our conversations, Valentina often stressed that her character had changed since she had started practising religion. As she described it, her individual transformation had a social-relational objective. Her aim is to change her way of being with others; this kind of transformation can radiate out into society. Valentina describes herself as having had bad character; she got offended easily and would immediately respond in an even more offending way to the person who had offended her. This was the challenge she had to face when she started actively engaging with Orthodoxy after the birth of her son:

> I started noticing that I was really changing. Now I would not allow myself to, let's say, do rude things. I prefer to endure (*terpet'*). I do not get offended. To get offended was my 'party trick' (*dlia menia koronnyi nomer byl*), my usual reaction. It is too easy to get offended. Now I somehow started thinking of the others. [...] When you do good to a person, be he the angriest person, he may insult you, but this is all. If you stay kind, then he will feel that something good has been done to him, his soul will respond to that. I think that this is a more promising solution, more correct. This means not to respond to evil with evil, but instead to do something good. [...] I started to think more of the people.

These words might sound like 'common wisdom'. In fact, they are the cornerstone of the teachings of Father Antonii, Valentina's spiritual guide. It has taken work and concerted effort for Valentina to incorporate them into her everyday behaviour. She described one of Father Antonii's techniques for learning to 'be good':

> Take a sheet of paper and make two columns. In the first one you write the names of the people whom you like, whom you find nice, the people to whom you do good without even thinking of it. In the other column, you write the names of those whom you do not like even to see, or of whom you think even worse, to whom you do not want to talk. And then you will start doing good to those whom you dislike. To the people whom you like, with whom you have good

relationships, you will do good anyway, because this is the call of your soul.

Such techniques, said Valentina, help you 'to be good with the others', and constitute 'the beginning of a powerful work on your human soul ... work that leads to your internal transformation, the work that brings you closer to God'.

Valentina strives to spread amiability (*blagozhelatel'nost'*) in people's relationships. She says that it happens that people treat her with hostility; she faces aggressive attitudes and disparaging words. Valentina reports what is a common experience in Russian society. She brought examples from school teachers from her son's secular state school. Several times, teachers complained about Kolia, charging him with all sorts of misdeeds, including a theft which he had not committed. Faced with the teachers' particularly aggressive tone, Valentina felt very sad and weak, but also determined. 'When these difficulties come up, one should not skirt them. One has to learn to overcome such difficulties. At the same time, one should not harm the others, but instead act without anger, with patience, with humility'. Instead of replying to the teachers with anger or frustration equal to their own, she would pray in silence until she overcame her own nascent anger. Then, she would ask the teachers to forgive her for the misconduct of her son. She believes that her amiability, patience, and humility touched the teachers. After a few such meetings, their attitudes had changed. They are much nicer with both her and Kolia. Valentina firmly believes that this experience shows well that amiability, patience, and humility are the vehicles of God's love, that they show the right path to the real objective: more peaceful human relationships.

Conclusion

Laywomen's participation in Orthodox schooling has significantly contributed to the mutual integration of the ROC and society. The structural disadvantages with which women are usually faced in Russia have been imported into ROC's parish schooling where they are reproduced on a perennial ground. Yet parish education, a new area of post-Soviet Orthodoxy, has been shaped from the very beginning as a specifically female area of expertise. Inequalities are inbuilt in parish education through its practical operation and through the personal lives of the women who devote the time and energy to allow the expansion of parish education. But inequalities are not directly voiced or addressed as such. The stress lies elsewhere. The women who undertake and support this work have designed it themselves as a moral-spiritual enclave. From this enclave, they actively work to let their ideal of enlightened and humanist Orthodoxy reach out to the wider society. They work as mediators of God's love.

Sometimes, Sunday school workers explicitly formulate their motivations and goals for pupils. But most of the time, they suggest them implicitly. Through their own ways of behaving, they patiently instil a worldview of love to pupils and parents. They can believe that their efforts make a difference because they know that millions of people painfully experienced the lack of humanity that accompanied the measurable and sociologically tangible post-Soviet transformations. This experience is largely acknowledged at the individual and collective levels; it is particularly salient in intersubjective exchanges among women. Women's longing for a better society and more sympathetic human relationships has become commonplace. For the parish school workers, this aspiration has crystallized as part of their commitment of faithful Orthodox.

Chapter 7
The Alchemy of Almsgiving: How a Persistent Social Problem Prompted New Ethics

Since the early 1990s, beggars have become part of parish life; they occupy the surroundings and entrances of most urban churches. An analysis of the ways in which parish clergy and parish workers approach this socially marginal group helps to unravel the specific nexus that connects the clergy and various churchgoers with non-practising people who are nevertheless part of church life. Beggars occupy the geographical margins of the church, and they are outsiders of the parish as a Eucharistic community. However, church insiders interact with them every day, and these interactions prompt novel ethical reflections. The transformation of priestly ethics has been stimulated by the dynamics of this aspect of street-level Orthodoxy, in a way that actively addresses economic distress and social stigma.

In this chapter, I consider why and how clergymen, church workers, and churchgoers distinguish between different groups of the indigent. How are views of deservingness negotiated in everyday interaction and talk? Contrary to the widespread romantic image of an uninterrupted Orthodox tradition of indiscriminate almsgiving to all poor, Ozerovo's parish actors make recourse to contemporary popular categories of 'good' and 'bad' poor.[88] They confront these categories, however, from soteriological belief, thus entering a process of what I call the moral valuation of things and actions. Scrutinizing the ways in which parish actors craft relationships to beggars, whom they approach mostly as a particularly unattractive group, is a way to study the production of everyday religious ethics. It is these ethics that express a relationship of responsibility towards society.

---

[88] Orthodox charities, such as the umbrella organization Miloserdie, related to the ROC's Synodal Department of Church Charity and Social Service, are no exception. The popular website miloserdie.ru prominently features the usual categories of good, deserving needy: orphans, the elderly, large families, disabled and sick children, disabled and sick adults, the homeless. Common poverty and social distress, as well as groups that are discriminated against on the basis of ethnic or gender belonging are not mentioned.

In Russia, social distinctions are made among the poor between those who are recognized, morally and legally, as vulnerable, and those who are deemed responsible for their poverty. These distinctions draw on Soviet and earlier layers of social history. The early post-Soviet welfare system, and with it the categories of population that were entitled to benefits, remained relatively untouched by the overall economic liberalization in the 1990s. But, as Julie Hemment (2012) argued, since the first presidency of Vladimir Putin, this continuity has been used somewhat paradoxically by the government to purchase consent over neoliberal restructuring of the welfare institutions. As a result, while the discourse about those who should receive help, and those who should not, has remained relatively unchanged, real state welfare support has suffered significant erosion.

This is the context in which the surroundings of Orthodox churches have become typical places for begging. Church almsgiving has become one of the most ordinary expressions of Orthodox compassion in post-Soviet Russia. It is also a node of intense questioning and tension. The role of the ROC as a provider of social relief raises issues such as the interplay between religion and nationalism, the unequal position of different religious institutions in contemporary Russia, and diverging notions of charity, as Melissa Caldwell (2010) demonstrated. By focusing on almsgiving, I consider charity an arena that is constantly animated by ethical issues. In the eyes of Orthodox priests, everyday dealings with often uncivil and smelly beggars are a trivial and charmless part of church life. But they are also the source of a vibrant ethical dilemma to which the priests are compelled to respond creatively. How should they express Christian compassion and yet still refuse to support begging as an unfit way of life? Priests (and others) craft pragmatic solutions to such questions every day. The church-beggar nexus reaches frail equilibriums that do not rule out uncertainty, hesitation, or contingency.

When confronted with begging, priests draw on several, sometimes contradictory, layers of the past. They emphasize and combine aspects of these layers in individually and collectively meaningful ways. They maintain 'traditional' Orthodox notions of spontaneous uncontrolled almsgiving, but these are coloured by late nineteenth-century ideas of target-oriented charity and by twentieth-century Soviet notions of work. The historicity of these ethics not only informs my interpretation, it also serves as a resource consciously and selectively mobilized by the priests themselves. This diachronic aspect is intertwined with a synchronic aspect: the immediacy of practice, concrete ethical decisions, and interactions reveal the complexity of priests' attitudes toward practical responses. Dealing with beggars is hardly 'trivial' after all.

In general, priests usually approve of giving money to passive beggars such as silent elderly women. They try to sanction younger ones who seem able-bodied from begging, but usually refrain from expelling them from the church premises. Their practical ethics involve simultaneous sanction and compassion. In this way they 'punish' the able-bodied beggars for pursuing a 'bad' way of life even as they respond to the beggars' demands in a 'charitable' and 'Orthodox' spirit. In doing so, priests realize themselves as ethical persons and assume a responsibility toward beggars and society.

Ethics, Morals, and Values

Ethics in the sphere of religion are approached here as a dynamic area of practice and interaction, distinct from morality. Or, as Douglas Rogers wrote in his study of Old Believer ethics in a provincial Russian town, 'The study of ethics should be distinguished from the study of morality and has interlocking social, cultural, and political dimensions' (2009: 15). Ethics, for Rogers, are best defined as a 'field of practice'. What can be grasped through individual 'moral narratives' (Zigon 2010) is important, but such narratives should be analysed in relation to practice, interaction, and historicity. Following Laidlaw (2002) and Rogers (2009), I use 'ethics' to throw light on practical processes, leaving 'morality' and 'morals' to designate more circumscribed sets of rules and codes (e.g. 'Soviet morals of work'). However, my approach differs from that proposed by Laidlaw inasmuch as my study of ethics is not exclusively an exploration of individual 'ethical projects' whose ultimate goal is self-perfection (compare with Zigon 2008). Inasmuch as charity is concerned, Orthodox priests are relatively unconcerned with achieving personal perfection. They try to act as righteous persons, but they are concerned with the consequences that their decisions will have on others. The ethnography of the relational and interactive nature of almsgiving therefore necessarily foregrounds the society-centred nature of ethics.

Nevertheless, there remains significant overlap between the above uses of 'ethics' and some anthropological uses of 'morality'. Michael Lambek (2000), for example, proposed that morality, in the anthropology of religion, could be best approached through the concept of 'reasoned moral practice'. Such practice, he wrote, aims to 'locate thought in the thick of immediate circumstances, in historicity, and in the constraints and opportunities of life' (2000: 318). This formulation sidesteps the opposition between static moral rules and dynamic practical action that is fundamental in the choice made by many authors to use 'ethics'. In many ways, 'reasoned moral practice' would describe well the emerging ethics of almsgiving, but it does not address well the question of the individual and collective dimensions.

Another useful approach that relies on 'morality' is found in Catherine Wanner's work with Ukrainian evangelicals (2007). In this study, Wanner argued that moralities are multiple, and exist at both individual and collective levels:

> While morality indicates commitment to certain principles, it also embodies commitment to a group that helps uphold them through shared discourses and disciplining practices, which, in turn, reflect certain understandings of good and evil, of virtue and vice. By connecting moral understandings to faith-based communities, we see how particular articulations of morality intersect with those of other social groups to shape an individual's commitment to various collectives and how these commitments change in tandem with particular socio-historical contexts (2007: 11–12).

Wanner's approach to the individual/ collective nexus applies well to the Orthodox ethics of almsgiving. I adapt it to this study by adding a distinction of the twofold role of historicity as historical background and consciously mobilized resource.

Studies of Christian and other denominations since the fall of the Soviet regime in 1991 have documented the selective but enduring social relevance of Soviet, pre-Soviet, and even older ideas, moral positions, and social configurations (e.g. Luehrmann 2005; Paxson 2005; Rogers 2008, 2009; Zigon 2008, 2011b; Agadjanian and Rousselet 2010; Benovska-Sabkova et al. 2010). As Wanner and Steinberg wrote, 'The Soviet experience itself has nurtured understandings of good and evil, agency and destination, and authority and submission that are part of the cultural and social landscape today. Religious life remains entwined with these and still older legacies – to be embraced, adapted, or challenged' (2008: 17).

These legacies constitute an 'ethical repertoire' (Rogers 2009), from which elements are selectively mobilized in response to current demands. Their importance becomes relevant especially when the social actors themselves index certain practices and thoughts to specific historical periods or figures. This is precisely what Orthodox priests do, and the reason why I pay special attention to some historical periods that my informants cited as frames of moral reference.

I combine this approach to ethics and morality in religion with a particular theory of value. One solution that Orthodox priests have crafted to resolve the dilemma of almsgiving – that is how to be charitable without affirming begging as a way of life – is to substitute the handout of money with other objects (especially food). Their gesture, so they say, addresses the problem of hunger (or other needs) but does not allow the beggar to profit.

The priests' dilemma is about how to act. They must give; they must be charitable. That much is clear from the overall framework of Orthodox teaching. But they are (somewhat) free to manipulate how and what they give, and what else they do as they give. This is the most creative part of their ethical resolution and the one which is the most immediately rooted in society and action.

It is for this reason that I take recourse to David Graeber's theory of value. He asked, 'What if one did try to create a theory of value starting from the assumption that what is ultimately being evaluated are not things, but actions?' (Graeber 2001: 49). For him, social value is realized in creative action, incorporated in some larger social totality, where 'Creative action … can never be separated from its concrete, material medium' (2001: 54). So it is with the priests. They use the things they give to modify the meaning of the giving, and thus to alter the relations between themselves, the Church, the faithful, society, and the beggars.

This dynamic approach to the value of things and actions provides me with an optimal frame within which to think about the creative and interactive nature of the ethics of almsgiving. The ethical valuation of things and actions in almsgiving is a critical, creative process that mobilizes, in direct and indirect ways, all the above-mentioned aspects of ethics: adherence to moral codes, creative reasoning and practice, historicity, and self-centred and society-centred orientations.

The Dilemma of Charity

By 2006-07, Orthodox parish charity was almost never a formal endeavour. In this respect parish-level charity differs widely from better organized Christian charities in larger Russian cities (Caldwell 2004, 2017). Nevertheless, the idea of helping the needy is deeply rooted in contemporary Russian Orthodoxy. Church almsgiving is the most ordinary and widespread form of Orthodox social support demonstrated in the vicinity of churches. In Ozerovo, beggars appear in the yards of Trinity Church and Saint George the Warrior as soon as the churches open. They are present around Saint Michael the Archangel too, but because it is open only for religious services, it attracts beggars only temporarily. I met beggars also at the churches in Ozerovo's smaller neighbouring localities, and in the big cities of Saint Petersburg and Moscow. Some data in this chapter comes from these other locations too, helping to draw the connections between street-level Orthodoxy in Ozerovo and the wider national scale.

Father Oleg is one of the most popular priests at Trinity Church. A thin man in his forties, of rural origin, he is known as a humble person and a good priest, as well as one of the most appreciated confessors. With the exception of the rector, he is the only priest at Trinity who has reached the rank of *protoierei*, the highest for a parish priest. He and his wife have three children – a large family by contemporary Russian standards. Although his salary is modest, he refuses large donations offered to him personally by well-off churchgoers. His humbleness and piety inspire respect among the churchgoers.

Father Oleg started practising Orthodoxy in the second half of the 1980s during perestroika. Like most churchgoers in Ozerovo, he did not learn about Orthodoxy from his parents who had worked in a state farm in the region of Tver. 'My parents', he explained, 'were believers, but never went to church. They did not speak of this [Orthodoxy]; there was no literature'.[89] During the last years of the Soviet regime, Father Oleg was carrying out his studies in agronomy; he started reading about religion and going to church. After graduation, he studied at the Orthodox seminary in Saint Petersburg and subsequently became a priest. Like most contemporary urban churchgoers, he finds that – atheism and anti-religious campaigns aside – the Soviet system had a better moral basis than the democracy of the post-Soviet period. 'We are free to go to church now', he said, and it is good that 'many young people go to church, no longer only *babushka*s', but 'perestroika was destruction'. During the Soviet period, Father Oleg explained, morality was higher: everyone had a job and the police arrested any panhandlers or other idlers hanging around.

One can easily disagree with Father Oleg's enthusiastic presentation of the Soviet past. But Father Oleg's nostalgic image of the Soviet moral atmosphere matters not as a true reconstruction of his feelings about the past. It should more accurately be understood as part of a deeply critical view of some aspects of post-Soviet life that he shares with many in the general population. Indeed during the 1990s and early 2000s, a feeling that 'democracy' had brought moral decline was widespread in Russian society. The presence of beggars prominently figures as evidence of this decline and, more importantly, as a compelling call for action. In a conversation that we had inside the church, Father Oleg initiated a commentary on beggars:

> I also face a dilemma. He begs. You have to give. But he is an idler, a sponger. There are disabled little old ladies. To them you can give. But the others, when we help them, we corrupt them …. But we cannot push them out. The Lord will say to us: 'Get out from the

---

[89] After the fall of the Soviet regime, popular Orthodox literature in the form of short books and pamphlets has played a crucial role for the promotion of Russian Orthodoxy.

Celestial Kingdom!' He [the beggar] must pray for every kopek, not to use it for vodka. Morality is like this now. Bad. Now there are these Uzbeks over here.[90] We get them used [to begging] and when they grow up, they will still sit here.

Father Oleg's dilemma is not one of a distant observer. How to act ethically vis-à-vis certain social characters is a pressing question for him. To answer it, he invokes the past, present, and future, as well as Orthodox and Soviet morals. In the same vein, how one responds to a beggar is imagined as having future effects. Father Oleg speaks of the possibility of expulsion from heaven, and voices the perspective of most somewhat-religiously engaged people in saying that, 'When you give [to a beggar] you corrupt him'. Giving alms works on the giver and the recipient; it creates good and bad persons; it shapes future and present selves. Giving alms is fraught with hazards, but the solution is not in avoidance. Father Oleg never expels the beggars. He lets them collect handouts, and feels compelled to modify his own response.

The rector of Trinity Church is also a man in his late forties. Unlike many other local priests, many of his close relatives are Orthodox clergymen. Additionally, he occupies the highest hierarchical position among the local churches, serving as rector of the deanery (*blagochinie*). He is the only priest in Ozerovo who owns a luxury vehicle. He drives a new gleaming black jeep with elegant leather interior – a nearly paradigmatic antithesis to Father Oleg's tired Soviet Zhiguli.

The rector distinguishes himself in relation to beggars too. Once, for example, I witnessed his harsh treatment of an unknown beggar who asked for help. I was standing on the stairs, in front of the main entrance of the church, chatting with the rector. A man arrived, unkempt and drunk. He asked for money and help. The rector became irritable, almost aggressive with him, and asked: 'Do you wear a cross around your neck?' The beggar immediately took out his necklace to exhibit the tiny cross hanging on it. Then, without saying anything, the rector went inside his office in the church. The beggar and I were left on the steps, wondering at the situation. After a minute, a young deacon came out with a small package of food for the man, obviously sent by the rector. The beggar took the package. He had hoped to receive some money, he said, but he was happy with the food. He departed; the rector did not return. It was clear that neither wanted to establish a relationship.

Able-bodied beggars are an everyday pragmatic problem that continuously raises the same dilemma: should they be blamed and expelled, or should they be offered support? The ways in which solutions are crafted

---

[90] At the time of this interview, there were Central Asian Gypsy children, accompanied by a few adult women, begging in the churchyard.

show the priests' twofold preoccupation: about their own realization as moral persons who 'have to give', and about the socially consequential effects of giving. In fact, acting righteously is an unstable construct that varies in interaction with differentiated groups of beggars and according to the subjective views of different priests. In the example above, the rector's anger and aggression are tied to this moment of decision making. The beggar was among the type that causes priests the greatest consternation: able-bodied but drunk, and forthright in his demands for assistance. The rector's question is targeted at finding out if he is yet the worst kind of beggar: that is, if he does not belong to Orthodoxy. Lucky for the beggar, he could answer that he does belong and thus 'deserves' charity.

Characters and Spaces

In post-Soviet Russia, begging is often linked to extreme urban poverty, social marginalization (Tikhonova 2003; Yates 2004), and homelessness (Stephenson 1996; Höjdestrand 2009). Kudriavtseva (2001) insisted that individual beggars in Russian cities are not necessarily needy persons; some ingeniously represent socially legitimate characters like a retired woman, the church poor, a single mother, a sick old woman, or a holy fool (*iurodivyi*, a typical figure of the Russian Orthodox tradition). Some researchers have approached the topic of begging by stressing that begging is a coping strategy, and by examining the processes of stratification within groups of beggars, their internal rules, and how they challenge the state order.[91] Taken together, such studies continue the social debate about whether or not beggars belong to society (and hold the same or similar moral values), or whether they are categorically a different kind of moral person, individually and collectively. I will not enter into this debate nor will I ask if begging is based on 'real' poverty and suffering. After all, a calculated demand for compassion does not exclude real need.

Instead, I describe the beggars' behaviour. To do so, I make use of two general categories: active and passive begging. The passive beggars sit or stand at the entrance to a churchyard or in the vicinity of a church. They are usually mute and immobile, silently addressing a demand to church visitors. Usually, the passive beggars are old women. I have never heard clergymen criticizing this type of beggar; rather the clerics point them out as exemplary recipients of handouts. They are referred to affectionately as 'little old ladies' (*starushki*), and are said to never cause trouble. They are seen as good poor. Their old bodies, quiet resignation, and passive attitudes legitimate their presence and expectation to receive help. According to

---

[91] For the case of China, see Fernandez-Stembridge and Madsen (2002).

Kudriavtseva (2001), such women often played the character of a retired woman (*pensionerka*): a woman deserving respect. Indeed, clergy and churchgoers are sympathetic to such women because they assume that the women worked while they were able to, and that it is the miserable pensions offered by the state that make it impossible for them to survive. They are among Russia's deserving poor because their social identity fits the dominant categories of Soviet and post-Soviet models of social welfare (Yates 2004: 233). By extension, other categories eligible for state welfare (e.g. invalids, veterans, and mothers of large families) – who worked while they were able – are usually considered to be deserving.

Plate 16. Elderly woman collecting alms at the entrance to a church yard.

Conversely, criticism of begging is directed at a particular target: active, mostly young and middle-aged beggars. Such individuals appear to be potential workers and their deservingness is constantly in question. It is these beggars who raise acute ethical dilemmas for parish priests. They can be called 'active beggars' and are often the most eye-catching.

In Ozerovo, active beggars stand next to the church entrance or in the yard. They move around, talk to church visitors, and try by all means to collect coins. Often, adult men – homeless and obviously alcoholic – stand next to the door. There are also groups of children accompanied by one or two women of Gypsy origin, who are the most mobile.[92] Most active beggars remain loyal to one church, at least for some time. There are individual beggars too, most often Russian men, who go straight into the church and address a priest or a church worker for money. Such beggars are passers-by; they never come back to the same church. Only this kind of beggar comes to Saint Michael the Archangel. Whether permanent or passer-by, active beggars are neither completely expelled nor openly accepted at churches. Their right to continue begging is a matter of permanent reflection and day-to-day arrangements by the clergymen.

Only the active beggars arouse interest, even resentment; only they constitute what the churchmen consider a problem to be solved. In Ozerovo, priests only allow begging outside the church, but this unstated rule is often broken at Saint George the Warrior. There, a group of three young locals, one girl in her late teens and two younger boys, aged 14 and 16, stand close to the main door. They are unavoidable for anyone who tries to enter the church. But they cannot really be removed from their spot because the church has no yard into which they can be dispatched. As people enter the church directly from the street, the group attracts their attention. Two other beggars are usually near the door too, a middle-aged woman and a man in his forties who is often drunk. They beg silently most of the time and remain immobile. The group of young ones is, on the contrary, far more active. They speak to the visitors, approach them for money and food, run back and forth in the vestibule[93] and sometimes inside the church, and joke and quarrel with one another. The girl and 14-year-old boy are siblings. All three live with their parents, but nevertheless resemble 'street children' in urban Russia – they lack parental control, use drugs, and live in poverty (Stephenson 2001). The girl is often drunk, her brother sniffs glue (the drug of the poor), and the other boy is frequently drunk as well.

The question, of course, is what to do about these young beggars. The responses have not been what one might expect. One former church worker tried to convince the young panhandlers to go to the city's residential school but her attempts proved unsuccessful.[94] No one else tried to 'normalize'

---

[92] I use 'Gypsy' instead of 'Roma' to focus on the perception that ethnic Russians have of these beggars. For an extensive discussion of the two terms in the Russian context, see Lemon (2000).

[93] I use 'vestibule' for the Russian term *pritvor* which, in the case of the churches, means a kind of airlock – a transitory space – between the big external door of the building and the inner door leading into the centre of the ritual space.

[94] Residential schools are widespread in Russia. Following the Soviet educational tradition, they host orphans and children from problem families. However, they tend to leave a durable negative mark on the social identity of their pupils.

them. No one tried to contact their parents. The status quo was tolerated. Already, clerics and church workers considered the young beggars incapable of change. They said, 'This is how they are, too used to living as they do'.

They did, however, sometimes engage the young beggars in church works. The teenagers had helped with some of the renovation work in formerly half-ruined buildings behind the church. The older boy had also cleaned up after a wedding in Trinity Church – work for which he received 100 roubles. And from time to time there had been similar work for one or all of them at Saint George the Warrior and at Trinity. But church insiders continued to consider the teenagers 'unwilling' to work, and thus a problematic kind of beggar.[95]

Ethics as Interaction

These young beggars are often discussed among clerics and the dozen or so members of the core community of the Church of Saint George the Warrior. In most matters, the core community strictly follows the rector, the charismatic Father Ioann (see chapter 4). Like Father Oleg, he is known for his humbleness and self-restraint. Father Ioann made a special decision concerning the small group of panhandlers. In March 2007, a placard appeared on the external door of the church:

Brothers and sisters!
Do not give alms in the entrance! Only on the church porch!
Blessing of Father the Rector

A similar placard was posted on the internal door. There were several explanations about what gave rise to the prohibition: one of the boys stole money from the shop cash box; visitors complained about the smell of alcohol and glue; the young group quarrelled in the church during a funeral ceremony (*otpevanie*). Eventually, the teenagers confirmed to me the latter story in a half-joking, half-guilty way.

After the placards were posted, the new rule was disregarded sometimes, especially during important feasts, when numerous visitors came.

The solution, like those that preceded it, did not remove the beggars from the vicinity of the church, nor did it change their behaviour. It only aimed at keeping 'bad' beggars at a certain remove. It still let them be a part of church life. The rector himself does not give alms to the teenagers, but neither did he repress, control, or ignore the beggars. He felt a relation with them, which was made surprisingly visible in a moment of tragedy: a third

---

[95] Kudriavtseva's (2001) informants used the word 'work' to describe their begging. My informants never used such a formulation.

sibling of the two sibling-beggars froze to death in the street one night. His siblings were deeply affected, and despite the accusatory comments that the young man should not have been wandering about so drunk, the priest took the unusual course of performing the funeral (*otpevanie*) free of charge (see chapter 5).

The most engaged church workers and churchgoers took their rector's position into consideration, but also developed their own opinions about almsgiving. The director of the choir at the Church of Saint George the Warrior is a man in his early forties. He aspired to become a priest but could not complete his training because he married a divorced woman. He is one of the prominent characters of this parish, known for his generosity and kindness. Like others, when commenting on beggars, he told me: 'We need them more than they need us. Giving to them is a path toward salvation, because God sends them to us'. However, one should not interpret his words as revealing a kind of utilitarian compassion convertible into salvation, for, as he explained to me, the way to salvation cannot be reduced to accomplishing acts of almsgiving. Almsgiving requires discrimination. At the very least, one must also hold that laziness and idleness should not be rewarded by charity.

How, in practice, should one decide whether to give or not to give? A woman in her fifties, who works as a ticket seller at the train station and sings in the church choir, told me in a critical vein that 'begging is a business now'. Most beggars, she thought, made calculated demands for compassion. But, she added, 'For the sake of your salvation, if you have a spare rouble, you had better give it'. As indicated in the preceding examples focused on priests, active churchgoers seek solutions in how and what to give, not whether or not to give.

The rector of Saint Michael the Archangel is the most radical in managing the problem of the active beggars. He is known for being the most demanding and hard with his parishioners. A man in his early forties, he is the only priest of the parish. He left his native Soviet Ukraine at the end of the 1980s to study in what was then Leningrad. Unlike most of the other local priests, he says that he was already a believer in his childhood. As mentioned above, beggars do not come to this church on a daily basis. There are clear structural reasons for their absence, but when I asked the priest why there were no beggars at the entrance of his church, he answered me, 'I forbade it. They beg for vodka'. Then he spoke of what happened when people, especially middle-aged men, knocked on the door of his house, just behind the church, asking for help. 'They approach me and they approach all the other priests. "Give me food", they say. I give them some. "Give me money to buy a ticket". But I know that they beg for vodka .... You open the door and a man (*muzhik*) stands there, strong and healthy. I tell him "I will give you money if you work here. There is a lot of snow. Remove it". He refuses'. Though spoken in harsher tones, this priest's response is in line with the others. He too is critical of contemporary beggars and conceives of monetary alms (for the able-bodied) only as a reward for beggars' commitment to work.

The differences come in how the priest twines together narratives of the past and present. He blames contemporary beggars for their absence of faith; yet, he maintains an idealized view of the 'good' beggars of the pre-Soviet and Soviet pasts. In his childhood, he said, the poor and the disabled accepted everything they were offered. They prayed and said 'in the name of Christ' (*Radi Khrista*), whereas now they ask for money only to buy vodka. Pre-Soviet and Soviet church beggars were, to his mind, good and faithful. As evidence, he showed me a recently published book about Orthodoxy, in which an old photograph taken before the 1917 Revolution showed two beggars: a man and a young boy. 'This is a blind man and an orphan child', he explained, 'They begged together and supported each other'. For him, beggars of the pre-Soviet and Soviet pasts were different but equally pious. In contrast, contemporary begging and almsgiving lacks spirituality: 'Now, there is one who throws out money and another one who takes it'.

In other conversations, this priest linked almsgiving to his overall perception that faith is generally fading in contemporary society. He criticizes those newly rich who invite him to bless their new houses and who take this act as magical protection, and those people who wish to get married in his church without cultivating the Orthodox faith in their heart. For him, beggars are just one among many kinds of faithless Russians who use priests to their own ends.

Another time, he stressed that 'In the Acts of the Apostles, Christ said that it is better to give than to beg'. Later, I found this same reference to Acts 20:35 in the chapter 'Property' in *The Basis of the Social Concept*, the most prominent recent theological document of the ROC. 'An owner of a considerable wealth does not sin if he uses it in accordance with the will of God to Whom everything belongs and with the law of love; for the joy and fullness of life lie not in acquirement and possession but in giving and sacrifice. St. Paul calls people "to remember the words of the Lord Jesus, how he said, 'It is more blessed to give than to receive'"' (ROC 2000). In this citation, there is no mention of begging. Instead, the passage is cited to discuss the merits of wealth and what the rich should do with their property. Here, the rich are instructed to share through 'giving and sacrifice'.

In conversation with me, the priest substituted 'to beg' for the original 'to receive' in the quotation from Saint Paul. In doing so, he altered the meaning of the passage to support his own critical view on begging. This substitution may not have been conscious or intended; but it testifies to the frequent subjective usages of authoritative references by parish priests in support of their opinions and decisions, typically voiced in the form of assertions starting with: 'As the Holy Fathers said' (*Kak sviatye ottsy govorili*). Although the positions of the individual priests are multi-referential morally and historically – and thus they subjectively emphasize one or another code, period, or figure – theology, traditional practice, Soviet morals, and post-Soviet discourses appear as shared frames of moral reference. Below, I review some recent and earlier theological views about begging and almsgiving, and historical moments that marked Orthodoxy's relationship to begging, and then I turn to discuss Soviet attitudes toward begging. In these cases, work appears as a structuring ethical category, differently involved in varying historical moral models of piety and deservingness.

Orthodox Almsgiving

Russian Orthodox theology has for a long time emphasized two spheres of righteous Christian life: charity and labour.[96] George Fedotov, a well-known Russian Orthodox theologian and historian[97], analysed a medieval collection of anonymous essays drawing on sermons of early Christian theologians that served as a guide to the moral life of laity and married clergy. He found that charity and labour were central. Moreover, redistribution of one's wealth to the needy and to the Church was not simply encouraged, but alms were 'normally prescribed as means of salvation' (1966: 80). However, Fedotov showed that despite the widespread representation of Christ as a beggar, in the Middle Ages 'Beggarliness or pious idleness [was] not the ideal', but rather 'labour, especially manual labour, [was] invested with a religious value and [was] even set on the same level as monastic renunciation' (1966: 78). In continuity with this tradition, contemporary Russian Orthodox theology usually insists simultaneously on the importance of charity and labour. *The Basis of the Social Concept* (ROC 2000) gives charity a prominent place in at least two chapters, 'Labour and its Fruits' and 'Property'. The first of these two chapters emphasizes that the 'Holy

---

[96] A strong tension between social work in the world and withdrawal in prayer has characterized the history of Russian Orthodoxy from its very inception (Kenworthy 2008).

[97] George Fedotov (1886-1951) left his native Russia in 1925. He was first based in Paris at Saint Sergius Theological Institute and later at Saint Vladimir Theological Institute in New York.

Scriptures point to the two moral motives of labour: work to sustain oneself without being a burden for others and work to give to the needy'.

The questions that logically appear then are: how to judge those who fail to sustain themselves and who become 'a burden for others'? And, if it is better to give than to receive, how bad is it to only receive? *The Basis* does not provide an explicit solution to the obvious tension produced between the obligation to be charitable and the uncertain moral judgment bestowed on those who neither have nor labour. Since 1991, the Church has made significant effort to instil official doctrine into mainstream practice. For instance, popular forms of Orthodoxy preserved under socialism outside Church control, are now labelled ignorance and paganism (compare with Sibireva 2009a, 2009b). Yet begging remains unaddressed by official pronouncement despite its conspicuousness in the vicinity of churches. Official theology sets up a code but remains silent on this ethical question (see also Kenworthy 2008: 46–47).

Indiscriminate almsgiving by clergy and laity was part of everyday urban and rural Russian life for centuries. At important Orthodox feasts, services were held in churches, public celebrations and entertainment took place, and the poor, as well as vagrants and beggars were invited into people's homes for a meal and a handful of coins (Bernshtam 2005: 282–86). Spontaneous, indiscriminate almsgiving to beggars was considered a worthy act and was widely practised. At least until the second half of the nineteenth century, poverty was not defined as a social problem.

There was, however, also a longstanding distinction about different kinds of beggars. Those who renounced wealth for the sake of piety were approved, but tramps who begged in order to make a living were disparaged (Golosenko 1996a and 1996b).[98] While holy fools occupy a special place in Russian Orthodoxy as ascetic characters (Fedotov 1966: 317–43), they often arouse suspicion too. The mid-nineteenth-century ethnographer and historian Pryzhov (1996) denounced the duplicity of some holy fools who impudently hoarded wealth but exhibited poverty.

The first repressive measures on begging appeared in Russia only in the eighteenth century, as part of the modernization reforms under Peter the Great. The emperor's efforts to replace chaotic almsgiving by organized, channelled charity were met with great resistance (Pryzhov 1996: 136). By

---

[98] Similar patterns of perception of beggars and tramps are prominent in Islam as well. For example, Ildikó Bellér-Hann (2008: 152–64) showed that during the nineteenth and the first half of the twentieth century, beggars among the Muslim Uyghur of Xinjiang were viewed as essentially religious characters; different forms of almsgiving were therefore considered to convey religious worth. At the same time, people blamed cheating beggars who presented themselves as pious mendicants.

the mid-nineteenth century, one strong strand of public opinion held that although almsgiving was an 'apparently pious' custom, it was in fact 'merciless and harmful' (Pryzhov 1996: 139; see also Golosenko 1996a, 1996b).

By the end of the nineteenth century, such ideas took a more defined shape and started to inform a new worldview: poverty and unemployment became categories of thought. Reforms were launched in order to respond to the increase of visible urban poverty aggravated by rapid migration from the countryside to industrial cities. Newly established work houses (*doma trudoliubiia*) – that first emerged in Saint Petersburg – tried to implement the idea that the able-bodied poor must be integrated into productive life and given a place to live (Lindenmeyr 1986). These initiatives were inspired by earlier west European reforms. However, in reality, the various types of such homes for the poor had very limited success.

Reform ideas had political strength, including those which introduced the categories of deserving and undeserving poor. Nevertheless, traditional almsgiving to all kinds of beggars, deeply rooted in Orthodox ethics, remained the most popular expression of the Russian ethos of charity in late imperial Russia (Lindenmeyr 1990). One of the key characters of this new movement at the end of the nineteenth and the very beginning of the twentieth century was Father Ioann of Kronstadt, a charismatic and influential Orthodox priest close to the Tsar's family. He created one of the first 'homes of industry' and wrote about the emergence of poverty relief in Russia. Although he shared many reform ideas, he never renounced giving handouts to beggars (Lindenmeyr 1986, 1996; Kizenko 2006).[99] More generally, until the 1917 Revolution the powerful belief that 'poverty is not a vice' remained untouched. Even after punishment for begging and almsgiving was imposed, public opinion tended to prefer 'pity' to punishment, marking a difference with western Europe where support for punishment had been growing since the Middle Ages (see Geremek 1987). Traditional Orthodox ethics of almsgiving were central in this resistance to Western-type ideas for social transformation. Even when new ideas gained ground, traditional forms of almsgiving continued (Lindenmeyr 1996).

The town of Kronstadt, where Father Ioann served, is situated on an island in the Gulf of Finland, several kilometres from Saint Petersburg. He was canonized by the Patriarchate of Moscow in 1990 as an all-Russian saint and became one of the most popular saints in Saint Petersburg Region.

---

[99] By the end of his life, the charismatic Father Ioann of Kronstadt was always surrounded by a miserable crowd begging for coins and food. This situation apparently took its toll, as he wrote in one of his diaries that he was sinking into tiredness and anger over the unceasing flood of poor (Kizenko 2006: 177–79).

Ozerovo is located in this same region. Sometimes, people draw on Saint Ioann's reputation, and claim that he would not give to active beggars. These people, they say, were among those whom he called the 'professional poor' (*professional'nye nishchie*). In fact, the evidence suggests that Father Ioann continued giving alms to all poor throughout his life. But his written philosophical views provide contemporary churchgoers with authority to champion the importance of work.

Soviet and Early Post-Soviet Morals of Work

Soviet ideology went much further than any imperial reform. In the new pattern, there was no place for religious charity and pity; only work mattered. Work became the only moral reference, and one of the supreme human virtues. 'The possession of the virtue of work ... was seen as the prerequisite for the rest of [the] positive human characteristics .... The rest of the "saintly character" of the Soviet ideal person was built around work' (Vladimirova 2006: 120).[100] Since the 1950s, the regime actively manipulated the category of work to repressive ends. The vocabulary of parasitism, strongly rooted in Russian colloquial talk since the Second World War, became particularly emphasized and anchored in law during the Khrushchev period in the 1950s and early 1960s, when special legislation against 'parasites' was adopted (Fitzpatrick 2006). Following a well-established Soviet tradition to punish vagrants, beggars, and prostitutes, this legislation extended the scope to all 'anti-social parasitical elements', including youth hanging around foreigners, those unwilling to work, those dressed in Western styles, people making a living from the informal economy, religiously active people (especially sectarians), pensioners who engaged in petty trade, and even housewives who did not have an official job. In addition, practising one of the institutionally recognized forms of work was essential for gaining access to the social security system (McAuley 1979). The laws against parasitism condemned all those who strayed outside of what was defined as regular and socially-useful work as leftovers from capitalism who 'impeded the Soviet march to communism' (Fitzpatrick 2006). The teleological bias of the Soviet rhetoric disappeared with the crash of the regime. Nevertheless, institutional and popular definitions of 'worthy' work remained in place (Rogers 2008), and were re-activated in new categories of state welfare (Yates 2004: 240).

In Ozerovo, the ongoing influence of Soviet ideology is tangible in the choice of many people to describe active beggars as 'parasites' (*parazity*).

---

[100] Although actual practices often differed widely from the ideology, the latter was profoundly incorporated into popular views (Vladimirova 2006: 126–34).

Such an invocation is far more common than references to Father Ioann of Kronstadt. 'Parasitism' continues to reference unworthy ways of earning money, motivated by laziness and immorality. Parasitism references its opposite too: the Soviet ideal of work as a central human virtue. Together, work and parasitism provide a frame for overall social ethics. For example, when begging is described as 'a business nowadays' (*eto biznes seichas*), the choice of the word *biznes* is not incidental. A post-Soviet calque from English, that is, from the West, the term became widely used in colloquial speech in the post-perestroika period to refer to non-physical work, most often commerce.

Biznes is a kind of work in that it generates income, but in the Soviet framework it is still an illegitimate and morally dubious kind of work. In the socialist period, labour was considered superior to commerce. Commerce, especially that beyond the control of the state, was associated with easy gain and cheating. 'Making profits from marketing was illegal in most circumstances' and private trading activities were considered immoral (Humphrey and Mandel 2002: 1). Today, the term *biznes* still often bears these semantic nuances, and carries strong connotations of calculation and profit-seeking. To equate begging with *biznes* therefore accomplishes many semantic leaps at once. It simultaneously recognizes and discredits beggars' efforts to 'work'. It overlooks the fact that begging is a physically demanding activity. And it suggests that beggars calculate and adjust their behaviour in order to arouse compassion.

This discrimination against *biznes* occurs while an entrepreneurial ethos of money-making within and outside of productive spheres has largely gained legitimacy in Russian society (Patico 2009). Be it the phrase 'professional poor' attributed to Saint Ioann of Kronstadt, the Soviet vocabulary of parasitism, or contemporary popular talk of begging as *biznes* – it is clear that 'religious' discourse is deeply suspicious of dishonest attempts to earn money and of inappropriate ways of using it. Vodka and accusations of immorality are profoundly integrated in the everyday philosophy of clergymen. Whether they invoke theology, Soviet ideals, or post-Soviet-styled criticism of *biznes*, a certain idea of deservingness stemming from notions of work underlies their views.

How is it that the question about the appropriate type of handout for able-bodied beggars is answered in the same way by all local priests? Neither age nor social background inflects their view. There is no official pronouncement from the ROC. The priests are certain that their position is borne out by biblical interpretation. They do not necessarily look for solutions in the scriptures.

Some do have a favourite quotation or saying that they invoke in private conversations and in sermons; such as Acts, things said by 'the Holy Fathers of the Church' or by Saint Ioann of Kronstadt. But, in general, priests prefer pragmatic solutions. For churchgoers and church workers, this is enough. What the priests do and say provides justification for their own actions if they need it. As they told me, 'The priest blessed (*batiushka blagoslovil*) giving them food, he did not bless giving them money'.

Crafting Ethical Responses: Accepting while Rejecting

Individual priests respond differently to the challenge that the very presence of beggars constitutes, but eventually they respond as a group with shared fundamental values. The idea of un-deservingness provides a common ground for the exclusion of active beggars. In practice, the clergymen support beggars. When we examine their politics of control over the space inside and outside of churches, we can conclude that priests want beggars to be part of church life. Unquestioned almsgiving may well belong to the pre-revolutionary and earlier past; however, the practice of almsgiving is still a vivid expression of charity. Instead of choosing between giving to beggars or rejecting them, the priests do both. They deal in the 'materials of ethics' (Rogers 2009) without resolving the ethical dilemma itself. They create object-centred choices for themselves – to offer money or food – shifting the dilemma away from themselves and onto the beggars. The question they ask is not whether they should give, but what beggars will do with the handouts. Graeber's (2001) theory of value stresses precisely this connectedness between things and actions. Drawing on his approach, it appears that a specific valuation procedure for things and actions underpins the priests' everyday ethics of almsgiving.

While giving coins to all beggars is a popular practice today, the clergy and many of the most engaged churchgoers of the three local churches condemn giving monetary alms to the able-bodied. It does not matter that the amounts given are small, and that beggars can hardly live off their collections. Alms money itself becomes distinguished: that given to 'little old ladies' is 'good'; that given to the able-bodied is 'corrupting'. These different monies (Zelizer 1997) are directly defined by the moral portrait of their receivers. Food donations have no such value differentiations.[101]

---

[101] There are parishes where the beggars are sometimes invited to share meals at the table of the church (*trapeza*). This was not practised by the parishes I studied – though food was occasionally brought to them outside.

The ethical competition between responding to the demand of the active beggar and penalizing him for his 'faults' is solved by moving the focus from the act of giving – the moral value embodied in almsgiving remaining untouched – to the nature of the gift and its potentialities for future actions. Graeber (2001) emphasizes that the value of the objects is, in fact, the value of the actions that one can accomplish with them, and that economic and ethical values are interrelated. Indeed, in church almsgiving, the economic value of money is always considered in connection to the ethical value of the monetary transaction: What kind of relationship does money mediate? To what kind of social character is it passed on? The ethical valuation of alms money occurs in the larger context of a society in which able-bodied beggars are most often stigmatized as idle, suspected of playing needy, and abusing people's compassion. The potential wider uses they could make of money fall under the same suspicion of abuses. Conversely, food can only be immediately consumed and there is little probability that one can exchange it for something else. In this way, when giving food, not only are the clerics accomplishing their Christian duty, but they also feel they are keeping the beggars' behaviour under control. Thanks to this object-centred choice, the dilemma between giving and refusing is neutralized, and the act of giving is no longer questioned. In the process, the priests index their thoughts and actions to different frames of historical and moral reference, a procedure constitutive of the elaboration of almsgiving as a simultaneous sanction and compassion. Through the ethical valuation that connects certain things to certain actions, they respond to the beggars and society. Thus, they go well beyond a self-centred project in which 'people's conduct is shaped by attempts to make of themselves a certain kind of person' (Laidlaw 2002: 327), placing the others as their centre of concern as much as themselves. These religious ethics are intrinsically relational, addressing a specific group and society at large.

Chapter 8
Secular Relatedness in Orthodox Churches: Grassroots Charities

In the 2000s, but also earlier, Russian Orthodox churches were transformed into an arena of secular social relatedness. This chapter presents a case study of charitable gifts that non-churchgoers make to anonymous others, whom they imagine mostly as the common needy. People of extremely various backgrounds use the churches as places for redistribution. I call this practice 'grassroots charities'. Most often, the donors as well as the church workers who take over the task of redistributing these gifts, completely ignore 'religious' motives. The underlying motivation they do recognize is to become 'useful' for others. The most intriguing element is the practical efficacy of their silent agreement and their common-sense knowledge that churches are the relevant place for redistribution. That is, the church is considered the most appropriate point of contact between anonymous donors and anonymous recipients.

Such anonymous grassroots charity has permeated street-level Orthodoxy. Its spread has been facilitated by the spontaneous initiatives of donors who – for the most part – are local inhabitants but parish outsiders. This grassroots charity is an important aspect of how people's desire to address poverty and social disjunction, and it has contributed to the mutual embedding of Church and society. In addition, the ethnographic study of these grassroots charities shows that even fully anonymous unreciprocated gifts express and actively make social relatedness. This finding calls into question an established position in most contributions to the anthropological theory of the gift since Mauss's foundational *Essay on the Gift* (1950 [1924]), according to which it is only the reciprocal exchange of gifts that engenders social relations. Finally, these charities bring out intrinsic relationships between the Orthodox Church and the Russian nation as an 'imagined community' (Anderson 1983).

Although most of the ethnographic detail presented here originates from my work in Ozerovo, I have encountered grassroots charities in different places in north-western Russia, including in several churches in Saint Petersburg. In spite of their pervasiveness, grassroots charities have remained undocumented in social scientific studies about post-Soviet Russian Orthodoxy. This is the reason why I depict the way they operate in Ozerovo in great detail.

A plethora of studies have demonstrated that in Russian society networks of support and informal exchange have a strong reciprocal and personal character. The use of personal connections was a clear feature of the late Soviet and early post-Soviet periods (Ledeneva 1998); such connections were important earlier too, when state resources were turned to serving personal ends (Grossman 1977, 1991). Post-Soviet Russians heavily relied on mutual help as well, especially between rural households from the same village (Rogers 2005) and within kin groups (Rousselet 2005). The ways in which Russians mobilize their acquaintances, neighbours, and relatives for making ends meet have received great attention in sociological studies conducted by native scholars (e.g. Fadeeva 1999; Gradosel'skaia 1999; Vinogradskii 1999; Lylova 2002; Shanin, Nikulin and Danilov 2002; Shteinberg 2002; Barsukova 2004). In various ways, these and other works all demonstrate that reciprocal support in the frame of personal relationships remains essential in the strategies of 'making do' for a large portion of the population.

This chapter examines a different logic of giving and receiving. Anonymous and unreciprocated acts of giving have been prominent in post-Soviet society too. They attest to feelings of solidarity and relatedness that are not circumscribed by narrower circles of kin, friends, colleagues, and acquaintances. Yet little is known about charitable giving or the circumstances that give rise to it in Russia, and less about the role of the Orthodox Church in it.

The Church has been criticized often by common people for its modest involvement in social care. Throughout the 1990s, only a few Orthodox charities were well structured and regularly funded in Russia. Their Protestant counterparts, in particular the proselytizing groups which entered Russia after the fall of the Soviet regime, were usually better organized, more efficient, and seemed to apply less discriminatory criteria in distributing aid (Caldwell 2004). Critics argue that the Russian Orthodox Church is self-interested, and not interested in alleviating suffering within society (Mitrokhin 2004). This critique is widely accepted because, as the 'national' Church, the ROC is expected to care for the national society: it is given little room to define or defend other interests (Caldwell 2010). Progressively, the formal charitable sector operating under the umbrella of the ROC has significantly expanded and diversified (see chapter 1). Yet even when the Church has done little as a whole, individual Orthodox churches have been involved in giving and receiving help at the local level. They do this in the absence of registered charitable structures and through activities which are not limited in their reach to those who identify themselves as parishioners. A more inclusive notion of charity is therefore necessary to account for these kinds of activities. As in the preceding chapters, charity can only be understood by extending a vision of the Church and its community to include people who come in touch with local churches in ways other than attendance and observance.

Because my initial project was to look at support, help-giving, and help-receiving inside parishes, I documented a range of practices, logics, and ways of speaking. The result is that two complexes of support can be identified. The first involves networks within the core parish community; these draw on both religious and secular views of sociality in giving and receiving help. The second complex consists of the grassroots charities. These depend on the church's existence, but reach out into broader groups of local dwellers. They involve people without requiring or announcing a religious commitment or component. Some grassroots charities, including some of the most spontaneous and informal forms of support, have already been outlined by Nikolai Mitrokhin (2004). Here, I examine the practical functioning of such support, and bring out the perspectives of participants. Doing so enables me to give attention to the peculiar and intricate configurations of secular moralities and religious organizations that have emerged in the post-Soviet context. The beginning is note that in Ozerovo, charities arose to replace the distribution of foreign aid. A few terminological details are in order first.

Insiders' Views on Giving Help

According to Russian-English dictionaries, the Russian word *blagotvoritel'nost'* is the equivalent of 'charity' and 'philanthropy'. *Miloserdie* means 'mercy', 'charity', and 'clemency'. Its adjectival form, *miloserdnyi*, means both 'merciful' and 'charitable'. Turning the direction of translation around, the English 'charity' is also translated as *blagotvoritel'nost'* and *miloserdie*.

In public usage, *blagotvoritel'nost'* is more common than *miloserdie*. Both terms, however, refer to a publicized, sometimes even grandiose, act of giving to help the needy. Both refer to acts through which one publicly commits oneself to support others. In other words, they refer to acts motivated by profound spirituality and moral purity. The giver (*blagotvoritel'*) is imagined as a person possessing such outstanding moral qualities. When the terms are invoked (as I found with my questions), they invariably call to mind the pre-Soviet era: a quasi-mythical period when such highly moral people existed. The terms *blagotvoritel'nost'* and *miloserdie* are too pretentious to describe current practices. When used, Ozerovo's inhabitants say that 'charity' does not really exist in their city.

With specific reference to the church, *blagotvoritel'nost'* is sometimes used to describe donations to help the needy, for church renovation works, or for the internal functioning of the parish. However, such donations are usually called sponsorship support (*sponsorskaia pomoshch'*). Referring to the donor as a *sponsor* connotes modernity and relieves the giver from the burden of moral purity. One can be a *sponsor*, too, without any religious motivation.

Nor are the activities that occur as part of the first complex of church-related support described as 'charity'. The most engaged members in the parish offer each other mutual assistance, and this help can spread throughout and beyond the parish activists. In colloquial language, such assistance is referred to as 'mutual help' (*vzaimovyruchka* and *vzaimopomoshch'*) or given no name at all. Like donations, these kinds of help cannot reach the epic levels of 'charity'. The grounds here differ, however; mutual help is totally invisible from outside the community of committed parishioners.

There is also invisible charity, performed by believers who wish their gifts and good actions to remain secret. Such gifts, appreciated only by God, may garner rewards for the giver in the afterlife. These gifts can also not be 'charity' because they are meant to remain hidden and unspoken; the donors consider themselves to act according to the Gospel's injunction that the left hand should not know what the right hand does (*levaia ruka ne dolzhna znat' to chto pravaia delaet*). Unlike sponsorship or mutual support, these gifts are explicitly conceptualized in Christian terms. Their giving has something of the moral purity associated with 'charity', but they are still not labelled as such.

Thus, there is no 'charity' in most Russian churches. But there are many forms of help. In addition to those already mentioned, which tend to concentration on financial or material help, there is abundant help in the form of spiritual services. Services provided by prayers, such as confession, the blessing of flats and cars, the distribution of holy water, prayers, and other religious rites are considered to constitute 'help' at least as much as food, money, and clothing. Sometimes these are considered more important. Indeed, I constantly encountered the conviction that 'real' support goes beyond offering items for everyday use, food, or health care. This idea is largely shared by priests, church workers, and regular churchgoers. For example, prayers are often requested by and for people who have little other interaction with the Church and little concern for its official positions. The names of acquaintances, friends, and family members, living and dead, are written onto slips of paper (the *zapiski*) which are then read out during prayers by priests and church workers. A specific request is not made on the *zapiski*, allowing God himself to decide how to best support the person for whom the prayer is offered.

And then, there are the grassroots charities. These are explicit, although not highly formalized, in their goal to direct material support to the larger public. These grassroots charities are far from being as inclusive and efficient as charities organized in larger cities (and often by foreign organizations): large-scale soup kitchens or clothing, housing, and health programmes. These much larger charities formally define, for example, who is entitled to assistance; precisely how the specific project works in terms of staff, and types of items and support provided; and their official authorizations (Caldwell 2004). Such formalization is absent from charitable efforts in Ozerovo's parishes. Nonetheless, in this city the invention of the local grassroots charities began with such foreign aid.

From Foreign Aid to Local Patterns

When considering the models of charity of the Roman Catholic Church and that of most established Protestant Churches, one might assume that a strong Orthodox revival would also lead to the establishment of stable and formal frameworks for Orthodox charitable activities. Yet local examples contradict this assumption. In fact, less formalization has been the dominant pattern in the post-Soviet period.

During the second half of the 1990s and in the very beginning of the 2000s, German charitable organizations and NGOs were particularly active in Russia. Ozerovo received humanitarian aid from its German twin-city. The aid benefitted various local institutions, such as homes for elderly and disabled people. The German Diakonie services, the main charitable organization affiliated with the German Evangelical Church (i.e. Lutheran Church), also sent humanitarian aid to be distributed through Trinity Church and the Church of Saint George the Warrior. Packages of food were also sent from Finland to the local Red Cross.[102] But the German aid was far greater in volume and is now remembered more clearly. When, in 2007, people in Ozerovo recalled this period of hardship, they mentioned that everyone had

---

[102] Ozerovo is situated in the historical region of Ingria. Before the 1917 Revolution, many Finnish speakers lived in the area. After series of disruptions in the Soviet period, the relations between Finland and Russia's ethnic Finnish communities are becoming stronger (see chapter 2). The Finnish humanitarian aid sent to Ozerovo after the collapse of the Soviet regime contributed to these strengthening ties.

received some type of material support from Germany. It was possible in those days to order a specific item, such as a coat, shoes, or other items, from the German charities, and even to specify the necessary size. Some received what they expected. Others received inappropriate clothing that they gave away to friends and acquaintances. In Orthodox milieus as well as beyond them, the name of the twin-city is remembered, but nothing is said about the Diakonie or its Protestant affiliation.

The Diakonie's support, however, was substantial. In 2000, Trinity Church received 11, 214 kilogrammes of clothing, shoes, books, and thermoses. In 1999, ten wheelchairs had reached the parish, and were turned over to the city's Committee for Social Protection. The parish archives hold detailed reports on the number of boxes and kilogrammes of aid received and re-given. The recipients included local inhabitants, other parishes within the deanery, a children's home, the local society of former children deported to Nazi work camps during the Second World War, a fund to support large families, and the local military detachment. The redistributed aid reached far beyond the city: the children's home that received aid is situated in a village (*poselok*) some ten kilometres away from Ozerovo. Many of the recipients – both institutional and individual – wrote letters of thanks to the rector of the parish. Some letters also mention 'the good people' who provided the packages. Staff at the children's home told me that all of the children had been clothed fully from the boxes of clothes and shoes they had received.

When the massive one-sided Western support ended, no similar initiative followed. For the clergy, as for all local inhabitants, the influx of foreign aid remained a central point of reference. This generous unilateral aid was seen as an ideal form of charity. At the time of my field research, the local positive memories were a strong reminder that Russia's public approved of such humanitarian aid, and that such charity was expected from the Russian Orthodox Church as well.

'The Cleaners Know Who Is in Need'

Shortly after 2000 the unilateral foreign aid ended, but the clergy did not undertake any initiatives to replace these programmes. Instead, foreign charity was replaced totally by local patterns of support. The supply of clothing was no longer such an acute problem in 2006–07, but a range of basic foods had become too expensive for many to purchase and people also suffered from the scarcity of affordable housing. There remained no trace of the central role that Trinity Church had played previously in providing clothing. There were no more visible activities of Church poverty relief. The only visible reminder of the association of churches with charity took shape in the churchyard beggars (see chapter 7).

Yet many people, both churchgoers and non-churchgoers, brought bags of clothes, shoes, and other used goods like dishes and baby strollers to the churches. It was the unnoticeable women, the church shop workers and cleaners (*svechnitsi* and *uborchitsi*), who received and redistributed these goods to the people they knew to be in need. This activity was not advertised. The workers themselves did not think of these activities as something valuable to the church. The priests were surprised when I showed an interest. One of them told me that the clergymen did not supervise this activity. 'The cleaners know who is in need', he said, indicating these redistributive activities; he did not need to be involved. Redistribution was of secondary importance and finding recipients was a totally informal affair. The church workers voluntarily took on the tasks of collection and redistribution. Surely these items (especially those of the best quality) reached their own kin, friends, and acquaintances first. But then, they spread into the networks of acquaintances. The arrival of bulky plastic bags of used goods was unceasing. They were more numerous on feast days, but still a regular feature of ordinary days. There were no official rules on how to distribute the items nor whom was deserving of them. There were no high ideals of charity and support associated with this redistribution.

Similar practices were carried out in other neighbouring parishes, with a similar lack of formalization. During a Sunday morning service in a neighbouring village, I inquired about the bulky plastic bags left in the entrance of the church. The female shop worker I had addressed immediately encouraged me to take for myself what I wanted. I was a completely anonymous visitor. Clearly it was possible to come to a church if one wanted to enter into the circle of the 'needy' to whom things were redistributed.

At other churches, people tried to give such bags of used goods and were refused. For example, at one church the priest refused all donations apart from those explicitly solicited by the church for its own needs.[103] He systematically redirected people who tried to leave things to a home for the elderly. For him, the bags were full of 'old clothes' and 'broken things' that nobody needs. The people who brought them were not donating, but merely acting according to the saying 'God, take what we don't like' (*Na tebe, Bozhe, chto nam ne gozhe*). Indeed, some of the donated items were really not useful anymore, but many were, and quickly found future users.

Churches are not the only destination for goods that are no longer needed or wanted. In Russia, similar initiatives are typical in kindergartens, elderly homes, and other social institutions. Parents of grown-up children, for example, take remaining clothes and toys to kindergartens. Social

---

[103] For a clerical point of view on charity, see Köllner (2011).

institutions are perceived as places that serve the needy. Pensioners, the disabled, and children appear to be natural recipients. In these other cases, post-Soviet donations continue Soviet practices and categories of the 'needy' (see Yates 2004; Hemment 2012). But why is it that churches have been added into the list of appropriate mediators between those who can give and those who receive? Why did people give them this role? In the first decade of the 2000s, as many people's material status improved, almost every local Orthodox church started to receive these bags. Bulky plastic bags full of used goods were left at the church by visitors and passers-by. It was unprecedented (as far as people could remember), unsolicited, and widespread.

It can be said that collective memory retained an association of churches with charity, and thus turned to them as a point of mediation. But it is also important to stress that the rising popularity of Orthodoxy in post-Soviet Russia has been accompanied by a takeover of the churches for non-religious purposes. The churches are open to everyone, and thus ideal for brokering new social relations. Moreover, the Orthodox Church has argued for – and in this instance gained – a special role vis-à-vis other denominations. Orthodoxy is promoted by the state as a 'Russian' religion in contrast to other denominations (especially those labelled 'sects'). The ROC is every Russian's church, regardless of his or her beliefs. Under such conditions of a public seeking spaces in which to manifest, local churches have become integrated into secular logics of support, sometimes against the will of the priest. Under pressure from the unceasing arrival of bulky bags, churches have become spaces of grassroots charitable efforts, whose practical modalities require a closer examination.

'People Bring, Others Take'

The churches are usually rather passive actors in the process of charitable redistribution. Priests are unconcerned, no formal structures for receiving or redistributing exist, and the whole process is handled informally by various church workers. However, the following example from Saint George the Warrior is a bit different. It illustrates, first, domestication of Western ways of providing charity and, finally, a total conversion to a local model with a higher degree of organization in comparison with the neighbouring parishes.

The church was undergoing reconstruction work (see chapter 3) when, in the middle of the 1990s, German humanitarian aid began to arrive. Ozerovo's 'twin city'[104] sent boxes containing clothes, shoes, and even

---

[104] It was probably the Diakonie Services that sent aid to this parish, as it did to others, but people spoke of the connection between the towns.

umbrellas and blankets, all used but in good condition. During several summers, too, young Germans came to help with the reconstruction. All of those who remembered the young Germans said that they were helpful and happy to be visiting Russia.

In the 1990s, the arriving packages were stored inside the church and distributed from there. First, those who worked for the reconstruction benefited from the packs, and after them all those who showed interest. By 2000, when the German aid ended, there were many items still undistributed. A shop worker told me how the church had used these items to begin its own distribution system.

Plate 17. Bags of donated clothes in the entrance of a church.

There is a small church shop, or *lavka,* in front of Saint George the Warrior, about 12 metres square. The building had belonged to the church before it was closed in the beginning of the 1930s. Then, in Soviet times, empty bottles were collected there. In the 1990s, the small building was returned to the church. By the end of the 1990s, it had been re-established as a normal church *lavka* selling various religious items, books, and booklets. At the time, the shop was run by Anna Ivanovna, a woman in her seventies. The shop worker who told me the story had been a friend of this lady.[105] As it came to pass, people coming into the *lavka* frequently told Anna Ivanovna that they needed shoes or other essential items, but had no money to buy them. Other people told her about household items in good condition that they did not need anymore. It occurred to the lady that the *lavka* could be used as an exchange point. She asked the clergy, and in particular the *starosta* who managed so many of the daily functions of this parish, if she could bring the undistributed German humanitarian aid into the shop. It had been encumbering the church, but could be displayed in the *lavka* and made available to those who might need something. She also asked if people who had useful items at home could bring them into the *lavka*. Anna Ivanovna's proposals were accepted, and it was thus that the *lavka* began its new charitable activities alongside the more conventional sale of religious objects.

Anna Ivanovna's initiative was well known and admired. I was told that a joke had circulated in her honour and testified to the popularity of the shop. It could happen that someone would admire another's coat (or other garment) that had come through the *lavka*, and the lucky owner would reply 'From Ivanovna', in the tone of a New Russian describing the latest Versace. This joke between acquaintances was a complex one, revealing also an ironic attitude to experienced economic hardship, and a deep awareness that they were 'making do' as others got rich.

At the time of my fieldwork in 2006–07, the *lavka* was well known across Ozerovo. It was open almost every day. Around 20 people came each day to buy a cross, a candle, or another religious item, to request prayers, or to inquire about rituals. Some people came in order to drop off clothes, shoes, dishes, or shelves from home. Others came hoping to find some donated things they needed for free. Despite the joke recounted above, the *lavka* had no name nor did its charitable service. The available goods were not even called *gumanitarka* (humanitarian package), as the former German and Finnish aid had been called. Nevertheless, almost every local inhabitant knew about this *lavka*; they expressed their approval for it, and many said that they had brought items there at least once. Although the church made no real effort to support these charitable activities, it did offer the use of the room and the assurance that the shop worker would look after donated items.

Perceptions of the *Lavka* Activity

It is tempting to look for deeply buried religious ethics as responsible for the process of integrating Orthodox churches into grassroots social support

---

[105] Anna Ivanovna had passed away before my arrival.

activities. One way of understanding the link between charitable activity and religious belief is to examine the actors' own interpretations by asking them whether they saw these activities as religious. Another method is to distance the analysis from these immediate responses by conducting it at a higher level and embedding the current logics in a historical perspective, and as part of a broader model of social self-representation. I will take this second analytic approach in the conclusion of this chapter, but for now I will examine the direct responses given to the question of the link between religion and charity, drawing on the case of the church shop.

Neither donors nor recipients of the *lavka* consider this charitable activity as religious. Similarly, parish workers and priests considered the *lavka*, like other grassroots activities, as an extremely modest and simple effort. They never spoke of such efforts as being based on a Christian motivation. Every time that I asked about charity (*blagotvoritel'nost'*) in this parish, I was told that, unfortunately, there was no such thing. The parish is considered poor and its parishioners are viewed as modest people; the clergymen, the parishioners, and other persons speak of it as a 'village parish' (*derevenskii prikhod*), implying that it is not well-off and survives thanks only to its parishioners (see chapter 4). The 'charity' of the *lavka* is completely subsumed under the secular motivations for gifting and logics of redistribution. 'People bring, others take' (*liudi prinostiat, drugie berut*) is the usual way in which it was described. Expressed in such terms, the *lavka* presented no particular pride for the clergy or church workers. They did not disregard the *lavka*'s activity. Rather, they saw it as vaguely good but insignificant, deserving only the lowest attention. Moreover, because the priests were not involved in the *lavka*, it did not occur to anyone that it could be a vehicle for acts of Christian compassion.

Gifting and the *Lavka*

In principle, the *lavka* was open to all. Anyone could donate items and anyone could take things for free. Donors and recipients were not clearly distinguished. Sometimes when people brought items to the *lavka*, they also checked to see if there was anything that they wanted. Such donors were not engaging in 'barter'; they had no strong expectation that having donated something, they would get something in return. For all donors, the major act was 'giving'. For all recipients, finding something was simply considered good luck.

People from various social backgrounds and of different ages brought items to the *lavka*. Women and men were equally represented. Some said that they brought a sweater, or shoes, or dishes, or a suitcase, because they wished to make a useful gift to others. Others emphasized that donating was a good 'opportunity to get rid of things' (*sposob izbavlenia ot veshchei*). Only one of the donors with whom I spoke, a woman, declared that she was motivated to give by her Christian faith, but she defined this as 'not especially Orthodox'. She said she often checked her cupboards at home hoping to find something to donate to the *lavka*. Some people said that they also took garments to the homes for the elderly and for disabled people. All donors were animated by the desire that their things should become useful again, rather than end up in the garbage.

Donors were interested in the future of the items they offered. Even those who said that they wished 'to get rid of things' were pleased when their donations were welcomed by the shop worker. A woman who brought in a plastic bag full of clothes, answered the shop worker's 'Thank you for bringing this' with a relieved, 'Thank you for accepting it'. The shop worker immediately refused garments that were too old and encouraged people to bring in only particularly useful and nice things. Thus acceptance of a donation was also a confirmation of the quality of the offering (and of the person; see below). When no one was in the *lavka*, people would leave their bags outside, but would often come back a few hours later to check that someone had taken them. Donors too were satisfied when they heard that their 'gift' had reached a receiver. Donors wanted to know that their donation had been 'useful' to another person. When they received such a confirmation, they felt that giving had been successful.

Privileged Recipients

In practice, the patterns of giving and redistribution reproduced some of the dominant social logics of discrimination and privilege, and of moral evaluation and judgment. Sociologically, there were several types of recipients. The diversity of social backgrounds of the recipients was less than that of the donors. There were no well-to-do recipients, instead they were usually people who were ostensibly poor, as well as people with low incomes who considered themselves to be neither particularly poor nor rich. Working people, especially women in their thirties, forties, and fifties, as well as pensioners (both women and men), usually selected one or two items that they liked. Those who visited the *lavka* in order to buy candles or another religious item, to request a prayer or a ritual, or simply to seek advice from the shop worker whom they considered competent in religious matters, often had a look at the donated items, and sometimes chose one or two pleasing objects. Sometimes, a person who brought an item would also choose another one to take home. These occasional recipients constituted one group of the common users of the *lavka*. They had access to all the things that were displayed, and the shop worker was open and friendly with them.

But not all recipients were granted equal access to the donated materials. The shop worker did not display all the donations that came in. Some she kept 'behind the counter' to offer to particular kinds of recipients. Her discretion, served to reproduce some widespread modes of discrimination and favouritism. A former factory and printing company worker, she had retired in 2004. Like many retired persons in Russia, she needed an additional income. As a trustworthy person, she was offered the job when Anna Ivanovna died. Although she was Orthodox, she was not an ardent believer and only rarely attended church. Like others from her generation, she was nostalgic about many aspects of Soviet life. This woman privileged some recipients she considered deserving, while disadvantaging others. The privileged ones were the shop worker's acquaintances, friends, and family members, including some of the most engaged parishioners. This privileged group, however, had no clear boundaries; it was rather a network of acquaintances, and could be entered into through conversation.

Frequently, a person who wished to bring something to the *lavka* first came and asked if the proposed donation would be accepted. When the answer was yes, the donor and shop worker would agree on a delivery date, and in the meantime, the shop worker would enquire among her closest contacts about who might be interested in the items. She especially called around concerning rare donations like baby strollers, or baby and children's clothes. If one of her contacts was interested, the shop worker would telephone the future owner as soon as the object arrived.

Sometimes the shop worker granted access to the goods behind the counter to unknown people. It was common for people to ask her if a desired item had arrived. In those cases, the shop worker made her own evaluation of the seeker. Did she or he really need this item? Did she or he deserve it? Was she or he righteous? In these situations, it was crucial for the person asking to demonstrate some convincing reasons to expect a 'favour'. The shop worker made her decisions according to widely accepted social criteria of worthiness: physical disability, work status, and – finally – moral qualities. For example, I witnessed one case of a blind woman who, because of her physical disability, received the requested garments directly at her home, carefully selected and delivered by the shop worker. Another woman, a single working mother ('She works a lot', the shop worker said), also received personally selected items at home. As in the church's response to the needs and desires of beggars, Soviet categories of worthiness premised on one's commitment to work played an important role in determining access to 'charity' in the *lavka*.[106]

A Procedure of Appropriation

In the very beginning of my fieldwork, when the shop worker considered me a special visitor, she offered me a long thick winter coat with the assurance that it had been donated by a 'clean woman'. As I understood later, the donor was an acquaintance of a friend of hers. What I took then for an exceptional event came out to be a rather usual practice. Since Marcel Mauss (1950 [1924]), anthropologists have acknowledged that, in a multitude of cases and societies, things that are donated are marked by the person of the donor. While in some cases the appropriation of a donated thing did not involve any mention of the donor, in other cases this was a prominent feature of goods redistributed through Ozerovo's grassroots charities. In particular, in the *lavka*, the transfer of donated items from a giver to a future recipient required a specific procedure. 'Cleanliness' was brought into the procedure as an intermediate category which allowed the transfer. The shop worker selected items of good quality for deserving recipients. For her, the quality of the item was raised by the moral portrait of the giver. When she offered good clothes to close contacts and deserving recipients, she often mentioned that an item 'was brought by a clean woman' (*chistenkaia zhenshina prinesla*) or that it 'was brought by a clean person' (*chistenkii chelovek prines*). As we know from Mary Douglas (1978), dirt and cleanliness are relative ideas. Indeed, the reference to cleanliness meant that the shop worker knew the donor, or that she considered him or her to be a good person. Thus, a positive moral judgment referring either to a close contact, or to an unknown but morally high-standing person, was voiced in terms of cleanliness. The donated objects appeared as an extension of the person; a moral portrait became instilled in the things that were given. Ultimately, this operation was meant to make the gift easily acceptable to the recipient.

When occasional visitors found something and decided to take it home, they often used the same phrases as the shop worker in order to acknowledge the donor's cleanliness, although they did not actually know who had donated the item. Admiring an item and saying 'this was given by a clean person' served as a kind of explanation for their choice and as an act of self-persuasion that the object was of good quality. The connection between the giver, the object given, and the receiver was built through these brief judgments of the donor's cleanliness. They signified a recognition and an acceptance of the moral self of the anonymous donor, and in this way they

---

[106] On work and Soviet morality, see also Yates (2004) and Vladimirova (2006).

helped to neutralize the tension existing in the process of appropriating other people's objects. On one hand, the donors seemed to desire complete alienation of the items they had given. When some of them came back to check up if somebody took their gifts, this was precisely because they wished their things to become other people's property. But on the other hand, complete appropriation did not seem immediately possible from the recipient's point of view. The appropriation required a special procedure of building a positive moral portrait of the anonymous donor through the category of cleanliness. The potential recipient achieved the transfer of the object by describing its cleanliness, a process which aimed at recognizing the worth of the donor.

Discrimination in the *Lavka*

In Russian society, 'Gypsies are hardly ever depicted as sincere players' (Lemon 2000: 4); they are considered 'slippery by nature' (2000: 226). At best, Gypsies' relation to money is suspect (Lemon 1998). Alaina Lemon's observations found a poignant resonance in the everyday functioning of the grassroots charities. The *lavka* welcomed all visitors; no one was prevented from entering and everyone could see the items on display. Scorn and latent conflict only became explicit when *some* visitors made a particular request or when their behaviour was considered inappropriate. The shop worker was clearly critical of those whom she called 'the Gypsies' (*tsygany*) and of those suspected of re-selling the free donations. Her negative opinion of these 'misusers' was shared by the leaders of the parish community. No one, however, took formal measures to limit access to the *lavka* or to the subsequent uses of goods taken from it. All this was accomplished informally, as in the example below.

One day, a young Gypsy couple entered the *lavka* and had a look at the clothes and shoes on display. Then the man turned to the shop worker: would she have a pair of shoes 'to sell' to his wife? The woman behind the counter became upset: how could the young man imply that she might be 'selling' shoes that had been donated to the shop? Everything, she replied, was on display. There were no other things available. In fact, at that precise moment, there were no shoes behind the counter. But the interchange is an important one because it indicates both that the Gypsy knew or had guessed at how the *lavka* functioned, and that he was not at all the right sort of recipient to gain the shop worker's favour. After the man insisted, the shop worker told him, in quite a firm voice, that the couple should go to the second-hand store where they could buy what they needed.

In this particular instance, the shop worker's reaction focused on the man's offer to pay, but the bigger problem was simply that he was Gypsy.

When the couple left, the shop worker commented on the idleness of Gypsies. They tried to acquire things for free. It did not matter to her that the young man had offered to pay for the shoes. This was in fact an offending offer to her. On another occasion, she told me that the Gypsies have no money and therefore they need to find goods for free, but 'One can see the golden teeth in their mouths'.[107] In other words, Gypsies have an irrational relationship to money. When they get it, they spend it frivolously, and this makes them poor. For the shop worker, it was totally natural that she should refuse to support such an absurd way of life by giving them things for free. Criticism of Gypsies erupted into the shop worker's commentaries even when Gypsy visitors did not offer to pay. Because Gypsies brought poverty on themselves, she did not think that they should be entitled to the free goods in the *lavka*.

But the shop worker never discussed why ethnic Russians should have recourse to the *lavka*. It was normal, she thought, to make free things available because 'Many have a hard life in today's Russia'. Ethnic Russians were subjected to personal moral scrutiny, and could find favour by looking either 'rich' or 'poor' (as long as they were 'clean'), but Gypsies were always treated with suspicion. They were 'the "wrong" social type' not only when they wielded money, but also when they lacked money (Lemon 1998: 45–46). Those who were of Gypsy origin always raised suspicion and resentment in matters of charity.

In addition to those perceived as Gypsies, the other group that was constantly criticized by the shop worker were those who were suspected of re-selling what they acquired from the *lavka*. Five or six of the regular *lavka* visitors were said to sell what they took. Of course, none of them openly declared that they engaged in such activity. In most cases, it was only their daily visits and the bulky bags they carried away that raised suspicion. What did they do with so many things, if not sell them? Nevertheless, the shop worker never impeded them from gathering the displayed items, and the priests were reluctant to become involved in the brewing sense of conflict. Gypsies and ethnic Russians took equal part in this 'unfair' trade.

The shop worker was sure that one woman was really selling the goods she took from the *lavka*. This was a Gypsy woman in her early thirties, originally from Moldova.[108] She was the mother of two young

---

[107] The shop worker's expression is a common one and it calls attention to the display of golden teeth as if they were a form of jewellery. In fact, gold was the common material for dental work in Soviet Russia. The statement is never meant by any who use it to be interrogated literally.

[108] In Ozerovo, all those identified as Gypsies (*tsygany*) by ethnic Russians say they come from Moldova, although many have been rooted in the same neighbourhood for generations.

children. She came to the *lavka* every day. The shop worker had an ambivalent relation with her. On the one hand, she denounced the young woman to me for her immoral behaviour. On the other hand, the shop worker supported the woman. She would hold aside clothes and other items that she knew the young woman could easily sell. And, as long as she sold the goods far enough from the *lavka* that nobody could guess their origin, she made no complaints to the woman. Once, the woman had set-up her selling point just outside the *lavka*, and this had made the shop worker extremely angry. People had begun to gossip that the *lavka* was selling things that people had donated. The shop worker could not tolerate such a situation, and sent the young woman away.

For the shop worker, re-selling donated goods was immoral. But, she admitted that the young mother could be pardoned because of her material hardships. The shop worker insisted that I should not give money to the woman; it was not good to encourage her to beg. The effort the woman put into re-selling the items she took seemed, from the shop worker's point of view, to qualify as work. Though the re-sale itself was immoral, the effort necessary to accomplish it brought legitimacy to the money it yielded. Sometimes the Gypsy woman did beg, and the shop worker heavily disapproved.

The shop worker's disapproval of the young Gypsy was also mixed with empathy. Humour indicated complicity between the two women. For example, the shop worker joked with the young woman that she lied so frequently to find reasons for requesting money and services that she forgot what she had said on previous days. 'I tell her: "Your birthday is six times per year!"', she laughed at her own half-critical and half-friendly remark. Sometimes the woman and her children helped the shop worker tidy the shop by sorting through and throwing out old and unpleasant clothes and other items. On those occasions, the shop worker offered candies to the children.

Nevertheless, the Gypsy woman told me that the shop worker did not like her. 'She advises people not to give me money', she said. The remark was a telling one, hinting at the complex motivations for cooperation between the two women and the limits of their apparent empathy. In practice, those who were needy were discriminated against in the grassroots charities, unless they foregrounded social relatedness. The Gypsy customers make this situation especially clear. While all unknown Gypsies were met with resentment, empathy became possible only by creating a closer relationship. Such a relationship did not completely erase the initial mistrust and scorn, but it facilitated exchange and support.

Conclusion

The ethnographic account I have given aimed at demonstrating the spontaneous and non-formalized giving, networking, and informal mechanisms of inclusion and exclusion that shape the grassroots charities. The current Russian high ideals about charity differ vastly from the realities of grassroots charities. While the idealized forms of charity rest on ideas of unilaterality and the distance between the charitable giver and the needy recipient, the grassroots charitable redistribution is made possible only by shared ideas of relatedness.

Two distinct, but often entwined, logics of relatedness are at work: the first one characterizes the process of distribution; it implies networking, various forms of reciprocity, moral judgment, and discrimination. In this logic, horizontal and hierarchical, inclusive and selective, personal and anonymous relationships are brought to bear in practical transactions. Numerous sociological studies emphasize the social significance of networking and informal exchanges in urban and rural Russia for the late Soviet and post-Soviet periods. What has attracted less scholarly attention is what constitutes the second logic of relatedness present in the grassroots charities: the spontaneous and often anonymous acts of altruistic giving. The donors act out of empathy and without much introspective self-examination of their deeper motives. The common motivation, even in the case of those who wish to 'get rid of things', is for their gifts to be helpful to others. Thus, instead of asking whether their acts are *really* altruistic or conceal shadows of interestedness, I prefer to trust my informants – following, then, John Davis (1992: 14–27) – and to argue that people become donors out of a mere desire to help. Discriminatory relationships and indiscriminate (most often anonymous) gifting combine to shape the overall model of charity in practice.

An intriguing element in this second logic of relatedness is the role attributed to and played by the Orthodox churches. As I showed above, no religious meaning is consciously attributed to the grassroots charities. These donations cannot be labelled religious 'pure gifts' (Parry 1986); they are not intended to address the transcendent in any way and even the clergy do not see any religious meaning in them. Neither do these donations show traces of almsgiving motivated by religious belief. Could we, then, advance the argument that traces of religious belief are embedded in the phenomenon of these modest donations, even though they are invisible at first glance?

A brief historical comparison between these grassroots charities and their possible historical precedents shows that the current practices do not reproduce earlier forms of giving in which religious belief was an underlying element. We can situate at the two extremes of a continuum the indiscriminate almsgiving, deeply rooted in pre-Soviet Orthodox culture and practised over centuries (Bernshtam 2005: 282–86), and the organized charities which emerged in the nineteenth century. Russia's 'homes of industry' are a prominent example of the nineteenth-century charities, inspired by scientific philanthropy. They hosted poor people, prostitutes, and vagrants and, by putting them to work, aimed at improving their employability and morality (Lindenmeyr 1986, 1996). Some of these homes operated under the auspices of the Church. In addition, there were a wide range of other religious and non-religious charities. As Lindenmeyr has argued, even charity is too 'frail' a concept to express the complex and multiple philosophies of giving that prevailed during the late imperial period (Lindenmeyr 1990: 689). Religious belief was pivotal to many pre-Soviet forms of support to the needy.

Religious belief is again important for some of the more recent Orthodox charities. However, it is deceptive to look for a revival of nineteenth-century models of giving in the shape of the recently created Church programmes. Revivalist discourses often surround such charitable initiatives. But these discourses are part of the performance of authenticity, since a particular representation of pre-Soviet Orthodoxy is meant to stand for an ideal of righteous religiosity. The grassroots charities themselves are an example of something radically different from all the nineteenth-century forms of almsgiving and philanthropy, and they also differ from any organized contemporary charity. They do not resemble the direct face-to-face relationships established in traditional Orthodox almsgiving, because they are indirect and anonymous most of the time, mediated by church workers, and their participants are rarely devoted Orthodox believers. Unlike almsgiving, they do not necessarily imply a hierarchy in the respective status of the giver and the receiver; in addition, the donor occasionally becomes a recipient of what other donors bring. Unlike the nineteenth-century initiatives, they do not rely on any idea about transforming society or reshaping the moral self of the recipient. They are something entirely new to the Church, or at least something that has not so far been acknowledged by historians.

If the donors do not expect any kind of reciprocity and there is no religious meaning attached to their acts, what relates them to the recipients of their gifts? The grassroots charities are an arrangement founded by the members of society, an arrangement that involves the churches in the practical enactment of a social ethos of relatedness. This ethos permeates the churches from below with the singular impetus of unplanned spontaneous acts of giving. It holds together an imagined horizontal community of those in need, a category largely coincident with the imagined community of ordinary Russians. Giving and receiving, often in anonymous ways, puts the emphasis on one's belonging to a specific but large group in society: the group of the common people who experience need and those who are aware of, and physically in contact with, the massive presence of needy people. This imagined collective of the needy is historically constructed and anchored in popular self-images. For example, Nancy Ries (1997) reports that, during perestroika, Russians overwhelmingly perceived themselves to be those who suffer but still make do. In the period of perestroika, the needy were to a very large extent defined as ordinary Russians who experienced chronic shortages of basic goods. More generally, the motif of material poverty and suffering is present in a large range of poetry and literature works. Hence, there is a lasting social self-representation of a community held together along horizontal lines of need. This self-image engenders concrete social dynamics, of which the grassroots charities are just one example.

Religious interpretations have sometimes given meaning to this self-image. One of the historically lasting ideological schemes in Russian Orthodoxy is the relation between physical suffering, poverty, and spiritual elevation. Traces of this were found even in the late Soviet period. For instance, Ries's rich description of 'Russian talk' during the perestroika years mentions implicit, and some explicit, references to Orthodoxy; poverty was considered a source of spiritual merit and some associations with sanctity were established (1997: 126–60).

But such religious conceptualization cannot be found in the grassroots charities. The latter are modestly pragmatic, not spiritually emphatic. On one hand, the use of the churches when manifesting this ethos indicates a lasting relation between Russian society and the Orthodox Church. But on the other hand, in the case discussed here, the ethos of relatedness is no longer articulated in terms of religious belief. When one turns to the larger public of those who use these charities and to the clergy, it is difficult to find any religious connotations. It is deceptive to search for traces of forgotten Orthodox teachings that could explain a phenomenon which is definitely secular. All donors share the conviction that the overwhelming majority of their fellow members of society face material hardship that they can help alleviate (although only partly). The practices of moral judgment and discrimination that accompany giving and redistribution do not overturn, but rather enforce, the sense of a community of equals. All clerics try to delegate the problem of the management of donations to their subordinates who 'know who is in need'. No religious belief or implicit religious meaning emerges. Although the grassroots charities are part and parcel of those dimensions of church life that are considered trivial and non-elevated, including by those who actively engage in them, they directly contribute to a distinctive mutual embedding of Church and society in post-Soviet Russia.

Chapter 9
Conclusion

The ROC plays a prominent role in public life in Russia and increasingly abroad, and its importance as a source of national identity in Russia is also on the rise. These marks of success stand at odds with Russians' insignificant levels of practice and their elusive manifestations of faith. In social-scientific approaches to religion, practice is usually taken as an indicator of devotion, and faith is normally sought for in a body of assertions. It becomes clear then that in Russia, only a tiny minority of the vast self-declared Orthodox majority can boast sustained practice and robust faith. When we focus on street-level Orthodoxy, however, we gain access to important aspects and dynamics of the bond between the ecclesiastical organization and Russian society.

My conclusions may not be representative for all of Russia. Some of the specific elements of urban life in north-western Russia may prevent such a generalization. However, there is much that can be generalized. Moreover, this ethnography of street-level Orthodoxy in the ROC should prompt reflection on the possibility for developing new approaches to understanding the continued influence of historically-established and well-recognized religious organizations even when classical forms of attendance and observance have eroded significantly. It is typical to treat the ROC, and Orthodoxy generally, as unique in its relations with state and society compared to the Catholic and Protestant churches. Is street-level Orthodoxy also unique to and in Russia? Perhaps. But, even this presupposed uniqueness can open up new comparative horizons. At the very least, it prompts a new question. In Russia, we need not ask if the Church and local parishes still matter in society. Clearly they do. The question is rather, how do they matter?

The Russian Orthodox parish as a subject of scholarly investigation has long proved challenging, and not only with respect to its post-Soviet intricacies. Understanding the eighteenth-century transformations of the parish posed challenges to historians too. Before the Great Reforms of the eighteenth century, the parish was the primary administrative unit of the Russian Church. As a religious organization, it fulfilled sacramental functions; more broadly, it served the spiritual needs of the laity. The parish was also a social unit, identified with the local territorial community (*obshchina* or *mir*). It played administrative and economic roles by connecting state officials to the local communities, by lending money to its members, and by typically allowing markets to take place around the church. Moreover, the laity felt deeply connected to their parish, not least because they elected their clergy. In short, the parish church served as the local centre of spiritual, administrative, economic, and social life, and was to a large extent subject to the decisions of the community members. Thus, for centuries, the parish embodied the strongest bond between the Church and the laity.

The series of reforms, first introduced by Peter the Great and pursued by his successors, among whom Catherine the Great and Paul I proved the most interventionist, radically transformed this situation. The parish clerics became the appointees of the bishops; markets had to be held on special places at some distance from the churches; lay entertainment was banned from the churches and their surroundings. The renovation of old churches and the construction of new ones had to be submitted for approval to the hierarchs who often disapproved of the initiatives. In order to receive an agreement, the laity had to provide sufficient evidence that they had enough resources to support their parish church and clergy. The latter measure aimed at limiting the phenomenon of clerical poverty that had led not only to dire poverty and starvation for some priests, but also to the emergence of clerical vagrancy. These and other reforms allowed increased control by the political and ecclesiastical authorities over the management of the parish, and earlier forms of parish self-government by the laity disappeared. As a result, the parish ceased to play some of its crucial social roles. Many historians have interpreted these transformations as the end of the deep connection between the laity and the Church, or more simply as the end of the parish. But this is not the only possible interpretation.

The historian Gregory Freeze (1976), for example, argued that the bond between parish and people had been modified – significantly. The parish was stripped from 'its broad set of "extrareligious" functions for the community' (ibid. 34), and 'was split off from the parallel secular society' (ibid. 50). In response, the bond between the parish and laity underwent a deep transformation, as the parish became concentrated on religious service. By focusing on transformation rather than rupture, Freeze opened the possibility to see changes occurring in the nature of society's relation to the religious organization itself.

Conclusion

In the twenty-first century, it is important to push our analyses of the social role of the Church beyond the documentation of structural change. As Freeze has done for the eighteenth century, it is important to assume that the existence (and increase) of local parishes means that they matter in people's lives. To attend services, take communion, tithe and donate, or register and celebrate life-cycle events within a church are only some of the ways in which a parish may matter. Whether the laity financially supports or neglects its parish(es) is similarly unimportant from this perspective: both possibilities point to a deeply charged relation between society and church.

The question to ask then is not whether, but how. How does the parish matter in society? I have tried to provide answers to this question for the post-Soviet case. I have proposed the notion of street-level Orthodoxy as a methodological and conceptual tool that can help open up the analytical boundaries usually assumed in studies of the parish. The concept of street-level Orthodoxy comes closer to representing the fluidity, overlapping, and permeability that characterize the connections between the 'inside' and 'outside' of church walls.

As in the earlier eighteenth-century transformations of the Church, the social distress and unfolding economic processes of the post-Soviet period are deeply intertwined with the operation of the parish. This intertwining is multi-stranded. For its part, the 'parish' is not one thing. It is rather an administrative unit, a church building, and a community of people. As a community too, it consists not just of clergy and active parishioners, but of a highly variegated laity coming into different kinds of contact with the church: a core community of active parishioners, formal and informal workers, droppers-by, beggars, and other needy – among others. A close examination of how social distress and socio-economic and gender disparities shape the parish every day led me to spotlight several ways in which the parish is deeply embedded in the surrounding society.

In the early twenty-first century, we can see the parish becoming a locus of social support, even as this image is rarely associated with the parish churches. Those who come into contact with the Church find, at the very least, an anchor and buttress for their social values and personal moral worth. Many seek, find, or create material support as well. Most who come are distinctively 'post-Soviet' persons: they still hold dear values related to work; accept as 'natural' (if not just) a variety of socio-economic inequalities (among which those related to gender are most visible); and discriminate among a variety of 'moral others' to the detriment of many groups, including Gypsies. These different groups of people also distinguish between the parish churches. For example, struggles of the past reverberate through unequal levels of material prosperity and diverging sources of prestige into the present. This inter-parish differentiation is part of common knowledge that is transmitted through memory cultivated by small groups of activists and, beyond, through local standard narratives and through widespread distinctive images of the different churches.

Some objections might still be made that the parish is not the best ground for examining the liveliness of contemporary Orthodoxy. In addition to the previously acknowledged low figures of observant parishioners and reforms that further distance the laity from parish governance, there is a proliferation of nomadic forms of Orthodox religiosity. Moreover, Orthodox media and social networks are gaining in public prominence. Do such ephemeral and virtual forms of Orthodox belonging not also point to the declining importance of the parish? I think not.

The main point that I have made throughout this book is about the integrative nature of street-level Orthodoxy. The thriving non-territorial and fleeting forms of participation in Orthodoxy represented by increased consumption of print, broadcast, and online media; pilgrimages; fairs; and Orthodox social networks are interrelated with the development of street-level Orthodoxy. They are not opposed to it. The many interrelations between street-level and non-territorial forms of Orthodoxy are hinted at in the biographical accounts of my informants. If anything, the non-territorial and fleeting or momentary forms of engagements stimulate more openness and fluidity at the parish level, sometimes in accordance with canonically sanctioned practice and sometimes with disregard for it. So it is that a single informant can be an informal worker at one parish, a dropper-by at another, and a regular visitor to a far-away Orthodox community headed by her chosen spiritual counsellor (whom she found through a book). Though she is an active parishioner nowhere, such an informant contributes to and gains from three parish communities. Moreover, her multiple engagements build her personal religiosity and her role as a 'religious person' throughout various social networks and relations.

The ROC's efforts to control parishes may well expand the domains of street-level Orthodoxy. From a formal perspective, the Church reforms adopted under Patriarch Kirill since 2009 have restricted greatly the possibility for the laity to intervene in parish affairs. Instead, bishops have been granted ever more power over parish decisions. But it should not be assumed that lay participation in parish governance has been decreased. The new restrictions do not address the many ways documented by my research that lay actors influence parish life on an everyday basis. Laypeople can and do manage pragmatic aspects of church life. They are the heads of the lay parish council, of course, but they also run the parish shops and schools; they write the church's bulletins and newspapers; they are responsible for 'grassroots charities' and the redistribution of various goods that appear at the church; they man the doors, clean the floors, and provide all of the other logistical guidance that moves (or hinders) visitors through the spaces of the church and its grounds. Laypeople also take up many of the procedures surrounding the canonization of new saints. The parish priests hold formal positions of responsibility over some of these activities, but many are simply unaccounted for, and priests themselves usually defer to the authority of those who take up practical responsibility for the various tasks.

Increased formalization of the official rules of the Church regarding decision making may encourage even more creativity in the sphere of actual lay participation. There are simply so many tasks to be accomplished that those that go uncodified may be taken up by anyone, and those that are assigned to particular individuals in excess of what they can (or want) to accomplish may also be taken up by others. From this perspective, formalization might just as equally deepen the flexible multifaceted roles of the laity within and at the margins of the parish, as prompt their progressive fading away under more authoritative direction. Indeed, the ROC's history indicates that the complex bond between local churches and the laity has long evolved under the conditions of rigid ecclesiastical structures. Deepening authoritarianism and rigidity from above, even when combined with steadily low statistics of attendance and practice, does not necessarily signal any lack of or disruption to lay participation in parish life. Instead, these may be the contextual factors in which its transformation will unfold in the future.

Russian Orthodoxy is a lively and controversial sphere precisely because formal Church organization, parish life, street-level, virtual and nomadic forms of religious engagement are not mutually exclusive, but closely interrelated. The logical and practical conclusion is thus that the most urgent theoretical challenge to understanding Russian Orthodoxy resides precisely in the need for adequate conceptual tools and models. The tools and models still to be developed must be able to account for the different and intersecting dimensions of these specific modes of religious engagement.

Bibliography

Agadjanian, A. 2011. Prikhod i Obshchina v Russkom Pravoslavii: Sovremennye Protsessy v Retrospektive Poslednogo Stoletia. In A. Agadjanian, and K. Rousselet (eds.), *Prikhody i Obshchiny v Sovremennom Pravoslavii: Kornevaia Sistema Rossiiskoi Religioznosti*, pp. 15–36. Moscow: Ves' Mir.

Agadjanian, A., and K. Rousselet. 2005. Globalization and Identity Discourse in Russian Orthodoxy. In V. Roudometof, A. Agadjanian, and J. Pankhrust (eds.), *Eastern Orthodoxy in a Global Age: Tradition Faces the Twenty-First Century*, pp. 29–57. Walnut Creek: AltaMira Press.

———. 2010. Individual and Collectives Identities in Russian Orthodoxy. In C. Hann, and H. Goltz (eds.), *Eastern Christians in Anthropological Perspective*, pp. 311–328. Berkeley: University of California Press.

———. (eds.). 2011a. *Prikhody i Obshchiny v Sovremennom Pravoslavii: Kornevaia Sistema Rossiiskoi Religioznosti*. Moscow: Ves' Mir.

———. 2011b. Predislovie. In A. Agadjanian, and K. Rousselet (eds.), *Prikhody i Obshchiny v Sovremennom Pravoslavii: Kornevaia Sistema Rossiiskoi Religioznosti*, pp. 7–14. Moscow: Ves' Mir.

Anderson, B. 1983. *Imagined Communities: Reflections on the Origin and Spread of Nationalism*. New York: Verso.

Barsukova, S. 2004. *Nerynochnye Obmeny mezhdu Rossiiskami Domokhozhiaistvami: Teoriia i Praktika Retsiproknosti*. Moscow: GU Vysshaia Shkola Ekonomiki.

Bellér-Hann, I. 2008. *Community Matters in Xinjiang 1880–1949: Towards a Historical Anthropology of the Uyghur*. Leiden and Boston: Brill.

Benovska-Sabkova, M. et al. 2010. 'Spreading Grace' in Post-Soviet Russia. *Anthropology Today* 26 (1): 16–21.

Bernshtam, T. A. 2005. *Prikhodskaia Zhizn' Russkoi Derevni: Ocherki po Tserkovnoi Etnografii*. Saint Petersburg: Ethnographica Petroplitana, Peterburgskoe Vostokovedenie.

Bogdanov, K. A. 1995. *Den'gi v Fol'klore*. Saint Petersburg: Bell.

Bourdeaux, M. (ed.). 1995. *The Politics of Religion in Russia and the New States of Eurasia*. Armonk: Sharpe.

Boym, S. 1994. *Common Places: Mythologies of Everyday Life in Russia*. Cambridge, Mass.: Harvard University Press.

Bremer, T. 2013. *Cross and Kremlin: A Brief History of the Orthodox Church in Russia*. Grand Rapids: Eerdmans.

Brooks, J. 1985. *When Russia Learned to Read: Literacy and Popular Literature, 1861–1917*. Princeton: Princeton University Press.

Caldwell, M. 2004. *Not by Bread Alone: Social Support in the New Russia*. Berkeley: University of California Press.

———. 2007. Elder Care in the New Russia: The Changing Face of Compassionate Social Security. *Focaal: European Journal of Anthropology* 50: 66–80.

———. 2010. The Russian Orthodox Church, the Provision of Social Welfare, and Changing Ethics of Benevolence. In C. Hann, and H. Goltz (eds.), *Eastern Christians in Anthropological Perspective*, pp. 329–350. Berkeley: University of California Press.

———. 2017. *Living Faithfully in an Unjust World: Compassionate Care in Russia*. Oakland: University of California Press.

Cannell, F. 2005. The Christianity of Anthropology. *Journal of the Royal Anthropological Institute* 11 (2): 335–356.

———. 2006. Introduction: The Anthropology of Christianity. In F. Cannell (ed.), *The Anthropology of Christianity*, pp. 1–50. Durham: Duke University Press.

———. 2007. How Does Ritual Matter? In R. Astuti, J. Parry, and S. Stafford (eds.), *Questions of Anthropology*, pp. 105–136. Oxford: Berg.

Carrier, J. G. 1995. *Gifts and Commodities: Exchange and Western Capitalism since 1700*. London: Routledge.

Carrier, J. G., and P. G. Luetchford (eds.). 2012. *Ethical Consumption: Social Value and Economic Practice*. New York: Berghahn Books.

Casanova, J. 1994. *Public Religions in the Modern World*. Chicago: University of Chicago Press.

Christensen, K. H. 2015. *The Making of the New Martyrs of Russia: Soviet Repression in Orthodox Memory*. Ph.D. dissertation, University of Copenhagen.

Chulos, C. J. 2003. *Converging Worlds: Religion and Community in Peasant Russia 1861–1917*. DeKalb: Northern Illinois University Press.

Clark, W. 2009. Networks of Faith in Kazakhstan. In M. Pelkmans (ed.), *Conversion after Socialism. Disruptions, Modernisms and Technologies of Faith in the Former Soviet Union*, pp. 129–142. New York: Berghahn Books.

Coleman, S. 2000. *The Globalisation of Charismatic Christianity: Spreading the Gospel of Prosperity*. Cambridge: Cambridge University Press.

———. 2004. The Charismatic Gift. *Journal of the Royal Anthropological Institute* 10 (2): 421–442.

———. 2006. Materializing the Self: Words and Gifts in the Construction of Charismatic Protestant Identity. In F. Cannell (ed.), *The Anthropology of Christianity*, pp. 163–184. Durham: Duke University Press.

———. 2011. Prosperity Unbound? Debating the 'Sacrificial Economy'. *Research in Economic Anthropology* 31: 23–45.
Curanović, A. 2012. *The Religious Factor in Russia's Foreign Policies*. London and New York: Routledge.
Davie, G. 2003. *Religion in Britain since 1945: Believing without Belonging*. Oxford: Blackwell.
Davis, J. 1992. *Exchange*. Minneapolis: University of Minnesota Press.
Dinello, N. 1998. Russian Religious Rejections of Money and Homo Economicus: The Self-Identifications of the 'Pioneers of a Money Economy' in Post-Soviet Russia. *Sociology of Religion* 59 (1): 45–64.
Dixon, S. 1995. The Orthodox Church and the Workers of St Petersburg, 1880-1914. In H. McLeod (ed.), *European Religion in the Age of Great Cities, 1830-1930*, pp. 119–141. London and New York: Routledge.
Douglas, M. 1978. *Purity and Danger: An Analysis of the Concepts of Pollution and Taboo*. London: Routledge.
Dragadze, T. 1993. The Domestication of Religion under Soviet Communism. In Chris Hann (ed.), *Socialism: Ideals, Ideologies, and Local Practice*, pp. 148–156. London: Routledge.
Dubin, B. 2005. Un 'fardeau léger'. Les Orthodoxes dans la Russie des Années 1990–2000. *Revue d'Etudes Comparatives Est-Ouest* 36 (4): 19–42.
Dubovka, D. 2015. Poslushanie kak Fizicheskii Trud i kak Dobrodetel': Semioticheskoe Nasyshchenie Proizvodstva v Sovremennykh Monastryriakh RPC. In J. Kormina, A. Panchenko, and S. Shturkov (eds.), *Izobretenie Religii: Desekuliarizatsia v Postsovetskom Kontekste*, pp. 63–81. St. Petersburg: European University at St. Petersburg.
Dunham, V. 1990 [1976]. *In Stalin's Time: Middle Class Values in Soviet Fiction*. Durham: Duke University Press.
Engel, B. A. 2004. *Women in Russia, 1700–2000*. Cambridge: Cambridge University Press.
Engelhardt, J. 2014. *Singing the Right Way: Orthodox Christians and Secular Enchantment in Estonia*. New York: Oxford University Press.
Fadeeva, O. 1999. Khoziaistvennye Strategii Sel'skikh Semei. In T. Zaslavskaia, and Z. Kalugina (eds.), *Sotsial'naia Traektoriia Reformiruemoi Rossii*, pp. 426–447. Novosibirsk: Nauka.

Fedotov, G. P. 1966. *The Russian Religious Mind, Vol. 2: The Middle Ages (The Thirteenth to the Fifteenth Centuries)* (ed. J. Meyendorff). Cambridge: Harvard University Press.

Fernandez-Stembridge, L., and R. P. Madsen. 2002. Beggars in the Socialist Market Economy. In P. Link, R. P. Madsen, and P. G. Pickowicz (eds.), *Popular China: Unofficial Culture and Globalizing Society*, pp. 207–230. Lanham: Rowman and Littlefield Publishers.

Filatov, S., and R. Lunkin. 2006. Statistics on Religion in Russia: The Reality behind the Figures. *Religion, State and Society* 34 (1): 33–49.

Fitzpatrick, S. 2006. Social Parasites: How Tramps, Idle Youth, and Busy Entrepreneurs Impeded the Soviet March to Communism. *Cahiers du Monde Russe* 47 (1–2): 377–408.

Florovsky, G. P. 1983 [1937]. *Puti Russkogo Bogosloviia*. Paris: YMCA Press.

Freeze, G. L. 1976. The Disintegration of Traditional Communities: The Parish in Eighteenth-Century Russia. *The Journal of Modern History* 48 (1): 32–50.

———. 1983. *The Parish Clergy in Nineteenth-Century Russia: Crisis, Reform, Counter-Reform*. Princeton: Princeton University Press.

———. 1996. Subversive Piety: Religion and the Political Crisis in Late Imperial Russia. *Journal of Modern History* 68 (2): 308–350.

Freiberger, O. (ed.). 2006. *Asceticism and its Critics: Historical Accounts and Comparative Perspectives*. Oxford: Oxford University Press.

Gal, S., and G. Kligman, 2000. *The Politics of Gender after Socialism: A Comparative-Historical Essay*. Princeton: Princeton University Press.

Garrard, J., and C. Garrard. 2008. *Russian Orthodoxy Resurgent. Faith and Power in the New Russia*. Princeton: Princeton University Press.

Geremek, B. 1987 [1978]. *La Potence ou la Pitié. L'Europe et les Pauvres du Moyen Age à Nos Jours*. Paris: Gallimard.

Golosenko, I. 1996a. Nishchenstvo kak Sotsial'naia Problema. *Sotsiologicheskie Issledovaniia* 7: 27–35.

———. 1996b. Nishchenstvo v Rossii. *Sotsiologicheskie Issledovaniia* 8: 18–25.

Gradosel'skaia, G. 1999. Sotsial'nye Seti: Obmen Chastnymi Trasferami. *Sotsologicheskii Zhournal* 1–2: 156–163.

Graeber, D. 2001. *Toward an Anthropological Theory of Value: The False Coin of our Own Dreams*. New York: Palgrave.

Greene, R. H. 2010. *Bodies like Bright Stars: Saints and Relics in Orthodox Russia*. DeKalb: Northern Illinois University Press.

Gregory, C. A. 1980. Gifts to Men and Gifts to Gods. *Man* (New Series) 15 (4): 626–652.
———. 1982. *Gifts and Commodities*. London: Academic Press.
Grossman, G. 1977. The 'Second Economy' of the USSR. *Problems of Communism* 26 (5): 25–40.
———. 1991. Informal Personal Incomes and Outlays of the Soviet Urban Population. In A. Portes, M. Castells, and L. A. Benton (eds.), *The Informal Economy: Studies in Advanced and Less Developed Countries*, pp. 150–170. Baltimore: Johns Hopkins University Press.
Gurova, O. 2016. Ideology of Consumption in the Soviet Union. In T. Vihavainen, and E. Bogdanova (eds.), *Communism and Consumerism: The Soviet Alternative to the Affluent Society*, pp. 68–88. Leiden: Brill.
Halemba, A. 2015. *Negotiating Marian Apparitions: The Politics of Religion in Transcarpathian Ukraine*. Budapest: Central European University Press.
Hann, C. 2000. Problems with the (De)Privatization of Religion. *Anthropology Today* 16 (6): 14–20.
———. 2007. The Anthropology of Christianity per se. *European Journal of Sociology* 48 (3): 383–410.
———. 2014. The Heart of the Matter: Christianity, Materiality, and Modernity. *Current Anthropology* 55 (S10): S182–S192.
Hann, C., and H. Goltz. 2010. Introduction: The Other Christianity? In C. Hann, and H. Goltz (eds.), *Eastern Christians in Anthropological Perspective*, pp. 1–29. Berkeley: University of California Press.
Hart, K. 2000. *The Memory Bank: Money in an Unequal World*. London: Profile Books.
Hedda, J. 2008. *His Kingdom Come: Orthodox Pastorship and Social Activism in Revolutionary Russia*. DeKalb: Northern Illinois University Press.
Hemment, J. 2012. Nashi, Youth Voluntarism, and Potemkin NGOs: Making Sense of Civil Society in Post-Soviet Russia. *Slavic Review* 71 (2): 234–260.
Hessler, J. 2000. Cultured Trade: The Stalinist Turn towards Consumerism. In S. Fitzpatrick (ed.), *Stalinism: New Directions*, pp. 182–209. London: Routledge.
Höjdestrand, T. 2009. *Needed by Nobody: Homelessness and Humanness in Post-Socialist Russia*. Ithaca: Cornell University Press.
Humphrey, C. 2002. *The Unmaking of Soviet Life: Everyday Economies after Socialism*. Ithaca: Cornell University Press.

Humphrey, C., and R. Mandel. 2002. The Market in Everyday Life: Ethnographies of Postsocialism. In R. Mandel, and C. Humphrey (eds.), *Markets and Moralities: Ethnographies of Postsocialism*, pp. 1–16. Oxford: Berg.

Kääriainen, K., and D. Furman (eds.). 2000. *Starye Tserkvi, Novye Veruiushchie*. Moscow: Letnii Sad.

Karras, V. A. 2008. Orthodox Theologies of Women and Ordained Ministry. In A. Papanikolaou, and E. H. Prodromou (eds.), *Thinking through Faith: New Perspectives from Orthodox Christian Scholars*, pp. 113–158. Crestwood, NY: St Vladimir's Seminary Press.

Kenworthy, S. 2006. An Orthodox Social Gospel in Late-Imperial Russia. *Religion and Society in Central and Eastern Europe* 1: 1–29.

———. 2008. To Save the World or to Renounce It: Modes of Moral Action in Russian Orthodoxy. In M. D. Steinberg, and C. Wanner (eds.), *Religion, Morality, and Community in Post-Soviet Societies*, pp. 21–54. Washington, D.C.: Woodrow Wilson Center and Bloomington: Indiana University Press.

Kharkhordin, O. 1999. *The Collective and the Individual in Russia: A Study of Practices*. Berkeley: University of California Press.

Kiernan, J. P. 1988. The Other Side of the Coin: The Conversion of Money to Religious Purposes in Zulu Zionist Churches. *Man* (New Series) 23 (3): 453–468.

Kizenko, N. 2006. *Sviatoi Nashego Vremeni: Otets Ioann Kronshtadtskii i Russkii Narod*. Moscow: Novoe Literaturnoe Obozrenie.

———. 2013. Feminized Patriarchy? Orthodoxy and Gender in Post-Soviet Russia. *Signs* 38 (3): 595–621.

Klassen, P. E. 2001. Sacred Maternities and Postbiomedical Bodies: Religion and Nature in Contemporary Home Birth. *Signs* 26 (3): 775–809.

Knox, Z. 2005. *Russian Society and the Orthodox Church: Religion in Russia after Communism*. London: Routledge.

Kobets, S. 1998. The Subtext of Christian Asceticism in Aleksandr Solzhenitsyn's *One Day in the Life of Ivan Denisovich*. *The Slavic and East European Journal* 42 (4): 661–676.

Köllner, T. 2011. Built with Gold or Tears? Moral Discourses on Church Construction and the Role of Entrepreneurial Donations. In J. Zigon (ed.), *Multiple Moralities and Religions in Post-Soviet Russia*, pp. 191–213. New York: Berghahn Books.

———. 2012. *Practising without Belonging? Entrepreneurship, Morality, and Religion in Contemporary Russia*. Berlin: LIT.

——. 2013. Businessmen, Priests and Parishes: Religious Individualization and Privatization in Russia. *Archives de Sciences Sociales des Religions* 162: 37–53.

Kormina, J. 2008. Ispolkomy i Prikhody: Religioznaia Zhizn' Pskovskoi Oblasti v Pervuiu Poslevoennuiu Piatiletku. *Neprikosnovennyi Zapas* 3 (59). Available online, http://magazines.russ.ru/nz/2008/3/ko11.html, accessed on 29 June 2017.

——. 2010. *Avtobusniki*: Russian Orthodox Pilgrims' Longing for Authenticity. In C. Hann, and H. Goltz (eds.), *Eastern Christians in Anthropological Perspective*, pp. 267–286. Berkeley: University of California Press.

——. 2011. Rezhim Pravoslavnoi Sotsial'nosti v Sovremennoi Rossii: Prikhozhane, Palomniki, Setiviki (na Primere o. Zalita). In A. Agadjanian, and K. Rousselet (eds.), *Prikhody i Obshchiny v Sovremennom Pravoslavii: Kornevaia Sistema Rossiiskoi Religioznosti*, pp.189–211. Moscow: Ves' Mir.

——. 2012. Nomadicheskoe Pravoslavie: O Novykh Formakh Religioznoi Zhizni v Sovremennoi Rossii. *Ab Imperio* 12 (2): 195–227.

——. 2013. Canonizing Soviet Pasts in Contemporary Russia: The Case of Saint Matrona of Moscow. In J. Boddy, and M. Lambek (eds.), *A Companion to the Anthropology of Religion*, pp. 409–424. Chichester: Wiley Blackwell.

Kormina, J., and S. Shtyrkov. 2011. St. Xenia as a Patron of Female Social Suffering: An Essay on Anthropological Hagiography. In J. Zigon (ed.), *Multiple Moralities and Religions in Post-Soviet Russia*, pp. 168–190. New York: Berghahn Books.

——. 2015. Eto Nashe Iskonno Russkoe, i Nikuda Nam ot Etogo ne Det'sia: Predystoria Postsovetskoi Desekuliarizatsii. In J. Kormina, A. Panchenko, and S. Shtyrkov (eds.), *Izobretenie Religii: Desekuliarizatsia v Postsovetskom Kontekste*, pp. 7–45. Saint Petersburg: European University at Saint Petersburg.

Kościańska, A. 2009. The Power of Silence: Spirituality and Women's Agency beyond the Catholic Church in Poland. *Focaal: European Journal of Anthropology* 53: 56–71.

Kudriavtseva, M. 2001. Dramaturgiia Poproshainichestva. In Voronkova V., O. Pachenkova, and E. Chikadze (eds.), *Nevidimye Grani Sotsial'noi Real'nosti*, pp. 37–49. Saint Petersburg: Center for Independent Sociological Studies.

Kuraev, A. 2006. *Tserkov' i Molodezh': Neizbezhen li Konflikt?* Saint Petersburg: Russkii Ostrov.

Ładykowska, A. 2011. Post-Soviet Orthodoxy in the Making: Strategies for Continuity Thinking among Russian Middle-Aged School Teachers. In J. Zigon (ed.), *Multiple Moralities and Religions in Post-Soviet Russia*, pp. 27–57. New York: Berghahn Books.

Ładykowska, A., and D. Tocheva. 2013. Women Teachers of Religion in Russia: Gendered Authority in the Orthodox Church. *Archives de Sciences Sociales des Religions* 162: 55–74.

Laidlaw, J. 2002. For an Anthropology of Ethics and Freedom. *Journal of the Royal Anthropological Institute* 8 (2): 311–332.

Lambek, M. 2000. The Anthropology of Religion and the Quarrel between Poetry and Philosophy. *Current Anthropology* 41 (3): 309–320.

——. 2008. Value and Virtue. *Anthropological Theory* 8 (2): 133–157.

Lambert, Y. 1985. *Dieu Change en Bretagne: La Religion à Limerzel de 1990 à nos Jours*. Paris: Editions du Cerf.

Lankauskas, G. 2009. The Civility and Pragmatism of Charismatic Christianity in Lithuania. In M. Pelkmans (ed.), *Conversion after Socialism. Disruptions, Modernisms and Technologies of Faith in the Former Soviet Union*, pp. 107–128. New York: Berghahn Books.

Lapidus, G. W. 1978. *Women in Soviet Society: Equality, Development, and Social Change*. Berkeley: University of California Press.

Ledeneva, A. 1998. *Russia's Economy of Favours. Blat, Networking and Informal Exchange*. Cambridge: Cambridge University Press.

Lemon, A. 1998. 'Your Eyes Are Green Like Dollars': Counterfeit Cash, National Substance, and Currency Apartheid in 1990s Russia. *Cultural Anthropology* 13 (1): 22–55.

——. 2000. *Between Two Fires: Gypsy Performance and Romani Memory from Pushkin to Post-Socialism*. Durham: Duke University Press.

Lindenmeyr, A. 1986. Charity and the Problem of Unemployment: Industrial Homes in Late Imperial Russia. *Russian Review* 45 (1): 1–22.

——. 1990. The Ethos of Charity in Imperial Russia. *Journal of Social History* 23 (4): 679–694.

——. 1996. *Poverty Is not a Vice: Charity, Society and the State in Imperial Russia*. Princeton: Princeton University Press.

Lipsky, M. 2010 [1980]. *Street-Level Bureaucracy: Dilemmas of the Individual in Public Services*. New York: Russell Sage Foundation.

Loader, C., and J. C. Alexander. 1985. Max Weber on Churches and Sects in North America: An Alternative Path toward Rationalization. *Sociological Theory* 3 (1): 1–6.

Luckmann, T. 1967. *The Invisible Religion: The Problem of Religion in Modern Society*. New York: Macmillan.

Luehrmann, S. 2005. Recycling Cultural Construction: Desecularisation in Post-Soviet Mari-El. *Religion, State and Society* 33 (1): 35–56.

——. 2011. *Secularism Soviet Style: Teaching Atheism and Religion in a Volga Republic*. Bloomington: Indiana University Press.

Lylova, O. 2002. Neformal'naia Vzaimopomoshch' v Sel'skom Soobshchestve. *Sotsiologicheskie Issledovaniia* 214 (2): 83–86.

Mahmood, S. 2001. Feminist Theory, Embodiment, and the Docile Agent: Some Reflections on the Egyptian Islamic Revival. *Cultural Anthropology* 16 (2): 202–236.

——. 2005. *Politics of Piety: The Islamic Revival and the Feminist Subject*. Princeton: Princeton University Press.

Makrides, V. 2005. Orthodox Christianity, Rationalization, Modernization: A Reassessment. In V. Roudometof, A. Agadjanian, and J. Pankhurst (eds.), *Eastern Orthodoxy in a Global Age: Tradition Faces the Twenty-First Century*, pp. 179–209. Walnut Creek: AltaMira Press.

Malinowski, B. 1984 [1922]. *The Argonauts of the Western Pacific*. Prospect Heights: Waveland Press.

——. 1926. *Crime and Custom in Savage Society*. London: Paul Kegan, Trench, Trubner & Co.

Manning, N., and N. Tikhonova (eds.). 2004. *Poverty and Social Exclusion in the New Russia*. Alderhsot: Ashgate.

Mauss, M. 1950 [1924]. Essai sur le Don. Formes et Raisons de l'Échange dans les Sociétés Archaïques. In M. Mauss, *Sociologie et Anthropologie*, pp. 143–279. Paris: Presses Universitaires de France.

McAuley, Alastair. 1979. *Economic Welfare in the Soviet Union: Poverty, Living Standards and Inequality*. Madison: University of Wisconsin Press.

McMahon, P. 1994. The Effect of Economic and Political Reforms on Soviet/Russian Women. In A. Aslabeigui, S. Pressman, and G. Summerfield (eds.), *Women in the Age of Economic Transformation: Gender Impact of Reforms in Post-Socialist and Developing Countries*, pp. 59–73. London: Routledge.

Medvedeva, K. 2015. The Landscape of a Religious Workspace: The Case of a Russian Christian Orthodox Sisterhood. *Russian Sociological Review* 14 (2): 70–81.

Meehan, B. 1993. *Holy Women of Russia: The Lives of Five Orthodox Women Offer Spiritual Guidance for Today*. San Francisco: Harper.

Meyendorff, J. 1995 [1960]. *L'Église Orthodoxe Hier et Aujourd'hui*. Paris: Seuil.

Mitrofanova, A. 2005. *The Politicization of Russian Orthodoxy: Actors and Ideas*. Stuttgart: Ibidem.

Mitrokhin, N. 2004. *Russkaia Pravoslavnaia Tserkov': Sovremennoe Sostoianie i Aktual'nye Problemy*. Moscow: NLO.

Morris, M. A. 1993. *Saints and Revolutionaries: The Ascetic Hero in Russian Literature*. Albany: State University of New York Press.

Naletova, I. 2010. Pilgrimages as Kenotic Communities beyond the Walls of the Church. In C. Hann, and H. Goltz (eds.), *Eastern Christians in Anthropological Perspective*, pp. 240–266. Berkeley: University of California Press.

Nazarov, A. A. 2006. *Ekonomika i Religia Rossiiskoi Imperii. Konfessional'naia Politika v Sisteme Ekonomicheskikh Reform*. Moscow: Paradiz.

Obadia, L., and D. C. Wood. 2011. Economics *and* Religion, Economics *in* Religion, Economics *of* Religion: Reopening the Grounds for Anthropology? *Research in Economic Anthropology* 31: xiii–xxxvii.

Orsi, R. 1996. *Thank you, St. Jude: Women's Devotion to the Patron Saint of Hopeless Causes*. New Haven: Yale University Press.

Oxfam. 2014. *After Equality: Inequality Trends and Policy Responses in Contemporary Russia*. Available online, https://www.oxfam.org/sites/www.oxfam.org/files/file_attachments/dp-after-equality-inequality-trends-policy-russia-100614-en.pdf, accessed 29 June 2017.

Paert, I. 2010. *Spiritual Elders: Charisma and Tradition in Russian Orthodoxy*. DeKalb: Northern Illinois University Press.

Papkova, I. 2011. *The Orthodox Church and Russian Politics*. New Yok: Oxford University Press.

Parry, J. 1986. The Gift, the Indian Gift and the 'Indian Gift'. *Man* (New Series) 21 (3): 453–473.

Patico, J. 2002. Chocolate and Cognac: Gifts and the Recognition of Social Worlds in Post-Soviet Russia. *Ethnos* 67 (3): 345–368.

———. 2005. To Be Happy in a Mercedes: Tropes of Value and Ambivalent Visions of Marketization. *American Ethnologist* 32 (3): 479–496.

———. 2009. Spinning the Market: The Moral Alchemy of Everyday Talk in Postsocialist Russia. *Critique of Anthropology* 29 (2): 205–224.

Paxson, M. 2005. *Solovyovo: The Story of Memory in a Russian Village*. Bloomington: Indiana University Press.

Pelikan, J. 2003 [1974]. *The Christian Tradition: A History of the Development of Doctrine. The Spirit of Eastern Christendom (600–1700)*. Chicago: University of Chicago Press.

Pelkmans, M. 2009a. Temporary Conversions: Encounters with Pentecostalism in Muslim Kyrgyzstan. In M. Pelkmans (ed.), *Conversion after Socialism: Disruptions, Modernisms and Technologies of Faith in the Former Soviet Union*, pp. 142–161. New York: Berghahn Books.

———. 2009b. Introduction: Post-Soviet Space and the Unexpected Turns of Religious Life. In M. Pelkmans (ed.), *Conversion after Socialism: Disruptions, Modernisms and Technologies of Faith in the Former Soviet Union*, pp. 1–16. New York: Berghahn Books.

Pesmen, D. 1995. Standing Bottles, Washing Deals, and Drinking 'For the Soul' in a Siberian City. *Anthropology of East Europe Review* 13 (2): 65–75.

———. 2000. *Russia and Soul: An Exploration*. Ithaca: Cornell University Press.

Pilkington, H. (ed.). 1996. *Gender, Generation and Identity in Contemporary Russia*. London: Routledge.

Pina-Cabral, J. de, and F. Pine. 2008. On the Margins: An Introduction. In F. Pine, and J. de Pina-Cabral (eds.), *On the Margins of Religion*, pp. 1–10. New York: Berghahn Books.

Pine, F., and J. de Pina-Cabral (eds.). 2008. *On the Margins of Religion*. New York: Berghahn Books.

Pryzhov, I. 1996. *26 Moskovskikh Prorokov, Iurodivykh, Dur i Durakov i Drugie Trudy po Russkoi Istorii i Etnografii*. Saint Petersburg: Ezro and Moscow: Intrada.

Richters, K. 2013. *The Post-Soviet Russian Orthodox Church: Politics, Culture and Greater Russia*. London: Routledge.

Ries, N. 1997. *Russian Talk: Culture and Conversation during Perestroika*. Ithaca: Cornell University Press.

———. 2002. 'Honest Bandits' and 'Warped People': Russian Narratives about Money, Corruption, and Moral Decay. In C. J. Greenhouse, E. Mertz, and K. B. Warren (eds.), *Ethnography in Unstable Places: Everyday Lives in Contexts of Dramatic Political Change*, pp. 267–315. Durham: Duke University Press.

Rivkin-Fish, M. 2005. *Women's Health in Post-Soviet Russia: The Politics of Intervention*. Bloomington: Indiana University Press.

———. 2009. Tracing Landscapes of the Past in Class Subjectivity: Practices of Memory and Distinction in Marketizing Russia. *American Ethnologist* 36 (1): 79–95.

Rock, S. 2014. Rebuilding the Chain: Tradition, Continuity and Processions of the Cross in Post-Soviet Russia. In K. Tolstaya (ed.), *Orthodox*

Paradoxes: Heterogeneities and Complexities in Contemporary Russian Orthodoxy, pp. 275–301. Leiden: Brill.

ROC (Russian Orthodox Church). 2000. *The Basis of the Social Concept*. Available online in English translation, https://mospat.ru/en/documents/social-concepts/, accessed 27 June 2017.

Rogers, D. 2005. Moonshine, Money, and the Politics of Liquidity in Rural Russia. *American Ethnologist* 32 (1): 63–81.

———. 2008. Old Believers between 'Society' and 'Culture': Remaking Moral Communities and Inequalities on a Former State Farm. In M. D. Steinberg, and C. Wanner (eds.), *Religion, Morality, and Community in Post-Soviet Societies*, pp. 115–147. Washington, D.C: Woodrow Wilson Center and Bloomington: Indiana University Press.

———. 2009. *The Old Faith and the Russian Land: A Historical Ethnography of Ethics in the Urals*. Ithaca: Cornell University Press.

Roitman, J. L. 2003. Unsanctioned Wealth, or the Productivity of Debt in Northern Cameroon. *Public Culture* 15 (2): 211–237.

Rousselet, K. 2005. La Famille Russe. Configurations des Relations et Évolutions des Solidarités. *Informations Sociales* 124 (4): 76–83.

———. 2007. Butovo: La Création d'un Lieu de Pèlerinages sur une Terre de Massacres. *Politix* 77 (1): 55–78.

———. 2011. Constructing Moralities around the Tsarist Family. In J. Zigon (ed.), *Multiple Moralities and Religions in Post-Soviet Russia*, pp. 146–167. New York: Berghahn Books.

———. 2013a. Sécularisation et Orthodoxie dans la Russie Contemporaine: Pour une Hypothèse Continuiste? *Questions de Recherche* 42. Available online, http://www.sciencespo.fr/ceri/sites/sciencespo.fr.ceri/files/qdr42.pdf, accessed 29 June 2017.

———. 2013b. L'autorité Religieuse en Contexte Post-Soviétique: Regard sur le Fonctionnement des Paroisses Russes Orthodoxes. *Archives de Sciences Sociales des Religions* 162: 15–36.

Rozov, A. I. 2003. *Sviashchennik v Dukhovnoi Zhizni Russkoi Derevni*. Saint Petersburg: Aleteia.

Scott, J. C. 1985. *Weapons of the Weak: Everyday Forms of Peasant Resistance*. New Haven: Yale University Press.

———. 1990. *Domination and the Arts of Resistance: Hidden Transcripts*. New Haven: Yale University Press.

Semenko-Basin, I. 2010. *Sviatost' v Russkoi Pravoslavnoi Kul'ture XX Veka: Istoria Personifikatsii*. Moscow: Rossiiskii Gosudarstvennyi Gumanitarnyi Universitet.

Sergazina, K. 2006. Dinamika Vozrozhdenia Russkoi Religioznoi Kul'tury. In K. Rousselet, and A. Agadjanian (eds.), *Religioznye Praktiki v Sovremennoi Rossii*, pp. 106–125. Moscow: Novoe izdatel'stvo.

Shanin, T., A. Nikulin, and V. Danilov (eds.). 2002. *Refleksivnoe Krest'ianovedenie. Desiatiletie Issledovanii Sel'skoi Rossii.* Moscow: Moskovskaia Vysshaia Shkola Sotsial'nykh i Ekonomicheskikh Nauk.

Shevchenko, O. 2009. *Crisis and the Everyday in Postsocialist Moscow.* Bloomington: Indiana University Press.

Shevzov, V. 2004. *Russian Orthodoxy on the Eve of Revolution.* Oxford: Oxford University Press.

Shlapentokh, V. 1999. Social Inequality in Post-Communist Russia: The Attitudes of the Political Elite and the Masses (1991–1998). *Europe-Asia Studies* 51 (7): 1167–1181.

Shteinberg, I. 2002. Real'naia Praktika Strategii Vyzhivaniia Sel'skoi Sem'i: 'Setevye Resursy'. In T. Zaslavskaia (ed.), *Kuda Idet Rossiia? Formal'nye Institutsii i Real'nye Praktiki*, pp. 183–274. Moscow: Moskovkaia Vysshaia Shkola Sotsial'nykh i Ekonomicheskikh Nauk.

Sibireva, O. 2009a. Rural Orthodoxy: Parishes in Ryazan Oblast. *Kultura* 2: 4–5.

———. 2009b. Where Satan still Lives: Orthodox Subculture in Russia. *Kultura* 2: 10–15.

Stark, R. 2003. Upper Class Asceticism: Social Origins of Ascetic Movements and Medieval Saints. *Review of Religious Research* 45 (1): 5–19.

Steinberg, M. D., and C. Wanner (eds.). 2008. *Religion, Morality, and Community in Post-Soviet Societies.* Washingon, D.C.: Woodrow Wilson Center Press and Bloomington: Indiana University Press.

Stephenson, S. 1996. O Fenomene Bezdomnosti. *Sotsiologicheskie Issledovaniia* 8: 26–33.

———. 2001. The Abandoned Children of Russia – From 'Privileged Class' to 'Underclass'. In S. Webber, and I. Liikanen (eds.), *Education and Civic Culture in Post-Communist Countries*, pp. 187–203. Houndmills: Palgrave.

Tarabukina, A. 2000. *Fol'klor i Kul'tura Pritserkovnogo Kruga.* Ph.D. dissertation, Herzen State Pedagogical University of Russia. Also available online, http://www.ruthenia.ru/folktee/CYBERSTOL/books/Tarabukina/arina_tarabukina.html, accessed on 29 June 2017.

Thyrêt, I. 2001. *Between God and Tsar: Religious Symbolism and the Royal Women of Muscovite Russia*. DeKalb: Northern Illinois University Press.

——. 2010. Economic Reconstruction or Corporate Raiding?: The Borisoglebskii Monastery in Torzhok and the Ascription of Monasteries in the 17th Century. *Kritika: Explorations in Russian and Eurasian History* 11 (3): 490–511.

Tikhonova, N. 2003. *Fenomen Gorodskoi Bednosti v Sovremennoi Rossii*. Moscow: Letnii Sad.

Tocheva, D. 2009. Frontière Politique, Ethnicité et Clivages Sociaux: Un Exemple Estonien. In B. Pétric, and J.-F. Gossiaux (eds.), *Europa mon Amour. 1989–2009: Un Rêve Blessé*, pp. 136–146. Paris: Autrement.

——. 2014. Rupture Systémique et Continuité Éthique: l'Orthodoxie Russe Postsoviétique. *Ethnographiques.org* 28. Available online, http://www.ethnographiques.org/2014/Tocheva, accessed on 29 June 2017.

Utrata, J. 2015. *Women without Men: Single Mothers and Family Change in the New Russia*. Ithaca: Cornell University Press.

Vinogradskii, V. 1999. 'Orudiia Slabykh': Neformal'naia Ekonomika Krest'ianskikh Domokhaziaistv. *Sotsiologicheskii Zhournal* 3–4: 36–48.

Vladimirova, V. 2006. *Just Labor: Labor Ethics in a Post-Soviet Reindeer Herding Community*. Uppsala: Acta Universitatis Upsaliensis.

Wagner, W. G. 2007. 'Orthodox Domesticity': Creating a Social Role for Women. In M. D. Steinberg, and H. J. Coleman (eds.), *Sacred Stories: Religion and Spirituality in Modern Russia*, pp. 119–145. Bloomington: Indiana University Press.

Wanner, C. 2005. Money, Morality and New Forms of Exchange in Postsocialist Ukraine. *Ethnos* 70 (4): 515–537.

——. 2007. *Communities of the Converted: Ukrainians and Global Evangelism*. Ithaca: Cornell University Press.

——. 2009. Conversion and the Mobile Self: Evangelism as 'Travelling Culture'. In M. Pelkmans (ed.), *Conversion after Socialism: Disruptions, Modernisms and Technologies of Faith in the Former Soviet Union*, pp. 163–182. New York: Berghahn Books.

Wanner, C., and M. D. Steinberg. 2008. Introduction: Reclaiming the Sacred after Communism. In M. D. Steinberg, and C. Wanner (eds.), *Religion, Morality, and Community in Post-Soviet Societies*, pp. 1–20. Washington, D.C: Woodrow Wilson Center and Bloomington: Indiana University Press.

Weaver, D. 2011a. Neither Too Scientific nor a Spy: Negotiating the Ethnographic Interview in Russia. *Comparative Sociology* 10 (1): 145–157.

———. 2011b. Shifting Agency: Male Clergy, Female Believers, and the Role of Icons. *Material Religion* 7 (3): 394–419.

Weber, M. 1985 [1906]. 'Churches' and 'Sects' in North America: An Ecclesiastical Socio-Political Sketch. (trans. Colin Loader). *Sociological Theory* 3 (1): 7–13.

Wimbush, V. L., and R. Valantasis (eds.). 2002. *Asceticism*. Oxford: Oxford University Press.

Yates, S. J. 2004. *Living with Poverty in Post-Soviet Russia: Social Perspectives on Urban Poverty*. Ph.D. dissertation, London School of Economics and Political Science.

Young, G. 1996. 'Into Church Matters': Lay Identity, Rural Parish Life, and Popular Politics in Late Imperial and Early Soviet Russia, 1864-1928. *Russian History/ Histoire Russe* 23 (1–4): 367–384.

Yurchak, A. 2006. *Everything Was Forever, Until It Was no More: The Last Soviet Generation*. Princeton: Princeton University Press.

Zelizer, V. 1997. *The Social Meaning of Money: Pin Money, Paychecks, Poor Relief, and Other Currencies*. Princeton: Princeton University Press.

Zigon, J. 2008. Aleksandra Vladimirovna: Moral Narratives of a Russian Orthodox Woman. In M. D. Steinberg, and C. Wanner (eds.), *Religion, Morality, and Community in Post-Soviet Societies*, pp. 85–113. Washington, D.C: Woodrow Wilson Center and Bloomington: Indiana University Press.

———. 2010. *Making the New Post-Soviet Person: Moral Experience in Contemporary Moscow*. Leiden: Brill.

———. 2011a. *HIV Is God's Blessing: Rehabilitating Morality in Neoliberal Russia*. Berkeley: University of California Press.

Zigon, J. (ed.). 2011b. *Multiple Moralities and Religions in Post-Soviet Russia*. New York: Berghahn Books.

Index

accounting, *see* bookkeeping
Agadjanian, A. 7, 8, 10
alms 4, 121-5, 127, 131, 133, 137, 139-40; almsgiving 17, 86, 133-7, 139-40, 158-9
anthropology of Christianity 9
asceticism 45, 51-4, 62, 76, 114

baptism 34, 80n, 90, 93
baptismal 23
baptize(d) 23, 81, 112, 113
beggars/ begging 4, 11, 13, 19, 22, 41, 61, 91, 121-140 *passim*, 146, 153, 163
belief/ believing 3, 4, 9, 136, 148, 151, 158-60; becoming a believing person/ coming to God/ the Lord 112, 115; belief and social support 151, 158-60
benevolent work 12, 43-9, 108
bookkeeping/ bookkeeper 12, 13, 32, 37, 58, 59, 65, 79, 80, 94-7, 104
building 6, 13, 25, 27-8, 29, 36, 46, 63, 75, 92, 109-10, 149, 163, *see also* construction; reconstruction

Caldwell, M. 15, 122
candle(s) 2, 22, 48, 77, 81-6, 89-94, 102, 104n, 150, 152
canonization 67n, 68-75, 165
charity 6n, 17-8, 91, 121n, 122-3, 125, 128, 132, 134-7, 139, 141, 143-8, 151, 154, 156, 158-9, *see also* redistribution
Christensen, K. H. 68
Chulos, C. J. 6, 44
church shop 3, 13, 58, 79-81, 89-90, 93, 97, 104, 147, 149-51, 155, 164, *see lavka*; stall
commerce in the church 34, 38, 78-9, 81, 83-6, 89, 91-7

construction; of churches 10, 11, 34, 43-6, 80n, 162, *see also* reconstruction

donation 34, 35, 38, 40, 43, 50, 58, 60-2, 64, 79n, 80, 83-5, 91-7, 126, 144; food donations 139; of items 147-8, 152-3, 155, 158, 160
donor 141, 144, 151-5, 158-60

economic transformation 86
equity 19, 79, 89, 90, 97; ethics of equity 79, 89, 95
ethics 79, 121-5, 131, 136, 138-40, 150

Father Ioann (of Kronstadt) 136-8
Freeze, G. L. 162-3
funeral(s) 80n, 81, 90-1, 131-2

gender; disparity/ inequality 2, 4, 13, 14, 41, 99, 107, 163; in the church 19, 32, 49, 102, 121n; in the household 14, *see also* poverty
gift 52n; altruistic/ pure/ unreciprocated gift 16, 78, 78n, 87, 88, 96, 144, 158; anonymous 141; as opposed to commerce 79, 83, 84-7, 91-7; church built as a gift 44; gift of consolation and perspicacity 74; in almsgiving 140; of items for everyday use 141, 151-2, 154-5, 158-9; sacrificial gifting 79, 92; unsolicited/ benevolent gift 77, *see also* charity; donation

Halemba, A. 2n, 9, 10

Köllner, T. 80n, 147n
Kormina, J. 9, 15, 41, 68, 83n, 109

lavka 81, 149-57
love 17; Christian love/ love of God 115-9, 133

martyrs; new/ new martyr saints 57, 67-9, 71, 74, 75, *see also* canonization
Metropolitan Iossif (Petrov) 74n
Metropolitan Sergius (Starogorodskii) 68n, 74, 75
Moscow 6, 15, 21, 43, 75n, 84n, 93, 125
motherhood; single 19, 109-10, 114

parish; definition of 4-14, 161-5; differentiation among parishes 33-40, 57-76 *passim*, 82-3; economy of 33-40, 77-97 *passim*; in Ozerovo 30-3; in post-Soviet debates 7-11; in pre-Soviet times 5-6, 162; membership in 7, 10, 11, 31, 37-8; Statute of 7, 36, 37n, 38
Patriarch; Alexii II 34, 84, 86, 93; Kirill 18, 34, 38, 84n, 164; Sergius 74n, 75, *see also* Metropolitan Sergius; Tikhon 74n
Patriarchate of Moscow 21, 43, 68, 80n, 136
pilgrimage 1, 8, 9, 13, 15, 22, 24, 39-41, 53, 104, 164
poverty 14, 15, 17, 35-7, 49, 53, 62, 64, 89, 121n, 122, 128, 130, 135-6, 141, 146, 156, 160, 162; feminization of 107
prayer(s) 2, 8, 22, 53, 63, 65, 72, 75, 77, 80n, 81, 85, 92, 94, 134n, 144-5, 150, 152, *see also* candle(s)
price 59, 62, 80-5, 89-94, 96-7; posted prices 83n, 84-5, 86, 89, 93, 97; pricelist 83n, 84, 87, 90, 93; price-setting 78, 93
Protestant 15, 28, 29, 78n, 142, 145-6, 161; and social distress 15-7; denominations/ communities 15-7
Protestantism 16, 27

reconstruction; of churches 11, 33, 41, 43-52, 57, 58, 61, 63, 65, 74, 148-9
redistribution 35, 134, 141, 147-8, 151-2, 158, 160, 165, *see also* charity
relics 41n, 57, 63, 69-73, 76
Rousselet, K. 7, 8, 10, 11n
Russian Orthodox Church (ROC); beliefs and practices 53-4, 72-3, 91, 97, 133, 138, 148; church economy 4, 19, 22, 35-41, 77-80, 83-4, 88, 92, 95, 97; hierarchy of 12, 37-8, 69, 99, 100; income and tax status 35, 37-8, 50, 72, 83; in post-Soviet society 2, 3, 7-12, 141-2, 160-1, 164-5; in urban settings in European Russia 21; post-Soviet resurgence 33-4, 43-4, 68; poverty and social distress/ responses to 17-9, 37, 40-1, 121-2, 142, 146; real estate/ restitution of property to 35, 46; Soviet repression 68-9, 73-5, *see also* parish; street-level Orthodoxy
Russian Orthodox Church Abroad (ROCA) 68
Russian Orthodox Church Outside Russia (ROCOR) 68, 70n

Saint Lidia 69-73, 75, 76
Saint Petersburg/ Leningrad 5, 17, 21, 25, 26, 44n, 48, 60, 70, 72, 74, 92, 106, 125-6, 132, 136, 142
Saint Petersburg Region 15, 21, 25, 37n, 59, 136
Saint Xenia 15, 41, 72, 100

salary 1, 2, 12, 35-7, 47, 58, 80, 83, 87, 100, 104, 106, 109-11, 114, 126

school; parish/ Sunday school/ schooling 1, 2, 21-4, 51, 58, 60, 61, 73, 93, 99-119 *passim*; Sunday classes 1, 22, 104-5, 113, 115

self-restraint 53, 131

services; of the church 1, 2, 8, 10, 11, 28, 29, 41, 60, 63, 80, 125, 135, 144-5, 147, 162-3; payment for 35, 80-4, 89, 90-1, 94; price of 59, 83n, 86-7, 157, *see also* baptism; funeral(s); prayer(s)

Shtyrkov, S. 15, 41

social service(s) 16, 17, 89n

socialism 84, 111, 135

stall 72; church stall seller 12, 13, 104, *see also* church shop; *lavka*

starets 39; spiritual counsellor 64, 74

starosta 13, 46, 46n, 48-9, 66, 67, 150; head of the lay parish council 24, 46n, 59

street-level Orthodoxy; definition of 11-3, 15, 19, 33, 44, 74, 77, 97, 100, 121, 125, 141, 161, 163-4

Synodal Department of Church Charity and Social Service (ROC) 17-8, 121n

systemic transformation 86, 97

teachers 11, 32, 45, 46, 63, 65, 105n, 106, 118; Orthodox 2, 103-7; parish/ church/ Sunday school teachers 12, 13, 21, 22, 51, 57, 101, 105, 106, 113, 116

The Basis of the Social Concept of the Russian Orthodox Church 17, 133-4

volunteers 18, 48, 52, 106; volunteer labour 43

women; and sainthood 15, 71n, 72, 100; as beggars 123, 127n, 128-30; as cleaners 11-3, 102-4, 110, 147; as church workers 22, 47, 73, 96, 101-4; as religious travellers 59; church attendance 32, 50, 93-4, 100, 108-9, 114-6; church social support 151-2, 157; elderly 15, 32, 41, 94, 101-2, 123; in Catholicism 100n; in Orthodox models of the family 60, 109, 115; in Orthodox schooling/ parish education 19, 61, 99-101, 104-19 *passim*; in Protestant communities 16, 29, 102; ordination of 99n; Orthodox dress code for 22, 50, 66, 116; roles in the church hierarchy (official/ unofficial) 99, 101, 104-5, *see also* gender; motherhood; poverty; work

work; and begging 131-3, 138; benevolent work(ers) 12, 43, 46-9, 106, 108; bookkeepers 12-3, 32, 37, 59, 65, 80, 95-7, 104; cleaners 11-3, 102, 104, 110, 113, 146-7; doorkeepers 11, 50, 101, *see also* church shop, *lavka*; for the church 13, 22, 23, 31, 37, 50, 52, 61, 68, 73, 75n, 80, 89, 91, 93, 99, 102, 106, 108, 121, 131, 147-8, 151; on one's soul 118; paid and unpaid 12, 47-8, 58, 101, 106, *see also* volunteers; professional activity outside of church 25, 26, 30, 32, 36, 45, 47, 60, 63, 80, 110, 111, 115, 132; social work 17, 18, 134n; teachers 11-3, 21-2, 32, 45-6, 65, 100, 103-6, 113, 115-6, 118-9, *see also* teachers; value of 47, 52, 87, 88, 110, 117-9, 122, 129, 131, 134-5, 137-8, 163, *see also* construction, of churches

Zigon, J. 18

Halle Studies in the Anthropology of Eurasia

1. Hann, Chris, and the "Property Relations" Group, 2003: *The Postsocialist Agrarian Question. Property Relations and the Rural Condition.*

2. Grandits, Hannes, and Patrick Heady (eds.), 2004: *Distinct Inheritances. Property, Family and Community in a Changing Europe.*

3. Torsello, David, 2004: *Trust, Property and Social Change in a Southern Slovakian Village.*

4. Pine, Frances, Deema Kaneff, and Haldis Haukanes (eds.), 2004: *Memory, Politics and Religion. The Past Meets the Present in Europe.*

5. Habeck, Joachim Otto, 2005: *What it Means to be a Herdsman. The Practice and Image of Reindeer Husbandry among the Komi of Northern Russia.*

6. Stammler, Florian, 2009: *Reindeer Nomads Meet the Market. Culture, Property and Globalisation at the 'End of the Land'* (2 editions).

7. Ventsel, Aimar, 2006: *Reindeer,* Rodina *and Reciprocity. Kinship and Property Relations in a Siberian Village.*

8. Hann, Chris, Mihály Sárkány, and Peter Skalník (eds.), 2005: *Studying Peoples in the People's Democracies. Socialist Era Anthropology in East-Central Europe.*

9. Leutloff-Grandits, Caroline, 2006: *Claiming Ownership in Postwar Croatia. The Dynamics of Property Relations and Ethnic Conflict in the Knin Region.*

10. Hann, Chris, 2006: *"Not the Horse We Wanted!" Postsocialism, Neoliberalism, and Eurasia.*

11. Hann, Chris, and the "Civil Religion" Group, 2006: *The Postsocialist Religious Question. Faith and Power in Central Asia and East-Central Europe.*

12. Heintz, Monica, 2006: *"Be European, Recycle Yourself!" The Changing Work Ethic in Romania.*

13 Grant, Bruce, and Lale Yalçın-Heckmann (eds.), 2007: *Caucasus Paradigms. Anthropologies, Histories and the Making of a World Area.*

14 Buzalka, Juraj, 2007: *Nation and Religion. The Politics of Commemoration in South-East Poland.*

15 Naumescu, Vlad, 2007: *Modes of Religiosity in Eastern Christianity. Religious Processes and Social Change in Ukraine.*

16 Mahieu, Stéphanie, and Vlad Naumescu (eds.), 2008: *Churches Inbetween. Greek Catholic Churches in Postsocialist Europe.*

17 Mihăilescu, Vintilă, Ilia Iliev, and Slobodan Naumović (eds.), 2008: *Studying Peoples in the People's Democracies II. Socialist Era Anthropology in South-East Europe.*

18 Kehl-Bodrogi, Krisztina, 2008: *"Religion is not so strong here". Muslim Religious Life in Khorezm after Socialism.*

19 Light, Nathan, 2008: *Intimate Heritage. Creating Uyghur Muqam Song in Xinjiang.*

20 Schröder, Ingo W., and Asta Vonderau (eds.), 2008: *Changing Economies and Changing Identities in Postsocialist Eastern Europe.*

21 Fosztó, László, 2009: *Ritual Revitalisation after Socialism: Community, Personhood, and Conversion among Roma in a Transylvanian Village.*

22 Hilgers, Irene, 2009: *Why Do Uzbeks have to be Muslims? Exploring religiosity in the Ferghana Valley.*

23 Trevisani, Tommaso, 2010: *Land and Power in Khorezm. Farmers, Communities, and the State in Uzbekistan's Decollectivisation.*

24 Yalçın-Heckmann, Lale, 2010: *The Return of Private Property. Rural Life after the Agrarian Reform in the Republic of Azerbaijan.*

25 Mühlfried, Florian, and Sergey Sokolovskiy (eds.), 2011. *Exploring the Edge of Empire: Soviet Era Anthropology in the Caucasus and Central Asia.*

26 Cash, Jennifer R., 2011: *Villages on Stage. Folklore and Nationalism in the Republic of Moldova.*

27 Köllner, Tobias, 2012: *Practising Without Belonging? Entrepreneurship, Morality, and Religion in Contemporary Russia.*

28 Bethmann, Carla, 2013: *"Clean, Friendly, Profitable?" Tourism and the Tourism Industry in Varna, Bulgaria.*

29 Bošković, Aleksandar, and Chris Hann (eds.), 2013: *The Anthropological Field on the Margins of Europe, 1945-1991.*

30 Holzlehner, Tobias, 2014: *Shadow Networks. Border Economies, Informal Markets and Organised Crime in the Russian Far East.*

31 Bellér-Hann, Ildikó, 2015: *Negotiating Identities: Work, Religion, Gender, and the Mobilisation of Tradition among the Uyghur in the 1990s.*

32 Oelschlaegel, Anett C., 2016: *Plural World Interpretations: The Case of the South-Siberian Tyvans.*

33 Obendiek, Helena, 2016: *"Changing Fate". Education, Poverty and Family Support in Contemporary Chinese Society.*

34 Sha, Heila, 2017: *Care and Ageing in North-West China.*